MOTHERING
THROUGH
PRECARITY

MOTHERING THROUGH PRECARITY

Women's Work and Digital Media

JULIE A. WILSON AND
EMILY CHIVERS YOCHIM

Duke University Press   Durham and London   2017

Text designed by Courtney Leigh Baker
Cover designed by Mindy Basinger Hill
Typeset in Whitman and Avenir by
Westchester Publishing Services

Library of Congress Cataloging-in-Publication Data
Names: Wilson, Julie A., [date] author. | Yochim,
Emily Chivers, author.
Title: Mothering through precarity : women's
work and digital media / Julie A. Wilson and
Emily Chivers Yochim.
Description: Durham : Duke University Press, 2017. |
Includes bibliographical references and index.
Identifiers: LCCN 2016044713 (print)
LCCN 2016047429 (ebook)
ISBN 9780822363361 (hardcover : alk. paper)
ISBN 9780822363477 (pbk. : alk. paper)
ISBN 9780822373193 (ebook)
Subjects: LCSH: Motherhood—Economic aspects—
United States. | Mothers—United States—Social
conditions. | Nuclear families—Political aspects—
United States. | Digital media—Social aspects.
Classification: LCC HQ759 .W527 2017 (print) |
LCC HQ759 (ebook) | DDC 306.874/3—dc23
LC record available at https://lccn.loc.gov/2016044713

Cover art: Photo by Douglas K. Hill.

For our moms,
Mary Chivers and Ann Wilson,
and the boys,
Elliot, Oliver, Isaac, Chris, and Joe

CONTENTS

ACKNOWLEDGMENTS

A prominent theme that runs throughout *Mothering through Precarity* is the vital significance of the infrastructures we inhabit. Infrastructures are our conditions of possibility. They allow us to travel, connect, and get things done. Or not. This book would not have happened without many infrastructures.

First, our intellectual infrastructure: We are lucky to have a brilliant group of feminist media scholars who inspire, mentor, and support us, including Sarah Banet-Weiser, Elana Levine, Allison McCracken, Sujata Moorti, Carol Stabile, and Brenda Weber. Diane Negra championed this project in its infancy, and her unyielding faith that we were on to something important made all the difference. Much is owed too to Laurie Ouellette, who taught Julie to dwell in the pressure points of social life and whose own work and mentorship have played a huge role in the development of our thinking; to Bambi Haggins, who showed Emily that compassion and criticism can commingle; and to Susan Douglas, who guided Emily to appreciate popular culture's everyday pleasures while honing in on mundane gender wounds. This book has been immensely energized by Greg Seigworth, the Affect Theory Conference: Worldlings, Tensions, Futures (WTF), and everyone in Stream 11 ("Ordinary Affect and Everyday Life"): you provided so much inspiration in the very end when we needed it most. The final articulation is all you. Avi Santo, Jamie Henthorn, and Laura Portwood-Stacer, thank you for allowing us to share our work with your own students and peers. Sarah Crymble, Kamille Gentles-Peart, Hannah Hamad, and Alice Leppert, you are our buoys in this profession. Thank you for being there to listen, read, conspire, commiserate, and laugh.

Duke University Press has been a wonderful publishing infrastructure. So much is owed to Courtney Berger especially, who recognized early on the tensions and potentialities embedded in our project. Thank you for asking the tough questions, providing thoughtful guidance, and finding the right reviewers to take our ideas to the next level. Sandra Korn was instrumental in pulling things together and willingly answered many questions about the nitty-gritty of putting the book in its final form. Thanks to our project editor, Lisa Bintrim, and our copyeditor for their sharp eyes and savvy advice. We also want to acknowledge here Joe Deville and Greg Seigworth (an early version of chapter 2 entitled "Mothering through Precarity: Becoming Mamapreneurial" appeared in their coedited special edition of *Cultural Studies*, "Everyday Debt and Credit"), as well as Elana Levine (some of our arguments were initially developed in our essay "Pinning Happiness: Affect, Social Media, and the Work of Mothering," which was published in Elana's *Cupcakes, Pinterest, and Ladyporn: Feminized Popular Culture in the Early Twenty-First Century*). Their editorial insights and guidance along the way were formative.

Allegheny College provides a supportive and nurturing institutional infrastructure. To our colleagues and students in the Department of Communication Arts and Theatre, we love you and thank you for being so supportive of our partnership, research, and the directions these take our teaching. Many students have contributed to this project over the years through participating in our classes, reading groups, and independent studies. A special thanks to our research assistants and thinking partners over the years: Megan Bart, Daniel Bauer, Erin Brockett, Larissa Card, Rachel DuChateau, Allison Nettnin, Rochelle Rogalski, and Brigit Stack. Funding from the Andrew W. Mellon Collaborative Undergraduate Research in the Humanities grant and the Allegheny College Dean's Fund for Student/Faculty Collaborative Research was instrumental in supporting these partnerships with students. Big thanks to Jan Mailliard for assiduous administrative support. We also are grateful to the Allegheny College Academic Support Committee for providing funds for our research and a space to share our early thinking, and to Linda Bills for inviting us to give the 20th Annual Pelletier Faculty Lecture. And, of course, we are forever indebted to our friends across campus who have supported us unconditionally throughout this grueling process: you know who you are.

And then there are our families, nuclear and extended, chosen and kin. The late John Wilson and Bud Tompkins would have been proud to see this book in print, and we wish they were still here. BeJay Gronauer, Patricia Langreck, Eleanor McGough, Kathie Smith, Deborah Tompkins, and Cathy

Wilson, you have been loud cheerleaders in Julie's life, providing much needed fuel and support, especially in hard times. Julie's sisters, Dana and Katie Wilson, are forces of nature in their own special ways; their energy and brilliance animate Julie's life—so much of this is for them.

Jennie Lindenberger, Amber Hotchkiss, Kelly Burke, and Asha Graeb have offered gentle and steady care to the Yochim boys. Nancy Kohler has been a lifelong inspiration, and Nicole Krystoff and Bethany Lewis are Emily's abiding allies, wise and funny chosen sisters. Emily's brothers, John and Tim Chivers, are steadfast in their love and wit, and her late brother Colin Chivers still galvanizes her. Emily's smart and tenacious dad, David Chivers, inspires with his enthusiasm. Finally, Nancy and John Yochim and the entire Yochim crew: your easy love is a soft landing.

To our moms, Ann Wilson and Mary Chivers, our bedrocks, our back-bones. Ann, you are always there, watching from a distance or showing up to support us. You will never know just how much your unyielding pride and belief in Julie undergirds our work. Mary, we are ever grateful for your kindness and grace. You generously stepped in when we needed to retreat into our writing, and your abundant help with childcare—on regular Tuesdays, during conference travel with the babies, and all the times in between—has been instrumental to this book's completion. Thank you both for listening to us and caring for us as only mamas can.

To Elliot Yochim, Oliver Yochim, and Isaac Yochim, you have filled your mama up with joy and wonder, and your spirits anchor this book. Your gentle hearts and romping energies provided a constant reminder of what is at stake and why we write.

Our husbands have weathered this book right along with us. Joe Tompkins, thank you for, with "perverse pleasure," editing every single word, and for stepping in and caring for Julie when she couldn't care for herself. We are grateful (most of the time) for your loving cynicism. Chris Yochim, thank you for infusing our lives with humor and loyalty, and for so attentively nurturing Emily's domestic scene. You give the little Yochims a secure footing and a sure sense of belonging. To both of you: your love for each of us, and your unyielding support of our own partnership, is the greatest infrastructure of all.

Finally, this book would not be possible if it weren't for the mothers who shared their lives with us. Thank you for opening up and being vulnerable, so we could clearly see your own infrastructures. We have really tried to do them justice.

THE DIGITAL MUNDANE

Mothering, Media, and Precarity

CARLY

"It's been brutal," Carly told us when we met her at a neighborhood barbe-cue joint to talk about her everyday life as a mother of three girls.[1] Friendly and pragmatic, Carly ordered a salad and beer and chatted with us for over two hours, laughing easily as she detailed the day-to-day frustrations of parenthood and candidly describing her family's financial troubles. In just three short years, this thirty-four-year-old had married her husband, become a stepmother, had two daughters of her own, abandoned her "dream career," found (and lost) a job as a marketer, weathered her husband's two layoffs, and taken on three young babysitting charges to make ends meet. In the meantime, Carly's father, with whom she used to talk for an hour daily, had passed away suddenly, and her mother had suffered a small stroke.

Carly's evening out with us was a temporary break from her normal day of caretaking and, more broadly, from a life shaped by seemingly impossible options that have left her making weighty decisions in order to hold her family together. Indeed, Carly's adult life had been a complicated path—through corporate buyouts, insufficient maternity leaves, and touch-and-go childcare arrangements—to stay-at-home, work-at-home motherhood. Through it all, Carly turned to her online networks for parenting tips and emotional support, seeking advice about childhood illnesses and posting family pictures to Facebook to celebrate her good days with the girls.

Carly's life as a mother, marked by grave decisions and mundane engagements with digital media, is not unique. Over the course of a year, we interviewed and spent time with twenty-nine mothers, all of whom were trying to be "good moms" in a highly mediated and deeply insecure milieu. Many were scared and anxious; some embodied a hopeful confidence; all inhabited a sea of intensity and weight, as they felt responsible for bringing certainty to their family lives in deeply uncertain times. We heard stories about sudden job losses, health scares, and taxing struggles to balance care of self with care of family. We also heard stories about the pedestrian affordances associated with digital media, from the big savings available through online couponing to the domestic inspirations of Pinterest boards. *Mothering through Precarity* explores these everyday entanglements of digital media and women's work, showing the myriad ways mothers come to absorb the punishing tides of advanced neoliberalism at the level of everyday life.

Carly was one of the first mothers we interviewed. During our time together, we found Carly to be a loving, no-nonsense mother who thinks carefully about how to raise strong and respectful young women. She was also openly emotional, crying unselfconsciously when she talked about the insecurities and fears endemic to contemporary motherhood. Like many of the women we spoke with, Carly had not always imagined becoming a mother. In college she became passionate about radio and threw herself into training for a career in the field. She landed a job at a local radio station in her Rust Belt hometown and eventually became the assistant program director, "which was pretty much running the station"; she worked eighty-to ninety-hour weeks producing the morning show, logging programs, and making public appearances on weekends—all for very little pay. "I would work from three thirty a.m. to eleven at night," she told us. "Work. Work. Work. Work." On Carly's rare days off, her stepdaughter, Maddie, offered an early introduction to parenting. When she met Maddie at age two, Carly took to her immediately, and she relished her part-time parenting role, enjoying child-centered time at the zoo as well as child-free time at the bar. Eventually, Carly and her husband decided to have more children—a decision she recalls "jok[ing] about for years" before arriving at a "point where I didn't want to joke about it anymore." She didn't seem to regard this decision with reverence, though, telling us, "We all know there's no right time to have kids." In short order, Carly had daughter Amanda and then, to her absolute shock, became pregnant with daughter Rory when Amanda was just five months old.

Though Carly had intended to take a twelve-week maternity leave after having Amanda, her radio station was undergoing a major change and asked her to return after just six weeks. Carly and her husband slogged through this grueling schedule for a while, with Carly sleeping in her daughter's room—getting up every few hours to make sure she was breathing and to breast-feed—and then turning on the baby monitor for her husband before leaving for work early in the morning. Carly's husband took Amanda to the sitter, and Carly pumped breast milk in the conference room at work, enduring male coworkers' teasing—"Oh! The creamer's here!" She laughs about this ribbing now, saying, "I was in mom mode even, you know, at work. I'm like, 'I gotta take care of my kid. I've gotta pump. I've gotta do this!'"

Becoming pregnant with Rory right after Amanda—and while Carly was in the throes of a taxing job and early motherhood—was overwhelming:

> I was really beyond belief with her. Scared out of my mind that I was going to have a one-year-old and a newborn and yelling, "How on earth am I going to do this and a career and a husband and a stepdaughter?" And I was very overwhelmed with her. And I felt horrible. It wasn't that I didn't want her, but I did just feel horrible because everything was turning in my mind going, "I don't know if I can do this." So if there really wasn't a right time for me to have a kid, in my mind it was when I was pregnant with Rory. It just completely threw me for a loop. And that's when I had to start analyzing, OK, "You're going to work at four a.m. Let's get a nine-to-five job." So I left a career that I love. I left a career that I loved and dreamed about for my family.

With her husband in and out of work, Carly eventually landed a less exciting job at a local company that better accommodated the rhythms and demands of family, only to lose that job two years later thanks to a corporate buyout.

Needless to say, these early years of mothering were marked by intense uncertainty—fear that neither Carly nor her husband would find steady work, that managing work and childcare would be impossible, that things would fall apart. Of course, motherhood is always already a high-stakes and deeply precarious scene: giving birth, learning to care for little ones, worrying about children's safety, nurturing their potential.[2] Thanks to a deeply entrenched gendered division of labor and durable ideologies of "good" mothering, women still tend to assume personal responsibility for these precarious scenes, despite evolving gender norms and necessities around parenting and work.[3] Moreover, as Carly's rickety life suggests, neoliberalism introduces additional volatilities to nuclear family life that mothers also feel compelled to accept responsibility for and work to alleviate. In other words, today what is deeply precarious for Carly—and the purview of her women's work—is the viability of the family itself. Of course, liberal capitalism has always assaulted the viability of family for poor and dispossessed populations, especially for African Americans in the United States; however, neoliberalism is generalizing economic insecurity and familial destabilization across social strata, making precarity a more broadly, though still unevenly, shared feature of motherhood.

For example, when her family was on the ropes, Carly took it on herself to steer her family ship to steadier waters. As Carly surrendered her own dreams to focus on those she harbored for the family, the domestic sphere became a defensive, elastic space where she absorbed everyday shocks by constantly adjusting her aspirations, affects, and labors as a woman. In the face of unstable employment, she stayed optimistic, determined to do whatever she could to stabilize her shaky family scene. So when a friend posted on Facebook that he was in desperate need of a sitter owing to health crises within his own family, Carly saw an opportunity: "I told my husband, 'Well, if I'm going to stay home with the kids anyway, here's a chance to make a little something.' I don't break the bank by any means, babysitting. I mean, because they are old friends. And I don't charge them for days they're not there or if they're late, and I don't, you know, I provide food and all that stuff. . . . I'm bringing in something from it, but they're all just friends."

Carly has since taken on two other babysitting charges. She begins her workday at a quarter to seven—rolling out of bed every morning at six thirty to throw on sweatpants before the first child arrives—and does not finish until seven in the evening. Her days now follow a predictable routine, packed with affordable outings with the kids to the zoo, the park, and the children's museum, and she is careful to build in time for herself, using the kids' nap times to exercise on the treadmill while she watches her soap, *Days of Our Lives,* which she digitally video-records daily. Carly is also online often— sharing funny family moments on Facebook in hopes of giving her friends and relatives a good laugh or looking for answers to health questions, which she readily admits has made her "a beast of a hypochondriac."

We begin with Carly because she exemplifies, in so many ways, what we learned about mothering through precarity. As decades of neoliberalism unravel the social protections that have historically propped up white nuclear family life, mothers like Carly feel they must work more and more to merely "hold on" to family.[4] Like Carly, other mothers we spoke with had, in their own ways, become flexible and resilient, quick to adjust expectations, defer their dreams, and retool their labors for the well-being and security of their families. Crucially, these efforts are realized within the banal spaces of digital media culture: online environments consisting of local Facebook groups, couponing sites, mommy blogs, health and parenting sites, photo apps, casual games, and so on. Mothers' precarious lives are inseparable from what we call *the digital mundane.*

IN SEARCH OF MOTHERS' VOICES

We began this research in search of mothers' voices. When we spoke to Carly and other women, we were simply eager to hear their own stories about life as women in the recessionary Rust Belt, which has long stood in stark contrast to the cosmopolitan, postfeminist mise-en-scène of so much media and consumer culture. We wanted to hear about their everyday joys and challenges, their hopes and dreams, and the ways media facilitated, shaped, and intersected with their gendered lives and labors. Both our scholarly and personal interests led to this research. Emily, a feminist media ethnographer and mother of three young boys, spent her first year of motherhood up countless nights with a colicky baby and immersed in digital mommy culture; accordingly, she was eager to explore mothers' work and mothering communities online and off. Julie, while happily child free, had done previous research on women's work, neoliberalism, and digital media and was invested in examining how gendered labor was taking shape on the ground in our respective postindustrial hometowns.[5]

Inspired by previous feminist audience studies, early on we adopted what Ien Ang calls a "radical contextualist perspective," which refuses to separate media culture from "the intersubjective networks" and "concrete contextual settings" of everyday life.[6] Consequently, we set out to tell a story about how media are interwoven into domestic scenes, giving sense to daily rituals and inciting particular modes of engaging with the family and the self. It was a story that would begin (or end) not with specific media texts, genres, or practices but rather with the situated stories and messy lifeworlds of women like Carly.

Most of the mothers in this study hail from two communities. The first is Julie's hometown of Ryeland. The county seat in a staunchly Republican area of northwestern Pennsylvania, Ryeland is characterized by rolling cornfields and small dairy farms. Home to 13,000 people—27.8 percent of whom live below the poverty line (a percentage far above the county's and the nation's average of 15 percent) and 5 percent of whom are black (compared with the county's 1.9 percent)—Ryeland is an oft-maligned small town that fosters deep loyalties among its citizens. Once prosperous— local lore suggests the town saw zero unemployment during the Great Depression—Ryeland now offers dilapidated Victorian homes ripe for renovation and restored Craftsman bungalows near a private liberal arts college that sits on top of a hill above the town. The downtown struggles to keep businesses, while empty storefronts speckle the streets. A multiplex cinema located just outside the town's borders screens the latest blockbusters, and an active community theater supplements the sparse cultural offerings of the local college. The town's manufacturing sector is legendary, though it now struggles under the pressures of globalization. The hospital and the college are the leading employers in a postindustrial, service-driven, knowledge-based economy. Ryeland is also a town where ideologies collide: Mennonite families sell homegrown jam to relocated professionals, longtime residents work alongside college students at underfunded local service organizations, and Christian conservatives exercise together with bohemian mothers at the YMCA.

The second community is the nearby Hugo region, a sprawling metro-suburban space that is a thirty-minute car ride north of Ryeland. This is where Emily lives with her husband and three boys, in close proximity to their large extended family. Home to 100,000—75 percent white, 19.7 percent black, and 6.9 percent Hispanic—the decaying, postindustrial city swings liberal owing to the working-class union Democrats who largely

FIGURE I.1 Downtown Ryeland.

populate it. As with Ryeland, Hugo's poverty rate approaches 30 percent (while the broader county's rate is 18 percent), as it too is transitioning toward a service- and tourism-based economy. While some of the women in this project come from the city of Hugo, others hail from its surrounding suburbs, a sprawling community (with a population of 50,000) that circles the city with a wide range of single-family homes, soccer fields, and chain restaurants. Downtown Hugo comprises seventy blocks filled with small high rises, abandoned buildings previously devoted to heavy industry, and cheap local bars and eateries. The city's waterfront has recently been redeveloped for tourism, and festivals are held almost every week during the summer. Winters are hard, with heavy snowfall and long, gray days. Residents pride themselves on their winter driving skills, general hardiness, and summertime cheer. Down-to-earth and a bit gritty, this area is also home to vibrant underground music scenes and close-knit artist communities.

In the spring of 2012, we hung up flyers at local community colleges, preschools, and grocery stores inviting "mothers of young children" to talk with us about their experiences as mothers. We asked acquaintances and

FIGURE I.2. Suburban working-class neighborhood in Hugo.

the mothers we interviewed for referrals, and we also reached out to several mommy bloggers from Emily's networks.[7] Most of the women who volunteered to speak to us were in the throes of mothering babies and toddlers, though some had school-age children. Most were white, but one was African American and another identified as multiracial. While some mothers we interviewed enjoyed economic security, many were working class or precariously middle class. Two women were working-poor. Most were married, though relationships were sometimes strained; others were in committed relationships. All of the women were heteronormative in their orientation toward family, and all of them lived in some version of the nuclear family, individualized units bound together by economic and caregiving needs.

In interview sessions that ranged from one to three hours, we sat with mothers in bars, coffee shops, our offices, and their own homes, and we talked about life with young children. Our interviews began by asking them to introduce us to their families and continued with questions about the rhythms of daily life ("Tell us about a typical day, from morning till night"). Children sometimes skittered in and out of our conversations as mothers told us about what made them feel like "good mothers" and what made them feel "not so good." They described their fears and hopes for their children and listed, often in dramatic detail, the labors they perform on a weekly basis. Only after we had a rich sense of their lives did we ask about media: what websites they frequented, what television shows they watched, how much they watched or browsed, and why they made these choices. In this way, *Mothering through Precarity* is aligned with what Elizabeth Bird calls "generation three" media ethnographies, which follow media through everyday lives.[8] Indeed, our conversations ranged far and wide—exploring the virtues of streaming media while cleaning the house, husbands' ability to relax in front of the television and mothers' inability to watch without multitasking, and fears about sacrificing time with their children to devote more time to work or Facebook.

Emily also engaged in extensive participant observation in a local Mothers of Preschoolers (MOPS) group. A popular international Christian network of mothering communities, MOPS supports mothers of young children through the muck of parenting. From September 2011 to June 2012, Emily met regularly with this group, participating in twice-monthly meetings for two hours at a time with fifty women at a large church; she also attended multiple informal playgroups with about six members at their homes and local playgrounds, and hosted a small baby shower for one of the members. Emily also participated in several organized events, including a holiday cookie exchange and a MOPS fund-raiser—a rummage sale at a local church, where participants rented table space so that they could sell their own wares. At these large-group meetings, Emily put her young children in childcare with the other members' children and listened to speakers, watched demonstrations, made crafts, and participated in guided discussions about contemporary parenting.

The MOPS group facilitated conversations that cut to the heart of women's dreams and fears for their families. The two-hour meetings were highly structured: after the large group listened to a speaker, table leaders facilitated small-group discussions centered on caring for children and families. In less structured activities outside the monthly MOPS meetings, Emily came to know these mothers more fully as they spent a considerable amount of time together watching the children play and discussing children's behavior and personalities. This participant observation offered a glimpse into the daily conversations of a community of mothers, bringing to life some of the issues discussed in the interviews and formal meetings.

Five of the women we interviewed were members of Emily's MOPS group, and two interviewees were members of a different MOPS group in the region.

BEYOND THE "MOMMY WARS"

It is important to understand that, from the beginning, we conceived this research as a distinctly feminist political intervention rooted in mothers' voices. As Nick Couldry argues, critical work grounded in voice is ever more pressing in the context of neoliberalism, in which the marketization of all of life increasingly deems "ordinary" voices worthless. Couldry explains:

> Voice does more than value particular voices or acts of speaking; it values all human beings' ability to give an account of themselves; it values my and your status as "narratable" selves. . . . Articulating voice—as an inescapable aspect of human experience—challenges the neoliberal logic that runs together economic, social, political, and cultural domains, and describes them as manifestations of market processes. It challenges the silences and gaps that arise when decisions on one scale—market functioning—seem naturally to "trump" the potential exercise of voice on other scales. It challenges any form of organization that ignores voice, and rejects, as a starting-point, apparent forms of voice . . . which offer only the opportunity to compete as a commodity.[9]

Media studies becomes complicit with neoliberalism's suppression of voice to the extent that it tends to privilege the commodified voices of "market functioning": that is, the producers, representations, audiences, fans, and users considered most valuable to the media industries. For example, both media-industry and audience studies tend to narrow the focus to popular sites of "convergence culture" and thus often elevate the practices and tastes of producers and fans (and sometimes academics themselves).[10] As a result, the persistent and banal inequalities that make up everyday life for media users like Carly tend to take a backseat to the new horizons of industrial cultural production. In losing sight of "nonmedia people," that is, those constituencies who aren't usually regarded as primary media users, media studies risks extending the economization of our social world by rendering inaudible the voices that are not so readily accounted for within the increasingly corporatized, fast-paced landscapes of neoliberal academia.[11]

We set out to give voice to mothers in our own communities, to listen to their stories of mothering, media, and everyday survival. The mothers we spoke with do not constitute an audience per se, much less a cohort of fans; their voices do not emerge from urban centers, and they do not necessarily share the desires, beliefs, values, and investments of popular cultural intermediaries, much less feminists like ourselves.[12] But by listening to these voices, we hoped to illuminate the "silences and gaps" of everyday gendered life—their situated, concrete contributions to the social and political imagination. Indeed, while the mothers we interviewed certainly do not speak for *all* mothers, taken together their voices provide a snapshot of everyday life for some women.

We also hoped that our approach might disrupt the so-called mommy wars, a prominent gender discourse that pits mothers against one another. In 1990 *Newsweek* popularized the term in an article titled "Mommy vs. Mommy," effectively marking the difference between working and stay-at-home moms as "a feud . . . that defines an era." Since then, contemporary media culture has capitalized on this distinction—purportedly based on personal choices women make about work, family, lifestyle, and childrearing. While these "wars" were supposedly fought over mothers' orientations toward paid work, they now regularly get referenced in relation to mothers' decisions about everything from medical care to nutrition to sleep. At the same time, calls to end the mommy wars abound.[13]

But it is important to see that the mommy wars are themselves symptomatic of broader neoliberal developments that, as our research shows, are not easy to shake. As Nikolas Rose argues, "wars of subjectivity" emerge when the lifestyles, communities, values, and beliefs of individuals come to figure as the primary medium of governmentality.[14] As public conceptions of citizenship premised on democratic participation are replaced with privatized models of personal choice, the gendered practice of lifestyle cultivation—in the sense of "good mothering"—becomes an increasingly politicized affair. Accordingly, we are concerned that prominent ideological critiques of media and motherhood within our own field inadvertently contribute to the mommy-war mentality. For example, critiques of the "new momism" tend to follow mainstream media discourse in drawing lines of distinction between women based on personal choices, investments, cultural norms, and political orientations.[15] By contrast, we wanted to undercut this approach by "decentering" dominant media culture—particularly its obsession with the mommy wars—and instead set out to hear from mothers themselves about their daily rituals and routines, their everyday engagements with media.[16]

These commitments guided both our experiences with mothers and our collaborative research process. As we entered encounters with mothers, we tried to unsettle the inherent power relationships between researchers and subjects. Emily's "insider" status as a mother of three certainly helped to generate intimacy and trust on many occasions. Indeed, Emily, too, wrestles with how to make family "work," and while she is critical of predominant mothering media, she takes enormous pleasure in throwing elaborate birthday parties for her boys and taking on ambitious do-it-yourself home projects. Julie, on the other hand, might be considered a sympathetic "outsider" looking in who places herself in solidarity with mothers. While several of our colleagues suggested that Julie might not fully understand mothers' lives—that her outsider status might prevent her from writing an honest and thoughtful account—our collaboration easily crossed these lifestyle boundaries; through constant communication we cycled in and out of mothers' lives and through the theories that helped us capture and articulate their forms and sensibilities. Still, we found ourselves routinely surprised by how readily many of the women we interviewed—regardless of class status, lifestyle, or cultural sensibility—opened up to both of us. Our conversations were often profoundly emotional: sometimes mothers cried, and many shared intimate, at times painful, details of their lives. By the end we had a stark sense that, for most, mothering is a fraught affair defined by a matrix of affective intensities—from the immense love they harbor for their children to the overwhelming anxieties that animate their lives.

Ultimately, our commitments carried a specific "burden of authorship" that animated our writing: maintaining solidarity with the mothers and giving voice to their stories, while holding on to our own critical, political, and feminist sensibilities. Indeed, our greatest challenge was situating mothers' voices in ways that would both honor their singularity and highlight our own insights. Throughout our research, we strove to balance sympathy toward mothers' lives with an unsentimental view of the larger structures that impinge on them, in hopes of writing a story that might intimate new modes of collectivity and political horizons.

Our work was guided, first and foremost, by what Melissa Gregg calls "a desire for the mundane." In her article "A Mundane Voice," on Meaghan Morris's use of anecdotes and colloquial address, Gregg argues that Morris was driven not by a desire for master narratives but rather by a feminist orientation, specifically, "by an urge to hear how cultural changes land in the context of people's everyday."[17] According to Gregg, Morris's work hones in on what Brian Massumi calls the "this-ness": "an unreproducible being-only-itself," enacting what Morris herself calls a mode of "historical analysis attuned both to socio-economic contexts and to the individuating local intensities." Being attuned to the mundane means attending to the local affective intensities that give sense and shape to people's lives, for these local intensities are themselves singular examples of "how the world can be said to be working."[18] For Gregg, Morris's mundane is politically significant for its humility and the "honesty and concreteness" it brings to intellectual work. The mundane demands letting go of "preferred interpretative models" in order to see emergent forms and performances and the horizons for collective life they figure.[19]

This "desire for the mundane" led us to see mothers' everyday lives as compositions: more specifically, as swirling amalgamations of "ordinary affects." Kathleen Stewart describes ordinary affects as "the varied, surging capacities to affect and to be affected that give everyday life the quality of a continual motion of relations, scenes, contingencies, and emergences. They're things that happen. They happen in impulses, sensations, expectations, daydreams, encounters, and habits of relating, in strategies and their failures, in forms of persuasion, contagion, and compulsion, in modes of attention, attachment, and agency, and in publics and social worlds of all kinds that catch people up in something that feels like *something*. . . . They give circuits and flows the forms of a life."[20]

Ordinary affects happen in the mundane flows of everyday lives; they are "a kind of contact zone" where events, politics, strategies for living, and "flows of power" meet and are enacted.[21] As such, they help us to see how big forces fold into minute lifeworlds in multiple, shifting, and highly contingent ways, and how these might prime people to order and experience their lives. As Stewart suggests, "structure is prismatic. It takes place as singular events saturated with everyday violence. . . . Politics is not reducible to a communal consciousness or a neatly conceptualized ideology but takes place as intensities of all kinds and in various registers. Agency is not the clear and intentional act of a subject but an energetics."[22] For both Gregg and Stewart, the potential for new worlds is embedded within the ordinary affective movements of everyday life. Agency registers in emergent and situated senses of what it might be possible to do, be, and become in a particular time and place, in the "forms of living" that "are now being composed and suffered."[23]

Mothering through Precarity hones in on mothers' ordinary affective lives and, more specifically, the affective infrastructures that undergird their labors and give their lives sense, texture, and form. Affective infrastructures are akin to "structures of feeling," Raymond Williams's influential, though undertheorized concept that seeks to register the shared social sensibilities of possibility that are engendered by discourses of all sorts but are not reducible to their significations.[24] As Lawrence Grossberg explains, structures of feeling inhabit the "gap between what can be rendered meaningful and knowable and what is nevertheless livable."[25] While not reducible to discourse, ordinary affects are structured—readily captured and made to circulate. They materialize and surge within particular social and historical circuits. Affective infrastructures thus direct attention to the governed life of ordinary affects by locating the affects that make up mothers' everydays within the specific infrastructures that animate, channel, direct, and redirect them. As Lauren Berlant puts it, "one's infrastructures are one's obligation to show up to life a certain way."[26] They help us to understand how mothers' days get organized and prioritized, navigated and survived—in other words, why mothers "show up" for family "a certain way" in this time and place.

Ultimately, this focus on affective infrastructures reveals the quiet and everyday brutalities of advanced neoliberalism for the women we interviewed. We use the term *advanced neoliberalism* loosely to characterize the atmosphere in the postindustrial Rust Belt. Here the exuberant entrepreneurial freedoms of the postwelfare state have long since given way to the harsh demands of austerity. The proactive, empowered self is thus a resilient subject who must cultivate capacities to cope with the shriveling resources and broken promises that neoliberalism brings to social life. Communities are often so depleted—affectively, culturally, politically, and economically—that there's little left to do except adapt, adjust, and, as Ryeland's city manager put it, "try to keep things going." Meanwhile, amid ongoing sprawl, Hugo's population just recently officially dipped below

100,000, which means the city will no longer qualify for much-needed federal grants.

Grounded in the voices of women in these places at this time, *Mothering through Precarity* opens up critical insights into mother's lives and the ways digital media come to animate, shape, and sometimes jeopardize them. Focusing on mothers' affective infrastructures allows us to see how women keep moving through daily hardships while remaining optimistic about their family's prospects, even as their lives get more and more uncertain and unmanageable. By tracing the myriad ways mothers weather advanced neoliberalism at the level of everyday media life, we capture the affective compositionality of mothering through precarity.

THE DIGITAL MUNDANE

Our "desire for the mundane" led us to the digital mundane, that is, to the banal entanglements of media and everyday life through which mothers like Carly strive to stabilize their families. The digital mundane was something we discovered late in our research. After completing the interviews, we found ourselves vexed and uncertain about how to write a book about mothering *and* media. While mothers spilled vivid stories about their daily trials and tribulations, their accounts of media were comparatively dull and sometimes nonexistent. Carly was actually one of the few mothers who seemed eager to talk about television. While many mothers mentioned TV, it often figured as background noise, something they had on while doing other things like checking e-mail or visiting Facebook. Others considered TV primarily in relation to their children or husbands, but when it came to *their* lives, they often appeared surprisingly indifferent. This is not to say that they didn't watch TV, but that television wasn't something they seemed to want to talk about.[27]

Mothers did, however, have more to say about their engagements with digital media, but even these stories were few and far between, and often lacking in specificity and richness. We heard some stories about particular websites, like BabyCenter, an online corporate-run community for expecting or new mothers, and social media platforms, like Pinterest. But, by and large, mothers didn't focus on discrete digital texts, sites, platforms, or practices. They tended to discuss their digital lives broadly as affective experiences, explaining what it *feels* like to be perusing message boards or shopping online.

Ironically, mothers' mundane voices spoke to the "silences and gaps" of the digital mundane. Here, media don't necessarily stand out as particularly significant—as objects worth talking about on their own—but figure as something indistinguishable from the movements of everyday life. As mothers move through their quotidian routines, dipping into social media for quick moments of adult interaction, digital culture becomes a vital, though taken-for-granted, foundation for their days. Whether mothers are scrolling through Facebook for links that promise something (fear, happiness, entertainment), organizing children for post-able snapshots, or Googling health conditions or child-friendly crafts, digital media are seamlessly woven into the fabric of family and women's work, though these engagements might be hard to voice and articulate.

Indeed, as new technologies are embedded in everyday life in increasingly banal ways, *the mundane itself is always already digital*. Readily available and always present, digital media constantly hum in the background. They stand at the ready as naturalized means for social interaction, information gathering, and entertainment, infusing ordinary joys and challenges with the potentialities of digital affordances. The digital mundane circulates a vast array of tools for "good" living, helping to make hard lives feel livable and sometimes even happy, while also mirroring and multiplying the threats of advanced neoliberalism.

For mothers, the digital mundane figures as a highly gendered atmosphere. The churning updates of Facebook feeds; the endless flows of recipes, coupons, and warnings; and the unrelenting streams of maternal advice all work to constitute the digital mundane as a *mamasphere* that is constantly percolating with information, inspiration, and opportunity for mothers. The mamasphere is a network of networks, composed of millions of "mommy blogs," each offering personal reflections on the experience of mothering; corporate websites like BabyCenter that peddle parenting products and advice and promise community through forums and chat rooms; feminized social media platforms that specialize in domestic inspiration, from Pinterest to cooking and couponing sites; and mothering communities like Momastery, where struggling moms find vital forms of emotional and material support.

The mamasphere also intersects with and thrives on broader popular networks, like Facebook, Twitter, and Instagram, as mothers post and pass around the latest family photo, an inspirational meme, a birthday-party idea, or a piece of parenting news. Overall, the mamasphere is a contradictory web of advice, friendship, information, and entertainment, fueled by highly organized and interactive data-mining machines but also by the situated experiences of mothers. Indeed, the mamasphere comes to be only via the cooperation and contributions of mothers, who produce and inhabit its always-on, churning content as they navigate the complexities of contemporary motherhood.

For mothers, the mamasphere beckons with what Brian Massumi calls the "event-potential" of affect.[28] Indeed, digital networks are affective networks.[29] While ideologies teem online, it is affect that binds network cultures. As Jodi Dean puts it:

> Blogs, social networks, Twitter, YouTube: they produce and circulate affect as a binding technique. Affect . . . is what accrues from reflexive communication, from communication for its own sake, from the endless circular movement of commenting, adding notes and links, bringing in new friends and followers, layering and interconnecting myriad communications platforms and devices. Every little tweet or comment, every forwarded image or petition, accrues a tiny affective nugget, a little surplus enjoyment, a smidgen of attention that attaches to it, making it stand out from the larger flow before it blends back in.[30]

Mothers are thus drawn to online environments by the "tiny affective nuggets" that circulate and accrue in the mamasphere; their encounters promise ongoing modulation and attunement to precarious family scenes. These affective nuggets—a happy family photo, a shared link to a time line, a much-needed "like"—cannot, therefore, be separated from the ordinary affects that make up everyday life. They are part and parcel of the affective compositionality of mothers' lives, moving in and out, pushing and pulling, terrifying and inspiring. They give life form and sense. Affective networks may even engender what Zizi Papacharissi calls "affective publics": "networked structures of feeling" that may "drive powerful disruption, help accumulate intensity and tension, or simply sustain infinite loops of activity and inactivity."[31] Simply put, the digital mundane is the affective machinery of everyday life. It is where sensibilities are shaped, worked on, intensified, assuaged, and attenuated, where worlds are simultaneously opened up and shut down.

On one hand, the affective networks of the mamasphere are stable, predictable, and profoundly comforting, as algorithms seem to know mothers so well. Indeed, the mamasphere is highly customized to their everyday lives and targets them accordingly, creating a deeply gendered and racialized "digital enclosure" that is built on the same social and economic inequalities that make up everyday life.[32] As Ulises Ali Mejias argues, networks are nodocentric: "Nodocentrism means that while networks are extremely efficient at establishing links between nodes, they embody a bias against knowledge of—and engagement with—anything that is not a node in the same network. Only nodes can be mapped, explained, or accounted for. . . . [N]odocentrism constructs a social reality in which nodes can only see other nodes. It is an epistemology based on the exclusive reality of the node. It privileges nodes while discriminating against what is not a node—the invisible, the Other."[33] Mothers circulate through mothering nodes along paths paved and paid for by multinational corporations, data firms, and marketers.[34] These nodes are designed to compel and channel mothers' participation as corporate interests constantly look to optimize online sociality and the affect that fuels communicative capitalism. "Participation is thus both a form of violence and a form of pleasure," Mejias insists. "More than a desire, participation is an urge, a form of coercion imposed by the system. This logic is internalized, rationalized, and naturalized. Participation in the network is a template for being social, for belonging."[35] Put a bit differently, through mothers' own highly structured participation, the mamasphere engenders deeply quotidian and practically invisible affective communities premised on already-existing hierarchies of class, race, gender, and sexuality.

On the other hand, the mamasphere is erratic and mercurial, intimately bound up in the mundane movements of everyday lives. As network theorist Tiziana Terranova writes, "beneath the level of desktop applications such as browsers and email, the space of the internetwork is continuously although unevenly agitated, constrained and transformed by the movement of packets. . . . This movement is the condition within which Internet culture operates and it constitutes an important interface with the world of locality. The relation between the local and the global, the territory and the network is thus that of fluctuation, of an increased or decreased, obstructed or relayed flow."[36] The mamasphere is both local and global: at once deeply responsive to, and contingent on, particular lives but also determined by the invisible protocols of the global network itself. Hence, affect circulates via the movement of packets—those seemingly inconsequential mobile bits of data that undergird and constitute the network's form. The movement of packets is the humming atmosphere in which mundane localities con-stantly agitate, contract, and expand the global network. However, some movements end up punctuating mothers' lives: a simple comment may get posted, shared, or noticed, even accidentally, and temporarily fill life with feelings of joy, hope, inadequacy, or fear. In so many ways, life in the digital mundane is moody, spasmodic, uncontrollable.

Ultimately, approaching the affective networks of the digital mundane re-quires what Mark B. N. Hansen calls a *"radically environmental perspective."*[37] Earlier media systems were designed to tell and distribute human stories, and thus their primary modality of power was interpellation. Digital media systems are different. Driven by the invisible and unknowable workings of big data, their aim is to register the environmentality of the world itself. Their power stems from the system's ability to access a "domain of worldly sensi-bility," where one senses the potentiality of things while having no access to, or knowledge of, the system itself.[38] Subjectivity takes shape in the mundane entanglements of these unknowable systems; as Hansen puts it, "we can no longer conceive of ourselves as separate, quasi-autonomous subjects, facing off against distinct media objects; rather, we are ourselves composed as sub-jects through the operation of a host of multi-scalar processes."[39]

Following Hansen, the digital mundane requires seeing mothers' every-day lives as intertwined with the mamasphere's digital affective networks, which provide ubiquitous opportunities for encounters with the worldly sensibility of contemporary motherhood. As we show, the ever-beckoning potentiality of the mamasphere makes everyday family life livable in myr-iad ways, while also reinforcing the inequalities on which these lives are premised. Not surprisingly, the mothers in our study generally inhabit the mamasphere with deep ambivalence. While they certainly appreciate its par-ticipatory affordances, they are also unsettled by its frenetic movements, which tend to exacerbate the volatilities and hurts of daily life.

PRIVATIZING FAMILY HAPPINESS

In the following chapters, we explore how mothers live entangled with digital media, and how the mamasphere undergirds women's unrelenting efforts at holding together their families. For mothers, family feels precari-ous; it is up to them to absorb the shocks that threaten to tear it apart. In re-sponse to the generalized insecurities of advanced neoliberalism, mothers step up their affective labors, confronting the precarious status of the family with intensified and expanded practices of women's work organized around privatizing happiness.

In *State of Insecurity*, Isabell Lorey distinguishes three dimensions of the precarious: precariousness, precarity, and precarization.[40] Precariousness is the shared condition of human and nonhuman life that emerges out of inherent interdependencies and vulnerabilities. Precarity, on the other hand, is a product of social, legal, and political orders that hierarchize shared precariousness, differentiating between those bodies that warrant security and protection and those that do not.[41] So while mothers share the precariousness of motherhood, their lived experiences as mothers are shaped according to differential distributions of risk and insecurity. Finally, precarization refers to a mode of biopolitical governmentality specific to the rise and advancement of the neoliberal state. While poor, dispossessed, and otherwise marginalized populations have long felt the punishing effects of precarity, neoliberalism governs *for and through* widespread insecurity, that is, through precarization. Lorey explains that "contrary to the old rule of a domination that demands obedience in exchange for protection, neoliberal governing proceeds primarily through social insecurity, through regulating the minimum of assurance while simultaneously increasing instability."[42] Thus, white middle-class families, once stabilized by social protections, become subject to precarity and, like Carly's, get swept up in neoliberalism's tumultuous tides. For example, Carly's father supported his family with a small business he inherited from his father. Carly thus grew up in a comfortable two-story home down the street from a country club in a suburb outside of Hugo with a well-regarded public school, and her parents put her through college. Despite these economic privileges, Carly and her husband, like so many of the mothers we spoke with, still struggle to stay afloat.

As we argue, ongoing precarization incites new gender sensibilities that impinge on and intensify women's work and their experiences of motherhood. As Lorey writes, "precarization means more than insecure jobs, more than the lack of security given by waged employment. By way of insecurity and danger it embraces the whole of existence, the body, modes of subjectivation. It is threat and coercion, even while it opens up new possibilities of living and working. Precarization means living with the unforeseeable, with contingency."[43] More than a material situation of economic insecurity, precarity is an everyday sense of threat, vulnerability, and uncertainty that must be confronted and managed in the contexts of everyday life. For the mothers we spoke with, what is felt to be precarious is first and foremost the family itself, and so these women work eagerly and anxiously to securitize their familial scenes.

More specifically, as advanced neoliberalism unravels the social securities that historically have propped up nuclear family life, mothers come to organize their lives around *privatizing happiness*, assuming higher and higher degrees of material and emotional responsibility for their families' well-being and security. Sam Binkley argues that happiness is the "hinge" of neoliberalism: through taking on happiness as a personal, private enterprise, individuals come to accept responsibility for their lives and disembed themselves from the affective life of the welfare state.[44] Jennifer Silva calls the privatization of happiness a "mood economy" and documents how working-class adults develop new markers of adulthood and currencies of citizenship through emotional self-transformation.[45] In both of these accounts, the privatization of happiness is a process of affective realignment: to adjust to a world where nothing is, or should be, guaranteed, individuals cultivate their capacities for achieving highly individualized forms of happiness on their own through self-work.

We suggest, however, that, for mothers, privatizing happiness is a powerful gender orientation toward the work of mothering, whereby individual women assume responsibility for underwriting their family's "promise of happiness."[46] Since family as a predictable and stable path to the good life is no longer a given, mothers feel pressed to hone gender capacities to not only govern the home and raise children but also, at the same time, shore up the material and affective conditions of possibility for family itself. No longer able to rely on public institutions or inherited social and economic capital, mothers feel it is up to them to privatize happiness for their families on their own.

Indeed, while Carly's life as a work-at-home, stay-at-home mom was precipitated by exploitative maternity-leave policies and a corporate buyout, she largely came to terms with her situation by focusing on all of the new ways *she* can help her family.[47] As she does what she "needs to do" for the kids, the questions on her mind are not so much about whether she wants go to work or to stay home as about what she needs to do right now to keep her family safe and sound. Deeply concerned about Hugo's struggling school system, Carly decided to send her daughters to Catholic school. And, rather than harboring anger about leaving her dream career, Carly insists on her happiness, focusing on the benefits of her current situation.

For example, after both her daughters contracted swine flu, she told her husband, "'I'm so thankful that I'm home because I don't have to take sick days or personal days or vacation days to be home and deal with this.' I'm not losing any money or any of my time because they're sick. I'm here with them, and I know what's going on and I can be here." For Carly, privatizing happiness is at once a material (sending her kids to private school) and affective ("I am thankful that I'm home") process that gives sense and shape to her work as a mother.

Women's work thus figures as a crucial linchpin of neoliberalism, as the continued erosion of public social infrastructures hinges on women like Carly and their efforts at privatizing happiness. In practice, then, advanced neoliberalism proceeds largely *through* women, as it is mothers' affective labors as the naturalized caregivers and keepers of the domestic realm that underwrite precarization and make it possible.[48] As Evelyn Nakano Glenn argues, because mothering is imagined to be bound tightly to the "reproductive function," it is "seen as natural, universal, and unchanging. . . . In this model, responsibility for mothering rests almost exclusively on one woman (the biological mother), for whom it constitutes the primary if not sole mission during the child's formative years."[49] Glenn's work emphasizes the diversity of mothering experiences and mothering roles, but it also highlights the enduring circulation of ideologies that pinpoint women as the "natural" caretakers of children and work to maintain long-standing gendered divisions of labor.

Thanks to these entrenched discourses, mothers are the ones who ultimately come to compensate for lost jobs, underfunded public schools, decimated state budgets, and the volatilities all these bring to family life, as mothers constantly retool and expand their women's work—taking on more and more social responsibility with less and less social support—in hopes of bringing some measure of stability to their shaky family scenes. Put a bit differently, mothers today are saddled not only with long-standing gender regimes of social reproduction but also with the precarious status of family itself. The demands of precarization pile onto mothers' already unequal and overburdened gendered lives, intensifying and expanding what is at stake in their practices of care. Privatizing happiness is thus frenzied, always impossible, ever more exploitative gender work, as, of course, mothers alone cannot actually guarantee their families' well-being in a global neoliberal economy fueled by growing insecurity.

Orienting their labors around the precarity of family and its ongoing incitements to privatize more and more happiness, mothers feel that they must work constantly, and on myriad fronts, just to keep the promise of family alive. Not surprisingly, then, as neoliberalism intensifies the high stakes and heartrending work of raising children, it also sharpens the banal and painful gender inequalities that continue to undergird life in the nuclear family for most women. For example, Carly and her husband have had to work out a number of issues connected to the constantly shifting terms of their home and work lives. While he imagines her luxuriating in sweatpants and simply playing with kids all day, she envies his days of adult conversations and scheduled lunch breaks. She explained, "I mean . . . he's starting to. But I think I do harbor some animosity at the 'You need to come home and unwind' or 'You just drove home [two hours], and you need two and a half hours to unwind.' No! We have work to do. Get up." Though Carly's husband suffered several layoffs, he never left the paid job market. Now that he's returned to full-time work, the couple struggles to negotiate mounting labors and their need for rest. Carly explained her frustrations further:

> I wish that he would step up more, I guess, to realize that I've been doing this all day, and he wants to come home and go on Facebook, or go down and watch a show, or read the paper or something. And I don't have time for, I don't have time to do that. . . . I don't want to say he doesn't understand, but he needs his—quote, unquote—"time to unwind." And I guess I have mine when the kids are napping. But when he gets home at 5 p.m. or 5:30 p.m. and I'm trying to get dinner on the table, and, you know, it's a bad night, and Amanda has home-work, and I still have this kid here until 7:00 p.m. My mind is just blank. How do I keep up? And he just wants to veg. And I don't think it's fair sometimes.

Many of the mothers we spoke with described this gender scene. While Carly's husband, as well as most of the other husbands we heard about, seemed to expect downtime when they could disappear into television or online, mothers described turning to social media for very brief breaks in the interstices of care work and watching television only while multitasking. As we noted earlier, Carly catches up on TV while exercising during the kids' nap time. We heard many stories of this sort of husband privilege: men "veg out" while women feel compelled to keep working and working for the family. As we show, they feel that it is up to them to prepare for and handle the fallout from inevitable disasters, to ward off and mitigate everyday threats that loom. As the assumed keepers of the domestic realm, they are the "designated worriers."[50]

No matter what, though, Carly is determined to stay focused on her family amid banal impossibilities and everyday gender hurts, so she organizes her energies around creating happy family moments that her children will remember. She explains, "You stop what you're doing for your kids. And you're there for them. You know, in the younger years, you aren't going to get them back. If they want to color, color with them. If they want to do a puzzle, do a puzzle. This is what they're going to remember, not that you bought them a new stuffed animal or bought them a new shirt or whatever. You know?" Aware that they are not in a position to keep up with the promises of consumer culture, Carly is certain that her investments of time and love are what ultimately matter most for her kids. In the summer of 2012, Carly documented her daily family activities in four Facebook photo albums titled "Promise of a Fun Summer." She captioned these albums, "I have made a promise to myself to make it a memorable summer for my little ones (without breaking the budget). Here is a pictorial of our summer!" Every day she posted at least one picture of her children doing something fun—these ranged from the extraordinary (e.g., visiting children's museums and amusement parks) to the mundane (e.g., eating popsicles outside, collecting pinecones). For Carly, Facebook provides a readily accessible platform for lifting her family into happiness amid the precarity that envelops her family. Through mundane digital encounters—snapping and sharing images of summer fun—Carly stabilizes her shaky family scene, coding the volatilities and uncertainties of everyday life as happy moments.

For Carly, a large part of privatizing happiness is about constantly tuning her ordinary affects to the precarity of family. Interestingly, Carly's favorite mothering model is *Roseanne*, which she DVRs and watches in the evenings or while working out:

> She's brutal, but that show is probably the most true-to-life parenting show I've ever seen. She had to deal with some crazy issues. I've had to deal with some crazy issues. And you're not a perfect parent. Nobody is. And anybody that thinks there is—you're going to mess up and your kids are going to mess up and you've just got to, OK. But see, I love Roseanne. I seriously do. I think that she's real. You

know? If [my kids mess up], I feel disappointed in myself, and I think that's how Roseanne feels. Like, if they fail, she puts it on herself, she doesn't blame her kids. "What did I do wrong?"

For Carly, Roseanne is a hero, but not because of her working-class feminism; rather, it is for the way she is attuned to Carly's sensibility of privatizing happiness, a sensibility that reverberates in the responsibility Carly feels when her family scripts break down: "What did I do wrong?"

Carly also told us about being struck by stories of families weathering hardships and emerging as stronger, happier families. "I like the sob stories," she said of reading *Parents* magazine:

> Like kids that are born with a disability or were born with some kind of deformity, things like that. I feel for those kids, and it makes me extremely thankful for the family that I have. But at the same time, little stuff, like Rory was born with a hernia, she has to have surgery. . . . I'm terrified. And I blame myself because it's an umbilical hernia. I'm like, "That's where she was connected with me! It's my fault!" It's a minor operation. It's going to be a hell of a lot harder on me than it is on her. But I'm like, "Here's my kid that was born with a problem, and I've got my own sob story." But it's a minor sob story in the realm of . . . . But to see how these parents can take the negative and spin it into a positive and work with their kids and start these foundations and just try to advocate for whatever problem their kid has, it just amazes me. The love and the dedication of a parent to your child, no matter what is, just, it blows me away. It blows me away.

For Carly, "sob stories" tap into an abiding sense of insecurity, a feeling that she only narrowly escaped major health problems, and her ongoing fears that her children's health is on the line. But what truly strikes Carly in these stories is the way families remake hardships into happy stories that put on display both deep familial love and individual families' desire to mitigate other families' pain. These melodramatic narratives certify the family's happy potential, even in the face of looming threats and insufficient vital resources like health care.

Carly's efforts at privatizing happiness for her family are inseparable from the churning of the mamasphere, which at once nurtures and compounds these efforts. While Carly's Facebook albums of "summer fun" were profoundly affirming, other encounters in the digital mundane are agitating and deeply upsetting for Carly. Recently, her daughter Amanda, typically a happy and outgoing child, began crying daily when Carly dropped her off at school. This caused considerable angst for Carly:

> But it was really weighing on me because I couldn't figure out what was wrong. What is the cause of this? Why did it change four weeks into school? Why did this happen? She keeps saying it's because she misses me. Andrew and I started talking the other night, and I started crying. And I said, "Is it because I'm a stay-at-home mom? Is it because I was with her all the time and now I'm not? Should I have gotten a job and put her in day care? Or put her with a sitter so that she didn't rely on me as much?" He's like, "What are you talking about?!" And I'm like, "I don't know!" I'm looking for any possible scenario to make me figure it out. But I don't blame her, I blame myself for [it]. Like I said, I figured she would walk into kindergarten and own the place. She's outgoing; she's smart; she's funny; she just. . . . She's got everything going for her. And she's acting this way, and I'm saying to myself, "How did I fail her? What did I do wrong?" And it might not even be me. It may be a host of other things, but for some reason I'm internalizing it as "it is my fault."

In her desperate quest to figure out what was going on with Amanda, Carly turned to her digital networks, yet online parenting advice only exacerbated Carly's angst: "I wanted to throw up," she said, "because somebody's like, 'Get your kid checked for ADHD. Get them on medication. Someone's bullying your kid. Someone's touching your kid.'" Carly found these claims outrageous, preferring to think instead that her daughter might simply miss her or feel sensitive about lunchtime after having been reprimanded by the teacher. "Why can't it be a simple answer like that?," she asks. Why do we have "to jump to medicating and bullying and molestation?"

Here we see what Hansen elaborates as the "inherent or constitutive *doubleness*" of contemporary media.[51] As digital, interactive media register "the environmentality of the world itself," at practically any moment mothers can tap into a "digital nervous system" and "*make contact with the present of sensibility.*"[52] At the same time, though, this tapping is also a contribution that is captured and coded as part of a system. Hansen puts it this way: "we now live in a world where the very media that give us access to events outside the scope of our conscious attention and perception . . . are now typically events that simultaneously contribute to the growth of this very domain of sensibility."[53] Mothers like Carly turn to digital media to make sense of the world, and, in turn, digital media sense them, affectively heightening and computationally optimizing the present sensibility of precarity that brought them there in the first place.

Mothers are constantly attuning themselves to the demands of precarized family happiness in the digital mundane. They are elastic—ready to contract and expand, modulate and modify. Indeed, above all, mothering through precarity is about resilience. Resilience is an affective capacity for surviving, weathering, managing risk, and bouncing back. We can think of resilience as a form of what Berlant calls cruel optimism, for it is a mode of optimism that embraces, and even amplifies, the very processes of precarization that are wearing mothers like Carly down in the first place.[54] Resilience, in other words, has mothers willing their families to live a "non-death." As Brad Evans and Julian Reid argue, "it is only by 'learning how to die,' by willing the 'messianic moment' (to borrow from Walter Benjamin) in which death is read more as a condition of affirmation, that it becomes possible to change the present condition and create a new self by 'turning your world upside down.' Resilience cheats us of this affirmative task of learning how to die. It exposes life to lethal principles so that it may live a non-death."[55] Ravaged family lives might be "read . . . as a condition of affirmation"; painful losses and everyday brutalities could open space for reimagined worlds. But the cruel optimism of resilience bounces mothers back into the world as they know it, fostering returns to familiar familial scenes and the mounting, impossible work of privatizing happiness.

To be clear, we are not suggesting that mothers are ideologically duped by cruel optimism but rather that resilience is a profoundly vital mode of attaching and attuning in advanced neoliberalism. And, as we show, the bouncing back of resilience is inseparable from the churning affordances of the mamasphere. In short, the digital mundane hones maternal resilience, helping women to become the seemingly tireless and flexible happiness workers that precarization demands.

MOTHERING THROUGH PRECARITY

The following chapters work to articulate mothering through precarity as "a form of living." Each chapter hones in on a different affective register, tracing through mothers' own voices the prismatic structures that undergird their lives and the work of privatizing family happiness. The chapters should be read as distinct layers that necessarily echo and bleed into one another, as they seek to capture the compositionality of mothers' lives in the digital mundane.

Chapter 1 accounts for the historicity and government of maternal affect and capacity, tracing how mothers have come to inhabit their roles. Here we provide a sort of affective "history of the present" by situating the ordinary affects that make up everyday family life within shifting discourses of "good" mothering and the broader political-economic contexts that impinge on and animate them. More specifically, this chapter traces how mothers' lives have been affectively loaded up by liberal and neoliberal regimes of family government, especially by family autonomy and its government of mothers. In turn, the work of mothering becomes ever more rife with anxiety and impossibility, as social responsibility for nuclear family life comes to rest ever more squarely on mothers' shoulders: on their everyday decisions, labors, capacities, and practices of self. Mothers' growing loads are made livable, but also compounded, in the mamasphere; while the demands of privatizing happiness stretch and strain mothers' capacities and affects to their breaking points, the mamasphere helps mothers stay pointed, always and anxiously, toward family autonomy.

The next chapter elaborates mamapreneurialism as the primary sensibility of mothering through precarity. Complicating prominent accounts of the mompreneur, we delve into the nitty-gritty everydays of four mothers, exploring how they organize their family worlds through and around privatizing happiness. More specifically, to stabilize their shaky family scenes within the ongoing turbulence of advanced neoliberalism, these mothers are pioneering new ways to appreciate their families in a competitive world where the threat of familial depreciation always lurks and looms. We trace how women—from a comfortable middle-class mother who puts her business acumen and passion to work for her husband's small business in her time away from intensive caretaking to a conservative working-class mom who has turned to vigorous online marketing in the face of her family losing "everything" in the recession—stay oriented toward optimizing their families by tapping into the myriad and mundane affordances of digital media and becoming mamapreneurial.

Chapter 3 explores how affective circuits of precarized family happiness are intimately bound up with the communicative circuits of digital culture. Here we excavate the digital mundane as a potent contact zone quivering with an intense power to mobilize, route, better, and buttress mothers' lives. Put differently, this chapter is about how mothers come to sustain themselves through digital entanglements; as we show, it is encounters between digital flows and ordinary affects that engender the affective resilience required to mother through precarity. Here we elaborate three primary forms of digital entanglement that at once make possible and complicate mothers' lives: charge, commune, and code and recode. As we show, the mamasphere figures as a crucial affective infrastructure for mothers, making their lives feel livable and brimming with happy potential. However, it also keeps mothers "dog-paddling around" for happiness, even as its horizons continue to recede.[56]

The final chapter is about the modes of collectivity that animate mothering through precarity. More specifically, it is about the ways in which mothers come together to take on the work of privatizing happiness. Indeed, one of the most important ways that mothers weather precarity is through helping each other and sharing their loads. We theorize these interdependencies as *individualized solidarities*, as the aim of collectivity is the stabilization and valorization of individual nuclear families. Mothers feel and act in solidarity with each other, providing significant material and affective support in hopes of keeping one another on the path to privatized happiness. We dig deep into two mothering communities: MOPS (a grassroots, international Christian network devoted to mentoring mothers) and Momastery (an online mothering community that coheres around the microcelebrity of blogger Glennon Doyle Melton). As we show, these communities and the individualized solidarities they engender construct *resiliency nets*, catching mothers as other social safety nets around them fray. Providing aid that ranges from material supports—delivering meals in trying times, raising funds for families in crisis—to affective punches that incite mothers to stay invested in and optimistic about their nuclear families, these nets are organized for resilience.

These chapters are hard, heavy, and seemingly not very hopeful, so, in the conclusion, we reflect on why we wrote such an "unhappy" book. It is important to know that throughout our writing we wrestled with what to do with whatever you want to name the undeniable pull that mothers feel for their families, especially their children. This is perhaps the reproductive power that Adrienne Rich identified at the core of the *experience* of motherhood, that power that she argued must always be contained and controlled by the patriarchal *institution* of motherhood.[57] Ultimately, we decided to leave that maternal power unquestioned as simply that unshakable affective force that emerges from the precariousness and potentiality of motherhood itself and that compels mothers through their overloaded everydays by infusing them with intense forms of joy and pleasure. We wanted our book to show how this indisputable force is nonetheless historical and subject to assemblages of power of all sorts (not simply patriarchy): it gets channeled, worked on, and exploited in myriad ways and directions.

Put differently, we wanted the experience of reading *Mothering through Precarity* to throw into relief the contingencies and compositionality of contemporary motherhood, so that readers might clearly see, and feel, the loads of privatized family happiness and thereby find new openings for a world of socialized happiness. *Mothering through Precarity* is thus what the Institute for Precarious Consciousness calls "a new style of precarity-focused consciousness raising."[58] Through the voicing of mothers' personal pain and anxiety, we work to articulate the systemic and shared nature of what is felt to be a highly individualized and privatized gender experience. "The goal is produce the *click*—the moment at which the structural source of problems suddenly makes sense in relation to experiences."[59]

1 · MOTHER LOADS

Why "Good" Mothers Are Anxious

SHANA

"You'll hear me call myself a 'supermom,'" thirty-three-year-old Shana, a mother to two kids, ages five and two, told us. Shana is a self-proclaimed stay-at-home mom who works three part-time jobs in the interstices of her husband's career. Her approach to mothering is passionate yet grave: she regards her role as one of critical importance to her children, who need her to behave optimally so that they can feel secure and reach their true potential. Accordingly, Shana spends as much time with her children as possible, playing with them, teaching them, following their desires and imaginations, and always working to let them know they are loved for who they are. When spending time with other families, Shana gets frustrated if mothers show more interest in talking among themselves than in tending to their children: "My kid could fall out of a tree. They could be stealing toys out of another kid's hands. . . . I just can't sit back. I don't want anything to happen to them. I don't want them to feel like I just dumped them off. Yes, they need to play with other kids, but like . . . I should also be running around and playing with [them]. That's how I feel." She deliberately avoids frequent Facebook and e-mail checks by logging out of Facebook on her phone. "I really have to want to get in there to see something," she explained. "It's not dinging at me. I go to my phone when I need it or when I have the time, so that this way I can be with the kids." Shana readily admitted that this highly attentive approach to mothering was hard on her emotionally. Recalling her son's relentless desire to repeat a task until he perfects it, Shana reflected, "So [someone asks,] 'What did you do all day?' And you're like, 'Look, Jonah wanted to paint the same pictures for eight hours. That is what we did because that's what toddlers need to do.' But you want to stab your eye out, because as an adult you need more."

Shana is driven to be "the best mom," describing how "moving along in life, I'm realizing I'm type A. So not only am I going to be a mom, I'm going to be the best mom. . . . Of course I'm going to make my own baby food! I'm going to breast-feed; I'm going to pump. I'm going to . . . because that's the best thing to do. That's what good moms do." Shana turns to many sources for ideas about how to be the best mom. For a while, she subscribed to *Martha Stewart Living* and *Parenting*, scouring them for party ideas, recipes, and kids' activities that she planned to organize in seasonal binders. She soon abandoned this plan, realizing, "I spent all this time making this binder instead of playing with my kids." Instead, Shana now turns to Google for ideas as "a creative outlet" and prefers to follow her children's lead, abandoning prescribed plans in favor of supporting the kids' energies and desires.

In order to be "the best mom," Shana relegates her paid work—a financial necessity—to weekends, driving nearly an hour each way to take a shift at an outpatient treatment center outside of Ryeland. The situation is overwhelming: "I don't have weekends, like [other] people have weekends to catch up. That's when I work. All week I've got the kids by myself, and I'm running, running, running. On weekends, it does feel like a little bit of a break. I'm driving [there] without the kids; I'm driving back without the kids. But I'm exhausted. Exhausted."

In so many ways, and more than any other mother we encountered, Shana embodies the ideologies of intensive mothering: she embraces her role as the central caregiver to her children and orients her life around their needs despite her own professional aspirations.[1] However, Shana's intensive approach registers something more than ideology. It also speaks to the ever-heightening demands placed on mothers by the advancement of neoliberalism. As Ana Villalobos's ethnographic work makes clear, intensive mothering is a response to broader political-economic forces and the destabilizations they bring to everyday family life.[2] "Supermom" Shana is living out the quietly devastating consequences of neoliberalism as she takes on more and more for her family. Throwing herself wholeheartedly into the weighty work of raising healthy, happy children, Shana strives to be the best mom in an insecure world where the family's survival is felt to depend on her efforts.[3] For her, intensive mothering is not simply a cultural ideal but a gender orientation, where every second, decision, and affect matters. Put another way, it is a "structure of feeling": a sensibility of what is necessary and possible to be and to do as a mother at this time.[4]

This chapter accounts for the historicity and government of mothers' affective lives by situating Shana's and other women's narratives of family life and caring labor within shifting discourses of "good" mothering. Underscoring the broader social and political-economic contexts that impinge on and animate these discourses, we provide a sort of affective "history of the present" by tracing how mothers' lives come to be lived within a range of intensities connected to the ongoing precarization and privatization of family happiness. From the unrelenting demands of "mother love" to the pulsating overflows of the mamasphere, we pull apart the discrete affective loads that give form to mothers' lives. Layered together, these intensities constitute mothers' sensibilities of "good" mothering, inciting them to assume more and more responsibility for their families.

More specifically, we explore how mothers' lives get affectively loaded up by family autonomy and the government of mothers. Neoliberalism entails an ongoing intensification of mothers' lives; to maintain a self-determined, autonomous family in an insecure world, new knowledges and risks must be incorporated into everyday family scenes and managed via mothers and their efforts at privatizing happiness. Mothering becomes ever more rife with anxiety and impossibility, as social responsibility for family life comes to rest ever more squarely on mothers. Indeed, privatizing happiness entails a double movement composed of both the widening of what it takes to be a "good" mom and the condensation of responsibility onto mothers and their women's work. In so many ways, the churning communication of the mamasphere piles on and multiplies mothers' loads, exacerbating the intensities and volatilities of mothering through precarity. Women are thus primed for increasingly unsettled affective lives, as what is at stake is not only the health and well-being of one's own children but also the project and survival of family itself.

THE AUTONOMY LOAD

While Shana's husband, Max, was reticent to have children in a "crazy . . . effed-up" world, Shana believed that, as "intelligent and kind" people, they *should* have children because they could "raise [them] right, to actually contribute to society and make it better." Though she throws all of her energy into being "the best mom," she nevertheless feels woefully undervalued. Through tears, she told Emily that "if we actually valued motherhood," we would have "world peace." She elaborated,

> We wouldn't have as many problem kids. . . . I think schools would be better. We would be more involved. . . . I think communities would be safer. Because you'd have people home at all times. Someone to watch kids, but also your neighborhood. You know? The investment in the greater whatever. . . . You'd have healthier kids, too. You have moms that have to work because it's a single-parent [household] . . . or [because of] lost jobs, and so they're just working little odd jobs. So there's no one home with the kids. You're not going to send your kid out to play if you don't feel like they're going to be safe. Say you're living in the projects or a scary neighborhood, [or] even if you're in a great neighborhood, you don't want them running out on the street. No. [The kids] have to stay home until [their parents] get home! What kind of meals are they getting? Mom has to work until whatever time, and there's nobody there to make meals for them. It's quick and easy. You plop them in front of the TV, convenience food. You've got fat, unhealthy kids. You've got a parent that is home all the time that can do that sort of stuff. You've got a parent that's involved in the school. They know what questions to ask. . . . You know that people are supporting your teachers, so your teachers feel better. . . . I just think it would be better on a personal, like nuclear family [level].

While Shana attributes her desire to be a supermom to her "type A" personality, she also believes deeply in the power of individual, independent families—mothers in particular—who "raise their children right" to change the world for the better.

Of course, we might point to pervasive gender ideologies like the "new momism" to make sense of Shana's weighty view of mothering. As Susan Douglas and Meredith Michaels argue, the new momism is "a highly romanticized and yet demanding view of motherhood in which the standards for success are impossible to meet."[5] It asserts that "to be a remotely decent mother, a woman has to devote her entire physical, psychological, emotional, and intellectual being, 24/7, to her children."[6] While these omnipresent cultural discourses undoubtedly weigh heavily on mothers, the women we spoke to were also critical of such entrenched ideologies. For example, as she described how our culture should better value mothers, Shana added, "What we see is an ideal, the mom that can do it all. She can work, she can do whatever. But it's not valuing motherhood. It's making people perfect, just like that model on the cover of *Cosmo* is airbrushed to be perfect." While Shana rejects discourses of good mothering as perfect mothering, she nonetheless understands her role as a mother in demanding terms: the world is on her shoulders, for her contribution to the collective future rests on her willingness to focus on building a family life organized to produce smart, healthy, engaged, and happy kids. For Shana, strong, individual families held together by child-focused mothers will make the world a better place.[7]

Shana's loaded-up imagination of good mothering derives most fundamentally from family autonomy: an entrenched rationality of liberal governance that provides a highly gendered *grammar* for imagining family life. Family autonomy posits social order and the moral life of the nation as resting on the private, domestic sphere that is governed and tended to by individual mothers. As Wendy Brown argues, liberal rule premised itself on a tripartite social order, in which the state, the economy and civil society, and the family are posited as distinct and autonomous realms. Gender inequalities take shape within this social organization and the gender and sexual division it materializes.[8] Specifically, liberal social orders constitute the imagined "separate sphere" of the family—personal, private life where care is given and received and emotional bonds of love and obligation are forged—as the "natural" domain of women. This sphere ostensibly stands in sharp contrast to the economy, where male subjects ideally exercise individual freedom through competition and participation in the market.

Unlike the allegedly amoral state, whose function is primarily to ensure formal freedoms, the nuclear family is held out as "an anchor for man in civil society, tethering what is otherwise in a kind of perpetual agitation, and civilizing and temporizing an otherwise ruthless social ethos. . . . the seat of moral restraint in an immoral world."[9] "Women's work" thus was axiomatic in early liberal political ontology: tempering laissez-faire freedoms with the burdens of family love, it is understood as the condition of possibility for a free, open, and good society. Furthermore, in this liberal imaginary, maternal subjectivity is premised on family autonomy, which, in contrast to the ideal of individual autonomy imagined to ground democracy and the market, requires the caring work of mothers in the separate sphere of home. Rather than being governed by individual rights, then, the family is regarded within liberal political discourse as "a domain of *collectivity*," "governed by needs and affective ties."[10]

Family autonomy engenders affective infrastructures for inhabiting family life, producing highly naturalized gender scripts that give form, sense, and significance to domestic scenes and labors. Thus, as we see with Shana, mothers may experience the systemic gender subordination and exploitation at the heart of family autonomy less as domination and more as a weighty and vital practice of citizenship.[11] Shana told us that a culture that valued mothers would inspire "the other parent [to] step it up. Like, 'I have to work harder. . . . I have to make sure I earn money so that my wife can stay home. I have to do more around the house. . . . This is how I can help her out, to support her.'" Family autonomy thus shapes Shana's script for a happy family, a good life, and a strong nation. Ideally, men work harder and harder to earn for the family and support women in their roles as domestic governors. For Shana, valuing motherhood means supporting her in her care work and thereby creating a better world for her children as well as other families.

It is important to see that these affective infrastructures nurture sensibilities of gender belonging and citizenship that are deeply racialized and classed. Indeed, family autonomy is rooted in not only systemic gender and sexual oppression but also the accumulation of white wealth and has resonance for today's mothers who imagine themselves to be good mothers so long as they are following the scripts of family autonomy.[12] For example, in contrast to black and poor families, who are often presumed to require more state intervention and social control, Shana sees herself as an autonomous gender citizen, capable of individual and family autonomy.[13] The white, middle-class precepts and privileges of family autonomy echo throughout her description of world peace built on mothers' labors. If she and her husband, for example, didn't take on the project of raising responsible citizens, "what's left but all the wackos that just suck from the system? . . . And those are the people who are going to run the world; it's not going to get better." According to Shana, single mothers and mothers who are underemployed, "working little odd jobs" and living "in the projects," cannot fulfill the promises of family autonomy—it is primarily their kids who are overmedicated, overweight, and living on television and fast food. Indeed, threats loom "even if you're in a great neighborhood," but, to Shana's mind, "good moms" fend off these threats by focusing all of their energies on their children.

Family autonomy is a vital institution of the liberal capitalist state, one that was and remains structurally necessary to broader programs of freedom and rule and the economic and social hierarchies of class, gender, and race that enable and sustain them. Within the grammars of family autonomy, so much is presumed to ride on mothers, nothing less than the independence, security, health, and wealth of children and the nation. Mothers are to be self-reliant agents of homemaking and childrearing and social producers of autonomous individual beings and future citizens. Good mothering thus rests on an impossible social premise. After all, mothers, as individuals, cannot be responsible for the dreams and desires, the fortunes and fates, of their children, much less those of the nation, yet, thanks to family autonomy and its government of mothers, women like Shana readily embrace the autonomy load in the interest of gender citizenship and the deep love they harbor for their children.

THE GOVERNMENT LOAD

Calley, a thirty-four-year-old mother to two-year-old Simon, is a Christian stay-at-home mom who describes herself as "free spirited." She left a career in a creative field to stay home with her son, a decision that she always anticipated making and does not seem to regret. A member of the Hugo Mothers of Preschoolers (MOPS) group that Emily joined, Calley was always reserved during group meetings, sitting quietly in the small group while the other mothers chatted about family challenges. She frequently came late and left early, leaning on her in-laws to babysit Simon during MOPS meetings rather than placing him in the large-group childcare available for MOPS members. As became clear in our interview, mothering is complicated and foreign for Calley; when Emily asked, "Is there anything I missed?," Calley responded, "Not for me because anything else I would get into would probably just be more emotional. I don't really wanna get into anything that deep."

However, despite not wanting to "get into anything that deep," Calley's interview was a roller coaster of affects and contradictions. She readily described the everyday joys of mothering: "I really love my time with Simon. It doesn't matter what we're doing. I really enjoy just being with him and spending that time with him. It doesn't matter if we're reading a book or going for a walk or coloring. I enjoy all those things with him." But as the interview went on, things got more fraught. Calley's life with Simon also feels perilous and hard: he is frequently darting into the busy road adjacent to their house, grabbing at the knobs on the stove, and bolting away from her at parking lots and in stores. Calley rarely feels she is doing the right thing, frets intensely when he gets sick (even with minor illnesses), and looks constantly to others for insight into parenting correctly. Indeed, Calley spent much of our interview discussing multiple, and sometimes contradictory, strategies for making life with Simon easier: allowing him to "run in a field" to burn off energy, fulfilling more of his multiple daily requests, recognizing his individual personality and needs, and spending more time teaching him proper behavior. For example, at the time of our interview, Calley was trying to get Simon to stop watching *Baby Einstein* before and during mealtimes by including him in meal preparation.

Clearly, Calley's orientation toward motherhood is quite uneasy. She loves Simon intensely, but she also worries constantly, looks ever outward for advice on how to do things better, and harbors rage about the level of work and attention Simon requires. Calley was just one of the mothers we spoke to who was struggling to inhabit the affective infrastructures of family autonomy. More specifically, though, she was wrestling with the paradoxes and impossibilities of family government.

Government, according to Michel Foucault, is the primary modality of power within liberal regimes; it works on and through the freedoms—the affects and capacities—of individuals, guiding subjectivity "at a distance."[14] Rather than dominating or directly oppressing, government works as an enfolding of authority: "a folding of exterior relations of authority to sculpt a domain that can act on and of itself but which, at the same time, is simply the inside marked out by that folding."[15] In other words, government enables and activates, demarcating, through one's own incorporation of authority, the space and shape of freedom.

More to the point, mothers' capacities for family autonomy are guided by two intersecting modes of family and gender government. First is the government of children, whereby individual mothers guide their children's conduct and behaviors, as well as their dispositions and attitudes toward the social world. Through the adoption of specific goals and the implementation of practical techniques to achieve these goals, mothers put parenting philosophies to work, using them to guide their caring labors and maternal freedoms. However, the "good" government of children rests on a second form of government: the government of mothers, whose own freedoms as governors of children and the home must also be sculpted through an enfolding of "exterior relations of authority."

Consequently, women's work comes to encompass two unrelenting and entwined modes of affective labor. On the one hand, there is the caring work associated with proper government of children: establishing and maintaining family rules and rituals, providing cognitive development activities, promoting good health, developing an effective approach to discipline, showing adequate love and attention, and attending to mundane housekeeping tasks like laundry, cooking, and cleaning. On the other hand, there is the rigorous self-work attendant to the government of mothers: ongoing self-reflexivity and affective regulation of one's own life as a mother. After all, as we see with Calley, good mothers must be happy mothers regardless of their daily frustrations and deep fears.

While much has been written about maternal anxiety, we want to suggest that mothers' intense affective lives refract the broader paradoxes of family autonomy and, especially, the government of mothers.[16] According to the rationality of family autonomy, families must be self-reliant and individualized but also carefully guided and governed. As Nikolas Rose makes clear, nuclear families are to be self-producing and self-sustaining, beyond the reach of direct rule and yet, at the same time, readily "permeable to moralization and normalization from outside."[17] The government of mothers reconciles this paradox by opening up the private sphere of the home for external shaping and direction. Through the government of mothers, family could become "permeable" from a distance while still maintaining autonomy; experts might shape the scripts of "proper" family government, but mothers' individualized gender freedoms still constitute the private sphere of family sovereignty.

Thus, while the government of mothers neatly solves a structural paradox for liberal rule, it engenders maternal subjectivity as a necessarily fraught and contradictory terrain. Mothers are suspended between diverging sensibilities: the joyful yet grave responsibility of raising children and an inevitable feeling of lack and inadequacy. They are regarded as self-responsible agents of home and family life *and also* as potentially deficient gender subjects in need of perpetual government.[18] As Rose explains, "parental conduct, motherhood, and child rearing can thus be regulated through family autonomy, through wishes and aspirations, and through the activation of individual guilt, personal anxiety, and private disappointment. And the almost inevitable misalignment between expectation and realization, fantasy and actuality, fuels the search for help and guidance in the difficult task of producing normalcy, and powers the constant familial demand for the assistance of expertise."[19] In other words, the government of mothers proceeds through the incitement of maternal anxiety as the foreordained outcome of "inevitable misalignments" between the individualization and the normalization of the family. Calley lives caught up in the affective circuits of anxiety engendered by the government of mothers. For her, motherhood is often experienced as a series of permanent misalignments, which produce endless affective loops "inside" (of worry, fear, anger, and guilt) that in turn incite a constant need to import help from "outside."

Not surprisingly, when we asked Calley where she turns for parenting advice, she began to cry, betraying a profound trauma associated with the government of mothers. "You name it," she said. "For sleep [I've read] every book that's out there. . . . I own most of them. I've read them cover to cover." Bemoaning the advice of popular parenting guides like *On Becoming Babywise*, which advises mothers to "keep your infant on a very strict eating and sleeping schedule," Calley said, "[That book] was the biggest detriment to my parenting. . . . I never got sleep. It was horrible. Talk about starting off wrong. I mean, if you want to do it the stressful way, just ask me, because I've done it. . . . I didn't cry a lot. I was actually angry. I spent more time angry than crying. . . . [T]hat's the part that we needed to get away from is just not being angry. And I think we've come a long way."[20] She described putting Simon to sleep by bouncing him on an exercise ball for forty-five minutes every night, only to have him wake up as soon as she placed him in the crib: "That's where the anger came . . . in the amount of energy I put into it and then him waking up. . . . I was doing stuff I didn't need to do. I was following what they tell you to do, and that's why I would just throw it all out now." Indeed, much of Calley's work as a mother has been about "just not being angry." And while she declared that with a second baby, "I would just follow what the baby did and needed because [following the advice in *On Becoming Babywise*] added so much structure and stress rather than just enjoying the rhythm that they provide," she also described continuing to try to control Simon, maintaining strict discipline and learning how to do so from other moms: "I don't think that I'm teaching him as much as I need to be just about everyday stuff. I'll feel like he's not safe, and it's because we never taught him how to be safe. [I'm] just realizing that I don't invest as much as I need to in the stuff that's important, and I need to see other moms doing that, really, because it doesn't come to me naturally." For Calley, caring for Simon is far from simple. She loves her son, but family government and the work it takes to be a "good mom," a happy mom, also quietly shatter her.

Calley is not alone. One of the most consistent features of our interviews was mothers' overall reticence when it came to the topic of good mothering. While most had trouble recalling instances when they felt like good moms, many seemed eager to discuss instances of perceived failure. Like Calley, they were teeming with feelings of inadequacy. Even Shana, despite her self-assuredness in her capacities to be the "best mom," was driven by a deep anxiety that all of the love she gives her children won't be enough to ensure them a future of personal fulfillment and happiness. While working out or at work, Shana frets about "what I'm not doing" and worries that any uncontrolled expressions of anger or agitation toward her kids might dampen their unique spirits and potential. In this sense, we might say that the government of mothers engenders structures of feeling rife with tension and contradiction, which turn mothers' everyday family scenes into affective minefields. Through the government of mothers, family autonomy overloads mothers' lives with anxious responsibility, inciting them to keep working, reflecting, and realigning to meet its impossible demands. It is no wonder so many mothers struggle to land somewhere that feels "good."

THE MOTHER-LOVE LOAD

While all of the mothers we encountered were living out the consequences of family autonomy and its government of mothers, Shana and Calley especially were bearing the load of mother love, a privatized conception of mothering in which children's potentialities are imagined to rest on the minutiae of mothers' caring labor and their capacities for ongoing affective attunement to the needs of their children. Shana crystallized the mother-love load when she told us, "I'm hoping . . . that I'm letting them be who they wanna be. I'm hoping that I'm not guiding . . . forcing . . . them in any direction. I'm hoping that I'm gonna read off their cues." Admitting she still hadn't quite figured out her youngest daughter, Shana told us about being home with her oldest son, Jonah:

> Jonah was very much a thinker. He could do the same thing for six hours straight, where I wanted to stab my eye out, where he was painting. . . . He would paint the same color order: red, blue, orange, yellow, green, purple . . . and then he would do it again. Or the same six things . . . I want an apple and then an orange. And then he'd want a fish, and he had to paint them in the same order, or have me paint them, and tell me how to paint them. And he could do that all day.

Accordingly, Shana has to fight through boredom and frustration to adapt to her son's needs. She described one particularly stressful trip to Walmart to purchase a birthday present for Jonah's classmate. This brief trip required multiple moments of affective management: forewarning her children that she would not be purchasing toys for them, negotiating Jonah's toy-aisle tantrum when this rule was enforced, leaving their full cart in the store when the baby started crying as well, managing her own rising rage, strapping her children into the car, and then putting her head in her hands to breathe and calm down. Once she was calm, she proceeded to talk Jonah through her anger, working to teach him about both managing emotions and being grateful. She told him, "I will always love you. I will always love you. Even when I get frustrated. I told you we weren't getting toys, and you kept begging for toys. . . . What's frustrating for mommy is that you've forgotten all of the things that I've already done for you today. Instead of thinking that you are grateful for everything that you have and that you're happy." She then proceeded to teach him about all of the children, "particularly in our area, who don't have enough money for food." In the end Shana left Walmart without the needed gift, and she had to leave early for work the next day to make the purchase.

Shana captures the intensity of her mother-love frustrations in her comments about the hardest part of mothering:

I lose it on my kids. We all lose it on our children. Where Jonah's personality is sometimes so, just, high-strung, and you know if he was an adult you'd just want to slap him? Like, "Get a hold of yourself, kid!" And you can't say that. So, in the stressful times . . . [i]t's hard to take your breath and think, "Where is he? What is causing this?" And to talk in that calm voice, even if it means repeating a statement ten times. Um. That's hard. Because I'm realizing that how I respond in his moments of anxiety is what he's going to take on later as an adult and how he handles himself. So I just want to chill some things out.

Here we can see how Shana's fury lies in the difficulty she experiences walking the line between normalization—"Get a hold of yourself, kid!"—and individualization—"Where is he? What is causing this?" To walk this line, Shana must stay fully tuned to both her children and herself, navigating her own feelings in careful response to theirs.

Situated historically, Shana's sensibilities of mother love can be traced back to the rise of antimaternalism, which destabilized the ground on which mothers pursue family autonomy and ratcheted up the social impossibilities associated with the government of mothers. As Rebecca Plant suggests, while early liberalism was premised on a maternalist sensibility—"an outlook that defined motherhood as both a familial and civic act; enabled white, middle-class women to exert a morally charged influence within the public and private realms; and allowed mothers to claim the largest share of their children's gratitude and affection"—the rise of antimaternalism in the late nineteenth and early twentieth centuries sought to undercut that ideal, positing that mothers' roles should be construed more narrowly, demarcated by a highly feminized familial space.[21] Premised on a pathologization of women's sexuality, these new discourses focused on the intense government of mothers' dispositions and gave rise to a culture of "mommy blaming" where the outcomes of children were imagined to hinge on mothers' privatized affects and labors.[22]

In particular, early antimaternalist discourses were rooted in scientific motherhood, an approach that emphasized medical expertise and sought to replace situated maternal knowledge rooted in experience with domestic science rooted in behavioral psychology.[23] Mothers were thus encouraged to read parenting manuals and to regularly consult established *male* medical experts. Scientific motherhood aimed to professionalize and standardize mothers' practices of care, and, in doing so, it introduced new forms of patriarchal control into mothers' lives, while further problematizing the already hard stuff of raising children with its expansive field of "expert" advice.[24]

Starting in the 1920s, however, scientific motherhood began to give way to a new orientation defined by permissiveness. Barbara Ehrenreich and Deirdre English characterize this shift: "The behaviorists had seen the child as a piece of raw material to be hammered into shape. Its natural impulses—to eat when and what it liked, to play, etc.—had to be suppressed as firmly as bed-wetting and thumb-sucking. On the contrary, the permissivist proclaimed that the child's spontaneous impulses were good and sensible and that the child, instead of being a tabula rasa, actually *knew*, in some sense, what was right for itself."[25] Here what was required of mothers was not merely the consumption and implementation of scientific expertise but a greater sense of their children's unique desires, which was to be reconciled with established expert knowledge. To do this, good mothers needed to develop their so-called mommy instincts. Benjamin Spock was the most famous purveyor of the permissiveness approach, and while on the surface it seemed to empower mothers to follow their inner instincts, in reality it only heightened the anxieties and impossibilities attendant to nuclear mothering. As Plant notes, discourses of permissiveness not only bound mothers more tightly to their maternal responsibilities but also greatly privatized mothers' social roles by asking them "to adopt a more self-conscious and wary view of their maternal emotions."[26] Or, as Ehrenreich and English put it, "child raising comes unhinged from any external goal—an end in itself which will invite women to enter deeper and deeper into a shadow world of feelings and suspected feelings, guilt, self-analysis, and every nuance of ambivalence."[27]

Ultimately, this mommy instinct was imagined to represent a new kind of mother love based on an intensive mother-child bond that was to be formed in the early years of a child's life. Thanks largely to the work of English child psychiatrist John Bowlby, psychological discourses became increasingly preoccupied with mother love vis-à-vis ordinary maternal affects and "the minutiae of mothering."[28] Here the mundane, affective experiences of children at the hands of their mothers are what supposedly ensure a child's health and happiness. As a result, maternal subjectivity became increasingly fraught as a growing array of experts advised mothers on how to develop proper practices of mother love. As Rose explains, child maladjustment became linked to "love gone wrong," as allegedly "the forces of love could be used to promote subjectivity in children: increasing confidence, helpfulness, dependability, and thoroughness at the same time as averting fear, cruelty, stubbornness, and jealously."[29] Producing healthy, secure adults thus came to require more than vigilance and monitoring; it demanded an intensely hermeneutic mode of parenting, one that was about not only constant attention but the *right* kind of attention: a confident sensitivity capable of deciphering and fulfilling a child's unique needs.[30]

Today the mamasphere is peppered with scripts for staying in tune with children through mother-love attachments. For example, Rachel Marie Martin, author of the blog *Finding Joy*, offers this "Mom Truth": "Get down on [your children's] level. Look them in the eye when they talk to you. Learn to love what they love. It's easy in this fast pace tweet it Instagram it Facebook it racing world to lose the art of looking and communicating with those we love directly. Intentionally cultivate moments in your life where the social noise is quiet so that you and your kids can have space within the busy."[31] "The art of looking" and "space within the busy" are strategies by which mothers can come to know their children more fully and connect intimately in order to fulfill their deepest needs. In "A Letter to My Nursing Toddler" on the website *Mothering*, Megan Leary writes:

> You were tired. It had been a long morning in the car and then visiting with strangers. You rubbed your eye with one hand and said, "Nurse?"
>
> At home I would have scooped you in my arms and cuddled you close while you nursed yourself to sleep. Then I would lay you in bed and give you a kiss. But this time I reacted differently. You saw me look sideways at the room of strangers who have never been a part of your life and meant nothing to you. You saw me shift awkwardly in my seat. You saw me blush. You were confused. I hurt your feelings and you didn't understand why. I made you feel like I was embarrassed by you. I was. You took a step back. You looked around the way I had, wondering what made me nervous.
>
> I looked at your confused face and made a decision. I picked you up, pulled up my shirt, and nursed you. I kept my eyes on you because I didn't dare look at the room. I put a soft smile on my face so that you would know everything was okay. In that moment I made an unspoken promise to you to never make you feel ashamed for asking to nurse again.

Here, the mother's slightest reaction—shifting awkwardly in her seat—relays a whole series of troubling messages to the toddler, who now feels

FIGURE 1.1. The mamasphere is littered with scripts for properly practicing mother love. *Mothering*'s "A Letter to My Nursing Toddler" suggests that mothers must engage in constant and minute affective attunements to stay appropriately attached to their children.

ashamed, confused, and perhaps rejected by the mother. These affective attunements are the minutiae of mothering—the split-second decisions of mother love that come to weigh heavily when deemed responsible for children's normal development and future happiness.

THE EMPOWERMENT LOAD

For stay-at-home mom Kim, the key to finding peace in her role as a mother has been developing her own private mothering ethos and learning to navigate constant streams of advice. Kim is now content in her life at home with three little ones, ten-year-old Nate, four-year-old Timmy, and two-year-old Anna. Staying at home with them is, as she puts it, "a dream come true." Before Nate was born, Kim thought she "was going to be supermom. I was gonna do it all," but three months into her life as a working mother, Kim had "a nervous breakdown" and was diagnosed with postpartum depression. She quickly decreased her hours at her job, and by the time she was pregnant with Anna, Kim had vowed to do whatever it took to quit paid work altogether. "My one regret in life was that I had continued to work with the kids," she explained. "I was really tired of it being my one regret, and I wanted to change it, and I absolutely love being at home. I have absolutely no regrets whatsoever."

Unlike Calley, Kim is self-assured in her role as a mother, calling herself a "seasoned mom" and easily shrugging off the daily ups and downs of managing three children. But things at home weren't always so smooth, as Kim struggled for two years to get pregnant before turning to fertility treatments. As an infant, Nate was "sick all of the time," vomiting and crying constantly. She recalled, "People kept saying to me, 'All babies spit up.' And I was like, 'No, there's something wrong with this child,' and no one would believe me!" Her beliefs were confirmed only when Nate spit up in front of the pediatrician and the doctor diagnosed him with food allergies and reflux. She described how alone and frustrated she felt those days:

> I remember, he would just scream and cry and scream and cry, and I remember thinking to myself as I was standing over his bed with him screaming and crying because I couldn't take it anymore in my ear, like, why did I want this so bad? Why did I try so hard? For this? This

is crazy! And then the guilt of feeling that way! Because you love this little boy so much, but at the same time you're just at your wits' end and need help so badly. And, um, all of the "You should do this" and "This is how you do it" and "Oh, you need to have that baby put itself to sleep" and "You need to do this" and "You need to do that," instead of listening to what you know works best for you, which is what I do now as a mom, and it works out better for me!

For Kim, contentment with mothering comes only when she aligns outside advice with her inner voice: "I don't listen to what people tell me to do, unless it makes sense to me and it's in my heart what I know would work for me, which is why Anna does not put herself to sleep, because I like to snuggle my babies, and I will rock her until she falls asleep and I will put her in bed, and I love that time, and I know that it's so fleeting, it's gone so fast, and then they're so independent." "Listening to what . . . works best" for her empowers Kim to trust herself, capitalize on her lived knowledges, and be the mother she wants to be.

While the mother-love load continues to weigh heavily on mothers, it is important to see that the contemporary government of mothers does not necessarily pathologize women, inviting them "deeper and deeper into a shadow world of feelings and suspected feelings, guilt, [and] self-analysis" that Calley struggles to shake.[32] Indeed, because it is now up to individual mothers to sort through conflicting advice and, ultimately, to chart their own course to family autonomy, mothers like Kim are increasingly "empowered" to develop their own regimes of self-government and family government. They must learn, in other words, to follow what Shana calls her "mom gut":

> I didn't question being a mom; I knew I was going to be OK. I mean, I was worried about, I'd never breast-fed before, so I read the La Leche book cover to cover. And I knew when there were going to be growth spurts and this baby was going to nurse more, and I knew what page it was on and I flagged it, so that when he was eating like a champ, I went back so I could go, "He's following the book here." Always follow the book. I didn't read up [on] how to parent a child. . . . I don't want to say that I didn't get caught up in what the right way was, but there were so many conflicting, like, how to raise your child things. I just kind of wanted to trust my mom gut, you know?

Shana struggled mightily with baby Jonah, who was not a good sleeper, but while she yearned for strategies to help him sleep better, outside advice also frustrated her. "Everyone was trying to tell me, 'This is what you should do!'" She turned to parenting advice books. Some advised letting the baby cry it out, which made Shana "sick to my stomach. I'm like, this, this, I can't do this." Others advised babywearing and cosleeping: "Like, OK, attachment parenting? Some of this stuff sounds a little bit weirdo. I can't commit to all of it." Ultimately, unable to find advice adequate to her situation, Shana explained, "I went my own route. But when I had questions or wanted support, I would go and just kind of read a couple of different points of view and maybe pull tidbit[s] from everywhere but mush it together and make it Shana again with what went with my gut."

While mommy instincts are imagined to be embodied and natural to women, what Shana calls "mom gut" is different and has to do with an affective capacity for self-empowerment.[33] These capacities are animated by ethopolitical discourses that are, unlike earlier antimaternalist advice, premised on empowering moms rather than blaming them.[34] While antimaternalist discourse stressed mothers' need for guidance, rather than their resourcefulness (while still placing responsibility on mothers' affective labors), ethopolitical discourses of empowerment flip the script and elevate the personal sensibilities of mothers.[35] As both Kim and Shana suggest, self-empowerment requires knowing oneself and being confident to take the lead in family government, not only seeking out advice and regulating affects but also actively cultivating a highly individualized approach to family life through heightened capacities for self-reflexivity.

The rise of ethopolitical mothering thus goes hand in hand with the development of neoliberalism, in which "the sentiments, moral nature, or guiding beliefs of persons, groups, or institutions" become the primary "medium" of government.[36] The dismantling of public infrastructures of social support and security requires that citizens accept personal responsibility for their fates and prospects. Neoliberalism therefore touts a social world held together by self-actualizing citizens (as opposed to a social welfare state). For mothers, this means that family autonomy is to be guaranteed by their own "active practices of self-management and identity construction."[37] Of course, good mothers have long been responsible for family autonomy, but now they must actively produce their own regimes of family government by honing their "mom gut" and disembedding themselves from reliance on public authorities and resources through heightened self-reflexivity and gender empowerment.

Ethopolitical discourses liberalize maternal subjectivity: they promise mothers agency by granting them more and more autonomy over their selves and their families. In empowering mothers, they also promise to revalue motherhood and its weighty social responsibilities. Mothers are not sexually pathological beings but important gender citizens. Still, these discourses load up mothers' lives in new ways. Decisions about school, parenting, or health care become more and more consequential, as the family is imagined to hinge not only on the minutiae of mothers' affects and capacities but also on their broader lifestyle choices. Ultimately, through the ethopolitical government of mothers, women are empowered to privatize more and more happiness for their families, widening the scope of care to take on more social responsibility for their children.

For example, despite her intense frustrations with her highly attuned, responsive approach to family government, as well as her own professional ambitions to be working a high-powered job, Shana won't so much as consider putting her children in day care. She explained how she felt when watching young children from a neighborhood preschool:

> I think there's so much time in those organized settings that they have to do directional stuff, that managing stuff. And it's so cute: you see all the kids walking down the street from all the preschools, and they're all holding the rings. It's cute! They're all in a line, and they're all controlled, and you know that they're safe, but sometimes . . . they . . . I don't know . . . just the look on their face like, "This is what I'm supposed to do." Now, I don't want to say it's as far as being a machine, but it's, "Stay in line. We have to share the sidewalk now. Move over." Versus, really, like, "Do you guys see those trees? Did you see that bird? Did you see that one go by? That's called a blue jay."

Shana has determined that day-care children don't receive adequate mother love and therefore won't have the space to become "who they really are." That's her role, as a supermom, and as she told us, "If I'm going to do it, I'm going to do it 100 percent." For Shana, mothering is a challenging, empowering "test of personal capacities."[38]

Notably, part of Shana's ethopolitical load includes being self-reflexive about her life in the digital mundane. For example, Shana has to give herself permission to check Facebook while her daughter is napping. Relatively new to Ryeland, she struggles to find meaningful friendships that measure up to those in her previous locale. Facebook provides vital connections. Perusing pictures of old friends at a celebratory event "gives me a warm fuzzy, like I was participating," and friends' comments on her posts "make me feel loved." Despite finding Facebook a salve for lonely days, Shana rationalizes and restricts check-ins:

> So now the baby takes two-hour naps, and I have time to take care of that and do a little housework. And I'm like, "You know what? It's OK to go on Facebook." Like, when she's napping. So my house isn't totally clean, but that's the one time I go on Facebook and read a couple things from people. Or, at bedtime when Max is reading them a story, he hasn't been home all day. It's OK for me to check Facebook on my phone for five minutes. Otherwise, I really try to put it down so I'm not distracted by, by what? By someone's Facebook post. So are my kids cranky? . . . I've noticed that, yeah, when you're trying to get 10,000,000 things done, whether it's clean the house or check Facebook, the kids, you just have to be with them.

Despite its many affordances, the mamasphere thus becomes another load to bear.

THE MAMASPHERE LOAD

Taryn, a mother of two who worries constantly about her children's health and safety, told us how she lives "expecting the unexpected phone call from day care." "I guess my biggest worry is always just for their safety and knowing that they are developing," she explained. "You hear so many bad stories about kids just getting sick out of the blue, and, you just, I'm very thankful and grateful that I have two very healthy children. But if it could happen to them, it could happen to anyone, so, you know, I just hope that they will continue to grow." Taryn's worries about the health and development of her children do not emerge simply from atmospheric anxieties; Taryn suffered a miscarriage before her son Carter was born, "so when I got pregnant with him I just kind of found myself to be worried the entire pregnancy." What is more, during her pregnancy with her youngest daughter, Sarah, Taryn's doctor found "that something was abnormal" during chromosomal testing, and Taryn "freaked." While eventually "everything was fine," the scare, Taryn told us, "just kind of took me back. At no point do you just kind of

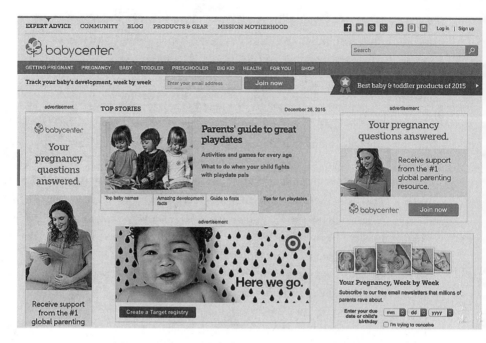

FIGURE 1.2. Johnson & Johnson's BabyCenter website, the self-proclaimed "world's partner in parenting," offers various digital tools promising to make parenting calculable and controllable for both moms and marketers.

sigh and enjoy pregnancy. To me at least, I just felt like there was always something to worry about with being pregnant."

Amid these swirling anxieties, Taryn turned to BabyCenter, a popular website for would-be, expecting, and new moms. BabyCenter offers mothers a vast assortment of digital "calculators, calendars, checklists, and worksheets [that] can help take the stress out of pregnancy and parenting." Owned by Johnson & Johnson, BabyCenter is an online hub that touts itself as "the world's partner in parenting." The site includes online message boards, advice columns, product reviews, and digital tools for tracking ovulation, scheduling vaccinations, predicting a child's height, and developing a birth plan. Other digital tools include "Is It Safe While I'm Pregnant?," "Baby Costs Calculator," "Symptom Guide for Children," and "Chinese Gender Predictor." It is crucial to see that BabyCenter's bread and butter, like that of all corporatized nodes in the mamasphere, is the commodification of the social, specifically the valorization of mothers' everyday hopes, fears, and desires for their children.

Indeed, the site ultimately aims to secure insecure mothers like Taryn as a predictable market, claiming, "No one offers deeper insights . . . into the minds of millions of moms. Learn what they're saying, thinking and buying—and the next big thing to anticipate." From "hand-pick[ed] influential voices from the BabyCenter Blog" to e-mails "timed to Mom's exact stage and with industry leading open rates," the site gives marketers tools for "connect[ing] with today's most powerful consumer" in a seemingly authentic, personal way. "No wonder our audience says we're psychic," the site brags.[39] By providing an array of tools and platforms germane to mothers' lives, BabyCenter incites their ongoing contributions and "free labor" to accumulate knowledge about its valuable user base, which can be sorted and sold on various data and ad markets.[40]

Promising to make parenting calculable and controllable for moms and marketers alike, BabyCenter sends regular e-mails to its users, detailing what they can expect in the present moment of development. As Taryn described it, "from the moment you find out you're pregnant you type in your e-mail address and it tracks your pregnancy week by week, and then it just kind of tells you how your baby is developing, and then once the baby is born once a week they send you an e-mail saying, 'Well, your baby should be doing this' or, during flu season, they'll send you an e-mail saying things like, 'If your baby has the flu, this is what could happen.'" The site also hosts online communities and message boards that provide a space to share photos, meet other moms, and find support, advice, and connection. Taryn at times found these extremely helpful, telling us that when Carter was being bitten by another child at day care, BabyCenter users assuaged her concerns. What "sounded excessive" to Taryn turned out to be "typical for kids of that age group." "It made me feel better that it wasn't sort of abnormal behavior, that type of thing."

Thus, BabyCenter has played an important role in Taryn's life as a mother, and yet she also felt troubled by its myriad affordances. While Taryn admitted to finding both the regular e-mails and the message boards useful, she grew ambivalent about them, explaining she could no longer read the weekly e-mails that kept coming "just because it's too much." She was especially annoyed by what she called the "blah blah blah" of BabyCenter's message boards. "It's just a competitive thing," she proposed. Reflecting on *Time* magazine's controversial cover story in 2012, "Are You Mom Enough?," which featured a lithe blonde mother breast-feeding her three-year-old son and debated the merits of attachment parenting, Taryn described "just being on Facebook and seeing the dialogue. Immediately, it just goes into this breast-feed or not breast-feeding thing, and someone says, 'I didn't do it.' And someone else [is] saying, 'Well, I think you should do it for the first year.' Blah. Blah. Blah. And it's just like it turns into an argument without fail, and it doesn't have to be that way."

As Taryn suggests, while the ethopolitical milieu empowers mothers to privatize more and more happiness (in Taryn's case, her pregnancies and children's health), it also politicizes mothering in new and often painful ways. As Rose argues, neoliberalism tends to generate "wars of subjectivity" that cohere around diverging lifestyles and values.[41] The so-called mommy wars emerge in this context, where citizenship is no longer underwritten by the state but rather "is multiplied and non-cumulative: it appears to inhere in and derive from active engagement with each of a number of specific zones of identity."[42] So, despite shared investments in family autonomy and nuclear family life, which have long drawn lines between good and bad mothers, good mothers are now necessarily situated in opposition to each other according to their espoused personal ethics and family lifestyles. Indeed, mothers' shared investments in family autonomy often disappear from view, as the politics of lifestyles and individualized approaches to the work of mothering become the new contested ground for gender citizenship and belonging.

Mothers negotiate these ethopolitical tensions in the digital mundane, and while they hate being pitted against each other by dominant culture, the mommy wars weigh heavily on them thanks to the churning, reflexive communication of the mamasphere and the "heated feelings" it circulates.[43] Parenting images and ideas culled from *other* moms' fraught domestic lives circulate relentlessly, engendering ever-morphing sensibilities about what "normal" and "good" might look and feel like for individual mothers. Maggie, for example, talked to us about how difficult it is to negotiate all the conflicting advice that often animates her Facebook feed, telling us, "I have a friend who is very opinionated about parenting on Facebook. And she's very opinionated, and it's always like if you did something with your kid, and she didn't agree with it, . . . 'You're not supposed to do that.' And I'm like, 'Who are you to tell me that?' . . . I just feel like you just have to do what you can, and the advice they give is always conflicting—there's always conflicting advice about everything. How to discipline, let your baby cry versus don't let your baby cry. All that stuff."

Some mothers try to counter these digital mommy wars by circulating articles critiquing these discourses, and they are rewarded with gratitude for resisting good-mothering demands. But the reflexive communication of the mamasphere is exceedingly capricious and also scolds mothers for such critiques. In her article "The Tyranny of the Bad Mother" on *Salon*, for example, Elissa Strauss writes, "Amid this struggle to reject the good mother, her naughty twin sister, the bad mother, has emerged. Born in the sanctimommy's shadows, the bad mother is everything the perfect breast-feeding, plastic-avoiding mom is not. Bad mommies don't obsess over things like screen time or nap schedules, they sometimes choose adult conversation or sex over being with their kids, and they don't feel guilty for serving rotisserie chicken and non-organic broccoli three nights a week." Bad mothers, Strauss writes, are "smug," and they "bully" stressed-out good mothers by discounting their deeply felt fears as silly. As the quest for family autonomy and "the almost inevitable misalignment between expectation and realization, fantasy and reality" sets them up for failure, mothers navigate these mounting impossibilities in the mamasphere, where passing around well-intentioned advice for other overwhelmed mothers only ends up producing more and more competing scripts for good mothering that unwittingly extend mommy-war sensibilities.[44]

Indeed, while Taryn sensed potential for different encounters online, she landed on the idea that "I guess it's just a female thing. . . . It just kind of seems like so many females pit each other against one another, and it's just so unnecessary." "It's not necessarily jealousy," she suggested, "but there's definitely something different about women than men. I just feel like it's that women can be so catty and judgmental over just everything— our weight, our appearance, our childrearing style—and men just aren't. I don't know what the root of that is. I wish I did, though." For Taryn, not only does BabyCenter intensify the politicization of motherhood and the mommy-war mentality; it also further naturalizes the broader regimes of gender exploitation that constitute users' everyday lives.

Sites like BabyCenter thus engender their own affective loads, reflecting the paradoxical affordances of digital media. Networks offer more freedom in the form of participation, information, and community, but they also produce more constriction and constraint. Platforms of participation are coded to elicit contributions that will optimize the network.[45] Though the always-on, highly corporatized interactivity of BabyCenter helps Taryn manage her mother loads, it also often feels like "too much," as it ceaselessly distributes unwanted information, communication, and affect into her work as a mother. At the same time, it shuts down potentialities for new connections and forms of living by keeping users cycling through "feed-forward loops," which intensify and multiply the very sensibilities and impossibilities that brought them online in the first place.[46]

Addie's experiences of mommy blogging also show these contradictory tendencies. Addie turned to blogging because she wanted to start "from scratch." An upper-middle-class white mother of one, Addie explained to us:

> I had two alcoholic parents. . . . My mom is amazing, but she also was sort of a wreck when I was growing up. My dad died when I was in college. . . . My parents were really fun. Like, there weren't a lot of rules. But I sort of grew up a little bit damaged as a result of my experience, and I didn't want that at all and, of course, carry a lot of that experience with me. So I sort of feel like I started from scratch a little bit in terms of developing some sort of philosophy.

Before becoming pregnant, Addie was a lifestyle blogger for a popular women's ad network. Certain that motherhood was going to be anxiety inducing for her and determined to create her own parenting scripts for her children, Addie decided to use her blog to develop "some sort of philosophy" to guide her as a new mother. Thus, blogging was an accessible and promising path to empowerment.

Mommy blogs have been heralded as a "radical act" by bloggers and feminist scholars alike, said to provide readily accessible reflection on the daily grind and banal joys of motherhood.[47] As Kara Van Cleaf argues, "blogging motherhood may feel radical because it allows for an up-to-the-minute, authentic, and less isolated take on motherhood, one that veers from the highly edited and airbrushed version found in other media, such as magazines or television."[48] Often culturally denigrated yet highly profitable for the ad networks they fuel, mommy blogs are thus written by mothers to help themselves negotiate the affective intensities of motherhood. The autobiographical form of the mommy blog enacts ethopolitical empowerment in documenting and reflecting on mothers' own experiences in conversation with other mothers. Distancing themselves from the myths and misdirections of dominant culture, mommy bloggers materialize their own privatized approaches.

Indeed, blogging provided both the content (streams of stories, advice, and information) and form (starting "from scratch") for Addie's maternal freedom and empowerment. Like Taryn, Addie turned to digital media to manage her mother loads, and, in hindsight, she seems grateful for these experiences, telling us that "looking back at some of her little videos of when Ginny was like one and two, and just seeing who she was then, and how it's not really that much different who she is now—I just love that." However, blogging also became its own sort of affective load for Addie, one she eventually gave up. She characterized blogging as "so anxiety provoking for me, I was researching all the time": "I was constantly seeking out advice from mothers and writing about it. And it was a mirror of my own anxiety. I was just trying to make sense of my experience and read about how others were doing things." Addie also described how she eventually "totally lost my voice." "I didn't have a voice anymore. I had a blogging voice. It's like a Twitter voice or a texting voice. It sounded like everyone else's, and I used to not write that way at all. And my work began to come with us everywhere. . . . I just wanted to stop writing. I felt like all of my posts were the same. . . . Then I was just DONE. I put in my two weeks' notice. I quit and have not written on my blog since, and I do not miss it one bit."

While Taryn was annoyed by the "blah, blah, blah" of BabyCenter's message boards, Addie felt her own voice had become something similar, just another voice in the mamasphere's pulsing communication. Taken together, Taryn's and Addie's experiences help to show how, online, the government of mothers overflows as a space of constant self-interrogation, evaluation, and communication about family life, parenting choices, personal ethics, and practices of self. Thus, while ethopolitical sensibilities fuel the flows of the mamasphere, online acts of empowerment quickly morph into scenes of heightened anxiety. One mother's freedom is another mother's judgment.

We can think of this mamaspheric overflow as a deeply gendered form of "infoglut" that doubles the government of mothers.[49] Indeed, Addie's anxious and ethopolitical sensibility of what it takes to be a good mom that sent her to digital media in the first place became "a mirror of my own anxiety," pulling her into digital circuits of self-doubt and uncertainty. Online, the government of mothers is environmentalized by networks, their nodes, and their churning communication, which is always beckoning, ready to entangle mothers in what Jodi Dean calls "the endless loop of reflexivity that becomes the very form of capture and absorption."[50] Mothers' ethopolitical freedoms are materialized digitally through participation in the mamasphere; however, this participation often only catches mothers up in the volatile affective infrastructures of family autonomy while contributing to their digital optimization.

Maggie was steering through neoliberalism's roiling waves after watching her old life fall apart. Highly educated and one of the more economically well-off mothers we spoke to, Maggie had once lived a fashionable life with her husband in Manhattan; upon deciding to start a family, they bought a house in the suburbs. Formerly a researcher at a hedge fund in the city, Maggie knew she would have to quit her job after having her first child, for even the hedge fund's "part-time" option would have kept Maggie away from home from six in the morning until eight at night at least four days each week, and likely more. Though Maggie settled comfortably into sub-urban life, keeping herself and the kids busy with playgroups and other activities, her husband lost his job in the financial services industry when their youngest was just six months old. The family hung on for ten months of uncertainty, blowing through their savings, until, lacking other options, they sold their home and moved in with Maggie's parents in rural Ryeland. Now Maggie's husband works long hours for an energy company, while Maggie has set herself to rebuilding their lives and raising her two young girls. Maggie described for us her current fears:

> I'm a planner, and I need stability, and that's been hard, because we don't have stability. There are things, like my husband hasn't decided if he likes this job, and we may have to move again soon. Or he's like, "You may not be able to stand living here, and I can find another job." So my parenting is always, like, I'm very careful about the way I talk to the kids, because I don't want to say something like, "Next year we're doing this." Or, like, the house we live in currently, they call it our house, but I'm always like, "We can't do that right now."

The uncertainty registered by her rented house deeply troubled Maggie, a self-described "control freak type [of] person." What should be a sign of family security indexed instead the precarity that rocked what was once a comfortable, certain world.

While ethopolitical discourses extend new sensibilities of freedom to mothers based on individual empowerment and autonomy, advanced neo-liberalism increasingly infuses nuclear family life and women's everyday decisions with the weight of precarity. Precarity is both a structure and an experience, defined today, on the one hand, by neoliberalism's systematic dismantling of social protections and safety nets of all sorts and, on the other, by what Kathleen Stewart calls the "precarious ordinary."[51] More than economic insecurity, the precarious ordinary is a structure of feeling, an everyday sense of dread and potentiality attendant to advanced neoliberalism. In the precarious ordinary, a child's illness or a broken car could send one skittering toward upheaval, and lingering everywhere are other disasters—accidents, affairs, bullies—that could surface at any moment and threaten family life. Maggie's sensibility of precarity compels her to carefully monitor the language she uses with her girls in an effort to manage their expectations and thereby keep them secure.

Advanced neoliberalism thus heightens maternal responsibilities, anxieties, and impossibilities, vastly expanding the scope and stakes of mothers' loads. More specifically, precarization transforms the affective labors of family government into what Marianne Cooper calls a "security project."[52] As families grapple with the realities of economic insecurity, they get organized for, and oriented around, security. However, as Cooper's work makes clear, families *do* security differently depending on their class and social position; in other words, there exists an inequality of security, as families are exposed to different orders of precarity and differential distributions of social protection.[53]

For example, Dana, a working-poor mother to three girls, ages eight, twelve, and fifteen, had recently moved to Ryeland to start over. On the heels of a painful divorce and bitter custody battle (which she lost), Dana was working toward an associate degree at the local community college. She expressed concerns about the safety of her three girls, who were living in a strange town and in a less-than-desirable subsidized housing complex:

> I worry about whether they're safe, where they're at. You know, they don't have cell phones, so when they're out and about with their friends, it's like, "OK, what are they doing? Who are they with? How far into town are they?" . . . [When they're with their dad, I worry,] "What's going on out at his house? Are they safe? Who's watching them?" They don't have a house phone. How am I supposed to get a hold of them? How are they supposed to get a hold of somebody? Just little things like that. And then with my oldest one, you hear about these thirteen-year-olds, and they're getting pregnant. I'm just like, "Oh my God." Those are my biggest worries. I mean, financial bills worry me too, but really when it comes down to it, at the end of the day I'm worried more about my children than my bills.

Dana's intense safety concerns were intimately bound up with social media like Facebook. She explained how she constantly monitored her daughters' accounts, logging in at random to assess communications and delete any suspicious new friends. "Not knowing who's really behind those pictures frightens me," she told us. "You see so many kids and so many people that pretend to be children, and it frightens me." Dana was also a survivor of domestic abuse and just getting by. As a self-proclaimed "fixer," she seemed optimistic about her prospects. Open and upbeat during our interview, Dana candidly offered up detailed stories about tense run-ins with her ex and frustrating experiences with local social service agencies.

Together, Dana's and Maggie's stories reveal how mothers share precarity yet inhabit it differently, as they take on very different security projects. Both love deeply, and worry intensely about, their girls. However, on the one hand, Maggie's "worry work" seems to overrun her emotional life, extending into mundane conversations with her daughters. As a white, upper-middle-class mother, she "upscales" her insecurity and magnifies uncertainty, trying to make the unknown visible at every turn in hopes of controlling it.[54] On the other hand, Dana's worries seem to stem primarily from the precariousness of motherhood itself. "Worried more about [her] children than [her] bills," she "downscales" her family's material insecurity, which, unlike Maggie's, is occasionally life threatening, much more than a sensibility.[55] Indeed, Dana's security work is rooted in positive thinking: she downplays the risks and threats she faces daily in order to survive them, while focusing on the physical health and safety of her girls.

Clearly, women's security projects hinge on different modes of affective labor and strategies for managing the insecurities and volatilities of everyday family life.[56] In middle-class families especially, the work of security is profoundly gendered, as it is mothers who emerge as the security guards and take on a disproportionate share of the "worry work." These mothers work what Cooper calls an "insecurity shift" that is about "holding on" to family amid uncertainties and unknowable risks.[57] It is up to mothers to steer the family ship to safety, to keep the family afloat and going.

For almost all of the mothers we interviewed, the security load keeps them oriented toward the fragility of their family scenes. They are not only vigilant managers of the minutiae of mothering but also vigilant assessors of the minutiae of present and potential threats to their family's security. Consider Elana. Mother to seven-month-old Jared and an administrative staffer at a local college, Elana told us that she compulsively checks her bank account—"I check my bank statement every day. I don't know why. Even when I know I'm not spending any money today, I still check my bank statement, my credit card, make sure my husband's not buying anything he shouldn't"—and that she worries constantly about her son's safety:

> I think maybe that my mind is thinking Jared twenty-four hours a day, even at night. When he started sleeping [through] the night, I still woke up on my own, and I was like, "Why is he not waking up? He's not breathing." So I run to his room just to check on him, I still do it sometimes, make sure he's not face first in the sheets. He moves so much that I'm afraid the sheets could come off the edge of the mattress . . . so if I don't hear him and it's like four in the morning and I wake up, I have to get up and check on him. I think the fact that, I feel like being a mom is a twenty-four-hour job even when they're sleeping, it's still a job to me because mentally I wake up and think, "Oh, is he coughing? Is he choking? Is he going to stop coughing?" I think . . . that you're a parent, you're at least a mom all the time, even when your husband's sleeping next to you. All you're thinking about is your son the entire time.

From bank accounts to sleeping kids, for Elana unknown disasters must be made readily visible and mitigated. While mothering is of course always already precarious, advanced neoliberalism heightens maternal sensibilities of precarity by materializing and magnifying a host of potential dangers to the family's security.

THE RISK LOAD

Mothers' everyday experiences of the precarious ordinary register a world of increasingly privatized risk: as governments and corporations continue to shed their own risk loads, individuals and families must constantly work to insure themselves against disasters of all sorts.[58] Put another way, privatized risk makes personal responsibility the new means of social insurance. Becoming largely incalculable in the hands of individuals, privatized risk requires folks to transform the various contexts of their everyday lives into insurance agencies.

Thanks to family autonomy and the government of mothers, women often come to bear the brunt of privatized risk, as their worry work is imagined to double as insurance for the project of family itself. Of course, maternal subjectivity has long been paradoxical: mothers have been both empowered to assume responsibility for the all-important work of child-rearing and constantly reminded of their inadequacy to the task. But the privatization of risk injects a new layer of impossibility into women's work. As Randy Martin argues, the logic of risk is itself profoundly paradoxical: it "presents not only the limit to what can be known in the present, but also the burden of acting as if one could know."[59] Risk folds the future into the present; it asks subjects to imagine their present lives according to the uncertain future one cannot, but nonetheless is compelled to, control: "Integrating the future into the present could only leave room for more self-doubt, which in turn expanded the arena in which risk could serve as life's barometer. So long as risk was everywhere, failure could be imminent at any turn for any possible venture, whether it be health, education, employment, investment, or personal affection."[60] As future dangers get folded into the precarious present, the privatization of risk injects even more impossibility into mothers' lives as they try to control the uncontrollable.

The privatization of risk is not simply about individuals assuming responsibility for economic, social, and health risks; rather, individuals *enact* the privatization of risk, *making space for it to happen* as they take on the myriad worries, sensibilities, and knowledges previously divided among experts and practitioners in various fields—education, health, finance, psychology, and work. As these social spheres collapse onto individuals, the latter take up the erstwhile responsibility of those spheres in order to enact the labor and knowledge attendant on them. Recall, for example, that Shana refused to consider placing her children in day care, citing her fear of its mechanized rhythms and highly managed mode of early childhood education. Rather than open her family up to perceived risks associated with institutionalized childcare with other kids, Shana took the daily care of her young children on herself, while also working upward of thirty hours a week, cobbling together part-time jobs to stay active and relevant in her field and keep up on her student loans.

The privatization of risk is furthermore exacerbated by and enacted within the digital mundane. News of school shootings, product recalls, and health warnings flow in and out of e-mail, dashing across screens, newsfeeds, and boards, while at the same time digital media appear awash in promises of sovereignty and techniques of risk management. Kim told us, "I use Google Chrome, so I have all the tabs open. . . . My husband laughs. My whole top of the screen is filled with tabs." Specifically, Kim keeps tabs on the weather "all the time," constantly monitors her son's grades through Edline, works on multiple continuing education courses at a time, and watches for any consignment sales she might have made. "A lot of [the tabs] are Google," Kim explains, telling us how she searches and shops online as well. For her, digital media are a machine for privatizing risk; online she can know "at any given moment" if her son has "tanked that test," while working to keep her own certifications active: "I'm afraid to let them lapse because God only knows what life can throw at you, so I keep [those tabs] open so I can work on those."

In this sense, mothers like Kim become "micro-vigilantes" in the digital mundane, constantly gathering data, assessing probabilities, making calculated decisions, and rationalizing ultimately unknowable outcomes.[61] Happiness becomes less about participating in a shared (white, middle-class) fantasy of the good life and more about hanging on to that fantasy for one's *own* family in a world of perpetual danger and contingency. Happiness is thus no longer merely the horizon or telos of family life but also the "hinge" by which individual mothers come to enact the privatization of risk in hopes of holding together their families.[62] Good mothering requires, above all, resilience and is measured by just how much risk mothers can take on and manage on their own.

As explored more fully in the next chapter, almost all of the mothers we spoke to were striving to be good mothers through taking on and enacting the privatization of risk for their families in the digital mundane. Caroline, though, described for us the shattering effects of this situation. When Caroline's eldest daughter was two and her youngest was a newborn, Caroline's mother suffered a devastating relapse of breast cancer. The combined stresses of the new baby and her mother's illness overwhelmed this self-described "planner," who turned to medical advice on the Internet in an effort to control her situation.

> I was clinically diagnosed as a hypochondriac. That's how I dealt with it. I spent a good six months not doing anything. I couldn't function. And I had to go on medication for a while. So, yeah, I legitimately went crazy because of that. . . . Like, I thought I was dying on a daily basis, and I didn't understand where this came from. Well, what my therapist said was, you know, there's this situation over here that I'm so involved in and I can't control it. The only thing I can control is myself, and I took all that inward and that's where I went with it. . . . It started by getting online and looking up my mom's symptoms and finding out what's wrong and calling her and saying, "Well, this is

what [the doctor] needs to do," and I got so consumed by that that I literally went crazy. . . . The more I started reading, and . . . the very first thing was mole checks. Check for a mole. . . . I had this tiny mole, and I was like, "Oh my God, that's melanoma; I'm gonna die." Called my doctor immediately. . . . And then it would go on from there, and I was able to link every symptom I had to this or that. . . . I dealt with it when I was pregnant a little bit too. Actually, yeah, that's kind of where it started, now that I think about it, when I was pregnant with Ella because I didn't know I was pregnant so I was panicking, what have I done? You know, of course I drank and I did all kinds of things, and I was like, "Oh jeez, I totally screwed up this baby." And then I thought I was having an ectopic pregnancy. I think maybe that part was normal mom scared, but it really escalated once my mom was sick.

Caroline's easy slip from "normal mom scared" to clinical hypochondria is certainly suggestive in its assumption that a panicky fear of "screwing up" one's baby or suffering an ectopic pregnancy is to be expected. And perhaps it is, for as mothers take on the risk load, women's work comes to require what Lauren Berlant calls a "wandering absorptive awareness and a hypervigilance" that, for mothers in particular, is always already bubbling with anxiety, responsibility, and impossibility.[63]

Buckling under more and more social responsibilities, mothers are overloaded and overrun as they teeter on the precipices of privatized risk and happiness. As the mamasphere perpetually cycles risks and reassurances, mothers inhabit ever more merciless affective infrastructures, orienting their daily lives and senses of self around fraying, unworkable scenes that cause steep frustration, fear, anxiety, or, in Caroline's case, worse. Chasing increasingly precarized promises of family autonomy, mothers stay tethered to ever-mounting mother loads and, perhaps more insidiously, to the pernicious idea that it is their responsibility, and theirs alone, to realize the impossible and securitize the family.

2 · MAMAPRENEURIALISM

Family Appreciation in the Digital Mundane

JENNY

In 2008 twenty-three-year-old Jenny; her husband, Dan; his five-year-old son; and their two-year-old son lost their financial footing when Dan was laid off from his well-paying job in the Wyoming oil fields. Jenny, a conservative Christian and committed stay-at-home mother, was just two weeks away from giving birth to their third son, and her extended family was across the country in Hugo. Forced to short-sell their home and give up their car, the family ultimately decided to move back to Hugo to start over. Five years later, Jenny nursed her newborn, their fourth son, in the kitchen of their rented 1940s Cape Cod home as she matter-of-factly described the punishing tides of advanced neoliberalism that wrecked her family's life:

> When the economy tanked and when everything went south, he got laid off, and at that point we owned a home, we had a car. I mean, life was a heck of a lot different than it is now. He lost, we lost everything.

And then he had been unemployed for a year and half. We were just, we had no help, we didn't know what else to do. We were trying to work our way up out there, but it just wasn't going anywhere so we moved out here to kind of start over. And my family's here, and we had help here.

By the time Jenny told us this story, her husband had found a job as a deliveryman and the family had settled into their new life. Though Jenny was optimistic, the memory of the past years was clearly fresh and painful. She explained, "It was just, it was so much. And it was insane. I don't know, I mean, by the grace of God we are still married. Because it, it's been hard. There's no doubt about it. It's been hard."

In response to losing "everything," Jenny transformed her work as a mother. No longer focused solely on childrearing and homemaking, Jenny's labors morphed and intensified as she sought out ways to boost the family's bottom line. Crucially, these efforts materialized in the digital mundane. Online, Jenny continues to pioneer numerous practical strategies for stabilizing and securitizing her family. She engages often and enthusiastically in online couponing and has run a pair of home-based businesses, first as a consultant for Thirty-One, a Christian direct-sales company specializing in handbags and totes, and more recently as a sales associate for Get Life. As a result, Jenny's life as a stay-at-home mom is no longer cordoned off from the world of paid work; thanks to digital media, it is an economic enterprise in its own right.

Indeed, we might think of Jenny as a "mompreneur." Increasingly, the mompreneur figures as a prominent figure in digital media culture. Blending entrepreneurialism with domesticity, mompreneurs usually run small lifestyle businesses out of their homes, often via the affordances of new communication technologies. Mompreneurs are thus shown as discovering a way to "have it all": they can be home for their children while still pursuing their own dreams as individuals through entrepreneurial work. In this way, the image of the successful mompreneur represents a powerful postfeminist fantasy that melds the requisites of neoliberal citizenship with traditional patriarchal values of family autonomy.[1] Of course, in the everyday experiences of moms like Jenny, things feel quite different.

This chapter pushes beyond the figure of the mompreneur to explore mamapreneurialism as the primary sensibility of mothering through precarity. Mamapreneurialism is not simply a postfeminist neoliberal fantasy:

it is a powerful gender orientation that provides a chassis for approaching the impossibilities and anxieties of contemporary motherhood. In our account, mamapreneurialism includes not only economic activities like couponing and work-at-home sales but also a battery of banal decisions, activities, affects, and labors that constitute mothers' everyday lives. Mamapreneurialism asks mothers to reinvent family life as a rationalized web of economized care, which in turn promises freedom, independence, autonomy, and security while allaying the affective and material volatilities of ongoing precarization.

More specifically, we show how the mamapreneurial sensibility emerges within mothers' intensified efforts at family appreciation, that is, increasing the human capital of the family. In the case of mothers like Jenny, it is not enough to be a "good mom" and follow the traditional scripts of family autonomy; rather, mothering through precarity requires securitizing the private sphere of family on one's own. In a world of increasingly privatized risk, individual mothers must underwrite the family and guarantee its survival through any danger or devastation that might visit it. As financial and other sorts of disasters loom, family becomes a security blanket that is fraying; it can readily depreciate or be depreciated, so mothers must work to continually appreciate it anew by becoming ever more mamapreneurial. As we show, these processes of becoming mamapreneurial are inseparable from the churning potentiality of the digital mundane, which incites and extends mamapreneurialism by providing an atmosphere of ubiquitous opportunity for appreciating the family.

This chapter drills down to the nitty-gritty of four women's everydays to explore how mamapreneurialism figures as the guiding sensibility of mothering through precarity. Here we attend to the totality and compositionality of specific mothers' lives, illuminating the myriad and highly mundane ways in which digital media come to figure in mothers' efforts at privatizing happiness. Sam is a busy, efficient working mom whose efforts at being "the best mom ever" are intimately tied to her highly rationalized approach to home life, including her "love" of online budgeting. Caroline is a comfortably middle-class stay-at-home mother who once harbored postfeminist, big-city dreams of a life in corporate finance. Now she puts her business acumen to work online for her husband's small business in her time away from anxiously working to raise two happy, healthy girls. Lisa is a work-at-home mother who orients all her labors around cultivating familial resilience. Thanks in large part to the affordances of new communication technologies,

Lisa is able to construct her home as a self-contained, self-reliant domestic enterprise in the face of global threats and shattering fantasies of the good life. Finally, Jenny's work for Get Life shows how digital media present expanded opportunities for melding the demands of care with those of family appreciation and enterprise. However, while Get Life provides a promising platform for shoring up her family scene, it also catches Jenny up in new circuits of affective modulation and cruel optimism.

NEOLIBERALISM AND WOMEN'S WORK

In *The Cultural Contradictions of Motherhood*, Sharon Hays asks, "In a larger social context that not only devalues intensive mothering but actually serves to undermine it, why hasn't this ideology been reconstructed to one more in line with the logic of instrumental rationality, profit maximization, and the practical needs of paid working mothers?"[2] As we show, intensive mothering is in fact aligned with the logics, practices, and movements of the market: the mamapreneurial sensibility is fundamentally about materializing the domestic sphere as an increasingly economized enterprise.

As many scholars have argued, neoliberalism is much more than pro-market economic policies and/or ideologies. Rather, it is, as Wendy Brown puts it, an "order of normative reason . . . extending a specific formulation of economic values, practices, and metrics to every dimension of human life."[3] Pierre Dardot and Christian Laval thus insist on understanding neoliberalism as the form of contemporary society: "it tends to totalize—that is, create a world in its own image through its power to integrate all dimensions of human existence."[4] Specifically, neoliberalism works to establish a social world premised on the logic of scarcity and the generalized competition for resources this logic demands.[5] Consequently, individuals must organize their lives around practices of self-appreciation in order to grow their human capital and ensure their individual survival in a dog-eat-dog world. Brown argues that neoliberalism is thus primarily about the economization of previously noneconomic spheres: "neoliberal rationality disseminates the *model of the market* to all domains and activities—even where money is not at issue—and configures human beings exhaustively as market actors, always, only, and everywhere as *homo oeconomicus*."[6] Scarcity, competition, valorization, and capital accumulation no longer only characterize economic markets; they constitute a social ontology. In other words, the market is now a *"subjective process,"* operating through and within the activities of competing human capitals.[7]

Put a little differently, generalized competition requires and figures a world of generalized enterprise. Graham Burchell describes neoliberalism as the "promotion of an enterprise culture," where "the generalization of an 'enterprise form' to all forms of conduct—to the conduct of organizations hitherto seen as being non-economic, to the conduct of government and to the conduct of individuals themselves—constitutes the essential characteristic of this style of government."[8] As Nikolas Rose explains, the individual is thereby incited to become "an entrepreneur of him or herself . . . to conduct his or her life, and that of his or her family, as a kind of enterprise, seeking to enhance and capitalize on existence itself through calculated acts and investments."[9] In his lectures on biopolitics, Michel Foucault shows how, as human capital, the individual is figured as an "abilities-machine" whose life must take shape as, and be rooted within, a network of enterprises.[10] Enterprise is thus the "universally generalized social model" that is to provide "concrete points of anchorage" for individuals; as Foucault puts it, "the individual's life must be lodged . . . within the framework of a multiplicity of diverse enterprises connected up to and entangled with each other."[11]

Mothers occupy an intensely fraught position in enterprise culture: they are, in many ways, excluded from it yet are ever more necessary to its operations. Thanks to the deeply entrenched grammars of family autonomy, the private sphere of family is expected to figure as the primary anchorage point for women. Hence, mothers cannot be true *homo oeconomicus*—competitive, self-investing, self-appreciating; rather, their abilities must stay tethered to and imagined within their role as *femina domestica*.[12] As discussed in the previous chapter, the government of mothers is ultimately about shaping mothers' capacities as *abilities-machines for the family*; this reflects the driving questions of contemporary parenting discourse, as formulated by Foucault: "What type of stimuli, form of life, and relationship with parents, adults, and others can be crystallized into human capital?"[13] Indeed, the goal of family autonomy is the production and valorization of the family's human capital. This production is premised on a long-standing gender and sexual division of labor in which mothers are imagined to exist as human capital for the family enterprise. As such, their labor as abilities-machines is oriented around *family* appreciation. Accordingly, mothers as individual human assets might work outside the home, but they may also stay home to focus on childrearing and homemaking. What matters most fundamentally is not the so-called mommy wars but their ongoing orientation toward the work of family appreciation, taking responsibility for constructing the domestic scene as their own private enterprise.

In this sense, advanced neoliberalism both intensifies and alters gender oppression in the nuclear family.[14] While women, in their traditional function as the (re)producers of workers and citizens, have always played a vital role in the economy and the state, neoliberalism reconfigures this relationship between the market and family enterprise in crucial ways. Neoliberalism's dismantling of social supports and public goods—from health care to education to recreation—hinges on the ongoing extension of women's work. Ongoing precarization relies on mothers' ongoing privatization of happiness—that is, their increasing responsibility for social care within the confines of their own families. Even as more women participate in the civic spheres of education and paid labor (albeit for less pay than men), more is required of mothers in the private sphere to appreciate the human capital of the family in a competitive, precarious world where resources are scarce and threats of familial depreciation are rampant. What is more, mothers are also called on to contribute to the buttressing of community life, picking up the social slack for slashed state budgets and the shuttered programs and schools they leave in their wake. Simply put, neoliberalism assigns to mothers the double burdens of family appreciation and community stabilization.[15]

At the same time, neoliberalism's reconception of the social and the self in terms of competition and human capital renders this intensified care labor increasingly invisible. As Brown puts it, "women both *require* the visible social infrastructure that neoliberalism aims to dismantle through privatization and *are* the invisible infrastructure sustaining a world of putatively self-investing human capitals."[16] As such, systemic gender exploitation intensifies but becomes more and more illegible as such. Consequently, divergent, impossible logics animate mothers' lives: they must either become *homo oeconomicus* or "remain the unavowed glue for a world whose governing principle cannot hold it together."[17] In short, they must radically reorient themselves to care work or try to sustain a familial and social world that no longer holds together.

We show how mothers traverse these impossibilities by becoming mamapreneurial, that is, by economizing themselves and their mother loads as the "unavowed glue" for their families. In everyday precarious life, mothers cultivate distinctly maternal, albeit largely invisible, performances of *homo oeconomicus* as they strive to live their lives as privatized happiness machines for their families. Economic logics get refracted into practices of care in myriad ways in order to optimize a family scene that seems to be always already on the verge of breakdown.

This is intense and complicated work. Cultivating the human capital of the family is both an affective and economic endeavor, but as Viviana Zelizer argues, the relationship between intimate bonds and economic encounters is vexed, for financial exchange seems to undermine the authenticity and value of intimate relationships.[18] Poor families, especially poor African American families, have long been vilified both for supposedly lacking enterprise and for replacing authentic care with cold, calculating economic rationality (e.g., in myths about "welfare queens" having babies simply to increase their government checks). Wealthier mothers who are too invested in material gain are also cast as immoral, "bad" mothers. "Good families," by contrast, are meant to feel happy despite economic hardship, but they must also be financially self-reliant and avoid exposing the family to harsh moral criticism based on accepting various forms of public assistance (e.g., food banks or welfare). In advanced neoliberalism, mothers must therefore work to "appreciate" the affective and economic dimensions of family capital—work that requires working on one's happiness, for the family's emotional fate operates as a sign of the family's well-being even as precarization impinges on the family's capacity for "the good life."

THE MAMAPRENEURIAL SENSIBILITY

Mamapreneurialism emerges as a vital sensibility for navigating, and surviving, the mounting demands and structural impossibilities of mothering through precarity. It enables mothers to compose a life rooted in family appreciation—where risks feel more manageable, dangers more avoidable, promises more certain—by reorienting women's work around rationalization, flexibility, and resilience.

As we learned, mamapreneurialism incites many mothers to *rationalize* their practices of family government and care. Mothers often feel themselves responsible for ensuring family outcomes; to guarantee these, they meticulously calibrate the minutiae of their days. Everyday family life in this sense becomes increasingly rationalized and defined by mothers' practices of what Eva Illouz calls "reflexive selfhood"; as she explains, "a reflexive self has internalized strong mechanisms of self-control to maintain its self-interest, not through the blatant display for selfish competitiveness, but through the art of mastering social relations."[19] For mamapreneurs, reflexive selfhood is about appreciating the family through optimizing the intimate relations that define it. Keen to master the dynamics of the home, mothers seek to control domestic interactions, as if taming the intimate contingencies of the present will lock in the happiness of the future. Mamapreneurs thus come to appreciate their families through an "intellectualization" of domestic life.[20] This includes mothers' own labors, which are constantly subject to the instrumentalizing scrutiny of reflexive selfhood, as they ask themselves to justify what they have done, or can do, for the broader family enterprise.

While mothers hone their capacities for mastering relations and rationalizing the home, they must also be eminently adaptable, ready to let go and change course with little notice. In other words, economizing the home requires *mamapreneurial flexibility*: mothers must be able to adjust and retool their appreciation efforts, both within and outside of the home, in response to the demands of advanced neoliberalism.[21] Thus, mothers who aspire to work often find themselves in the home, while mothers who desire deeply to stay home are often catapulted into paid work. Their labor is flexible: it contracts and expands, often on demand, around the work of privatizing happiness. Mamapreneurs by and large comply with the shifting terms and limits of their work and family scenes and accept that choices aren't really choices when it comes to family appreciation.

Finally, mamapreneurialism has many mothers circling the wagons, drawing hard-and-fast lines between their individualized family scenes and the rest of the world. Internalizing ontological scarcity and competition, they double down on family autonomy and cultivate practices of domestic resilience, readying the family unit to survive the dangers of precarization. Brad Evans and Julian Reid argue that "the resilient subject is required to accept the dangerousness of the world it lives in as a condition for partaking of that world and accept the necessity of the injunction to change itself in correspondence with threats now presumed as endemic and unavoidable. . . . [T]hey adapt to their enabling conditions via the embrace of a neoliberal rationality that fosters the belief in the necessity of risk as a private good."[22] For mamapreneurs, resilience means resigning oneself to the precarity of family—accepting the realities of privatized risk as opportunities for appreciating one's own family. As care work becomes oriented toward adaptation and survival, family happiness becomes an ever more privatized and competitive enterprise.

Mothers become mamapreneurial in the digital mundane, where rationalization, flexibility, and resilience are environmentalized by the participatory architectures of the mamasphere. The mamasphere makes opportunities for family appreciation ubiquitous, providing the medium by which mothers become finely tuned abilities-machines for their families. Circulating an immense array of mamapreneurial tools for self-appreciation and family appreciation, the mamasphere wends itself through mothers' lives, churning out tips from advisors, trackers, coaches, and experts, seemingly always eager to help mothers take personal responsibility for their families.

In other words, mothers live in a mamapreneurial atmosphere. To take just one example, the popular blog *Modern Parents Messy Kids* (MPMK), run by Stephanie Morgan, a former doctor of audiology and mother to three young children, promises to "provide daily inspiration to thousands of parents on simplifying, connecting, and living well. Our motto, 'mindful living, effortless style' translates to creative playtime activities, stimulating parenting discussions, clever organizational tips, DIY projects and even some fresh style finds. At MPMK, we're all about being in the moment and doing our best to live the good life—whilst always allowing room for imperfection."[23] Mindful living, organization, crafting, and intensive parenting in the form of well-thought-out, mother-led playtime activities all come together here as a highly instrumentalized path to happiness.

For example, "Happy Family Habits," a series of ten posts about "building stronger connections 21 days at a time," offers mothers a plan for cultivating happiness-increasing habits that promise to optimize family scenes as happy ones.[24] Every three weeks (the time in which the average person can acquire a habit), the series offers a new "happiness habit" for readers to practice. In her introduction to the series, Morgan writes,

> Last week something kind of remarkable happened to me. I had one of those rare days where everything just seemed to be flowing. The kids and I were connecting, I was getting stuff accomplished without feeling frazzled or distracted, and the whole day through I felt . . . happy. It was so wonderful that once the kids were in bed that night I sat down and took a few minutes to reflect on what we'd done differently that day to make it so. . . . It's my firm belief that happiness is something that can be taught to our kids—and is also something that

needs to be practiced. Happiness is, quite simply, a state of mind. Furthermore, I believe, from practicing gratitude to carving out one-on-one time with the kids, there are intentional things families can do to be more happy together.[25]

Here happiness is something that must be carefully and intentionally constructed through practices of reflexive selfhood: "Share YOUR Story with Your Kids," "Put Your Gratitude in Writing," "Making Family Traditions," "Taking the Time to Teach Your Kids Something New," "Get Your Kids to Talk: Establish a Chatting Spot," "Teach Gratitude by Remembering to Thank Your Kids," and "Creating a Blessing Bag."

Going to museums, taking a walk in the neighborhood, and shopping at an Asian market instead of the American supermarket are technologies of family appreciation. Exposing children to new ideas, stimulating them, conquering boredom, and "strategically" "managing [children's] energy for 12 hours a day" are means to rationalizing happiness.[26]

Despite the intensification of affective labor they surely elicit, sites like MPMK help mothers traverse the twinned though often competing affective and economic demands of neoliberal family autonomy by presenting happiness as a mamapreneurial endeavor. In "Happy Family Habit #4: Staying Young (and Silly!) with Your Kids," contributing blogger Kristin Eldridge, a photographer, writes, "So, in raising kids, my husband is often the fun parent and I tend to be the one holding the fort down. Many of you moms will side with me. Someone has to keep this ship afloat. Over the past few years I've learned that there's a time to let go of the rules and what 'should be done.' There's a time when the goal of having FUN is more important than anything else. And being the organized mom that I am, I have a few tips on how to have fun."[27] As Eldridge suggests, the work of family appreciation often places mothers in this kind of double bind, where they must "hold the fort down," holding the family together and ensuring its prospects, while also moving always toward happiness. In order to navigate this double bind, she implores moms to get out of their kitchens and laundry rooms and into their kids' rooms and outside on the grass, to "say yes to impractical things," even though "you're the one who thinks about budgets and 'good buys.'" Indeed, for mothers navigating this double bind, the mamasphere provides a host of opportunities for converting the muck of domestic labor into exciting, exceptional ventures. From MPMK to feminized social media platforms like Pinterest, the mamasphere is per-

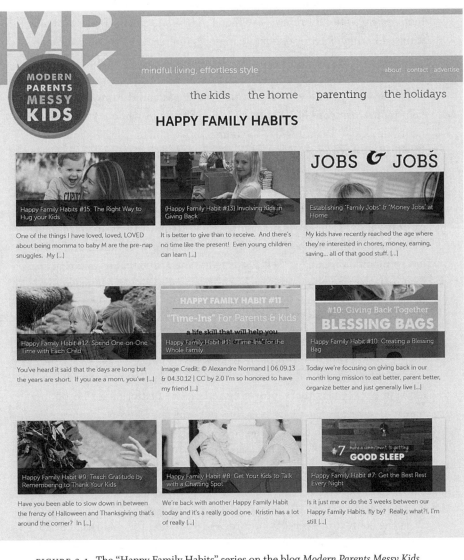

FIGURE 2.1. The "Happy Family Habits" series on the blog *Modern Parents Messy Kids* offers mothers instrumentalized strategies for cultivating family happiness.

colating with ideas for optimizing mundane scenes as sites of happiness accumulation.

While technologies for producing highly rationalized happy families abound, so too do technologies for producing highly rationalizing happy mothers. Online mothering communities like Power of Moms work on mothers' capacities for reflexive selfhood. As the site crows, "*Power of Moms* is the gathering place for deliberate mothers interested in growing through motherhood—not just going through motherhood. Our overall vision is to offer moms around the world the chance to 'network' with other moms who share their same values, motivations, hopes and dreams. We aim to help moms take care of the person inside the mom while taking care of their families."[28] To rationalize the home for happiness, mothers must methodically construct a lifestyle enterprise rooted in their personal ethic; at the same time, they must rationalize their own happiness in order to appreciate themselves. Thus, sites like Power of Moms figure family happiness and mothers' own human capital as a singular affair, offering Mind Organization for Moms (M.O.M.), a program to "help mothers organize their thoughts and time and projects so they can experience less stress and more joy"; a Bloom Program for "self assessment" and goal tracking; and retreats where mothers come together to learn "tried-and-true ideas to make their motherhood experience what they want it to be and help their families reach their potential."[29]

It is important to see that sites like MPMK and Power of Moms are not simply online sites hosting technologies of self-appreciation and family appreciation: they are also communities that incite and nurture communication between mothers, providing interactive platforms for becoming reflexive selves. The mamasphere thus not only circulates technologies of family appreciation but is also the environment in which mothers become mamapreneurial: through online participation, mothers become ever more rationalizing, flexible, and resilient. Put a little differently, the interactive networks of the mamasphere are constantly reflecting, registering, and inciting mamapreneurial activity.

In the context of everyday precarious family life, the mamasphere appears as an always open avenue to mamapreneurial success. Online, testimonies from work-at-home moms who have turned their personal passions for crafting, meal planning, couponing, and healthy eating into digital careers abound. For example, *The Digital Mom Handbook* promises to help mothers transcend the impossibilities that permeate their lives through

FIGURE 2.2. The Power of Moms path toward "deliberate motherhood" unites family happiness with mothers' human capital, cultivating mothers' reflexive capacities as a means to maximize family potential.

mamapreneurial reinvention. Authors Audrey McClelland and Colleen Padilla explain:

> Mothers have been looking for the middle ground for more than half a century. Staying at home and raising kids full time isn't it. Working full time and rushing home to tuck the kids in at 7pm sharp ain't it, either. Even part-time work outside the house can be scramble for most women as they try to "have it all" between 9am and 5pm. To work or not to work? That seems to be the bottom-line question for most women today.
>
> But we believe that equation is changing. In fact, we're living proof of that change.
>
> Both of us left the corporate ladder behind to stay home with our children. But instead of assigning us permanent stay-at-home status, this choice was the catalyst to our reinvention. . . . [W]e sat down at our computers one day, kids cooing in the background, and began to blog.[30]

The mamasphere promises a vast "middle ground" where mothers can readily reconcile the competing affective and economic demands of family appreciation. According to Charlotte Latvala, "today's stay-at-home mom (SAHM) may be a tattooed rock singer, the CEO of her own company, or a green-living activist—but they all have something in common: a deep desire to be there for every moment of their babies' lives—the good, the bad and the unbelievably messy."[31]

Work-at-home mamapreneurialism counsels mothers to find their "passion," posing questions such as "What did you want to be when you grew up?" or "Who is doing what you would love to be doing? Can you do this, too?"[32] Finding an appropriate passion through reflexive communication is vital, because, for mamapreneurs, work-at-home enterprise must be highly rationalized as a technology of the self, clearly oriented toward family autonomy, but lodged within the framework of self-enterprise. This is why *Mom, Incorporated* authors Aliza Sherman and Danielle Elliott Smith press mothers to consider lifestyle businesses, enterprises that will actually help them to materialize their motherly vision of a happy family and a better world.[33] Here mothers are prompted to imagine the totality of their lives as, in Foucault's words, a "multiplicity of diverse enterprises connected up to and entangled with each other," perfectly united by mamapreneurial flexibility.[34]

Online couponing, in particular, figures as a readily achievable mode of mamapreneurial labor. Couponing sites allow mothers to fit mamapreneurial endeavors around more traditional forms of caring labor. Couponing can be performed easily, yet exhaustively, in the interstices of everyday family life—in the car waiting for children or in front of the television late at night. These sites also foster familial resilience. The popular couponing site Fabulessly Frugal, for example, hosts a dizzying array of daily and weekly specials organized by retailers, as well as plenty of tips to help newcomers learn to "live fabulous on less."[35] Indeed, while popular media variously "praise and pathologize" enterprising activities like couponing, these practices more immediately promise opportunities for family appreciation in a competitive milieu, where the survival of family is felt to depend on mothers' own commercial spirit and their ability to prepare for the unknown economic disasters that loom.[36]

Distributing ubiquitous and myriad opportunities for family appreciation through mothers' everyday lives, the mamasphere operates a powerful affective infrastructure for privatizing happiness. As we show in the following stories, mothers often find immense gratification in becoming mamapreneurial, for economizing activities allow them to productively channel postfeminist sensibilities of capacity and reinvent the everyday gender oppressions and insecurities of precarity as profoundly vital practices of family appreciation. As Laurie Ouellette and Julie Wilson argue, digital media insert "new modes of media engagement into the domestic structures of women's work," refashioning mundane domestic labor as "an enterprising and self-empowering activity" that makes "the feminized labor of caring for others more compatible with the self-enterprising ethos demanded by today's neoliberal policies and reforms."[37] Yet mothers' labors are also doubled and intensified by the mamasphere, as its ever-flowing potentialities keep mothers cycling within the cruel optimisms of advanced neoliberalism.

SAM: THE MAMAPRENEURIAL FOURTH SHIFT

Educated, career oriented, and independent, Sam is a busy and efficient mother of three who has "a [book]shelf dedicated to being a mom and how to be the best mom ever." Though she never dreamed of having children, after marrying her family-oriented and deeply Christian husband, Sam left her career as a product engineer to move to his small, rural hometown and start a family. Her husband worked long hours at his small business, while Sam threw herself into taking care of the children, sacrificing material comforts so that she could afford to stay home because, at the time, she thought that a "good mom" was a "stay-at-home mom." She elaborated, "I'll be the stay-at-home, homeschooling mom who does scrapbooks and does all this other stuff. And I think that's an unfair assessment. I don't think . . . you have to be a stay-at-home mom to be a good mom, but for me I found that I do my best work when I'm focused, and I felt like I wanted to do my best work on my kids." Though she is skeptical of popular-media images of moms and wary of judging other moms' choices, Sam relentlessly assesses the wisdom of her own.

Sam is intent on optimizing family life, putting her "best work" into her children, tightly managing the family's time, and carefully calibrating the details of daily life to engender ideal outcomes. Sam's happy family life is an economized private sphere constructed by her carefully considered decisions and finely tuned plans. When we spoke, she had just returned to full-time paid work after ten years as a stay-at-home mom. Her detailed description of the family's daily schedule demonstrates her highly rationalized approach to family:

> So my day begins, I wake up at five thirty, and I don't use an alarm clock. I just wake up now at that time. And I usually spend about a half an hour drinking coffee and doing like some sort of morning prayer time. And then walking my dog. My kids' alarm clocks start going off at six thirty, and unfortunately they haven't gotten to the place where the alarm clock actually is meaningful yet. So I come in about ten minutes later and we do morning hugs and we pick out clothes and they all make their own breakfast now so they get started on that, and I go and wake up my husband and bring him coffee, and he is a really hard wake. He doesn't wake up well, so that's a long process so I just start him off, and my kids, they get on the bus at seven fifty. They all go to school together now, so between six thirty and seven fifty they each have a list of things they're supposed to do to get ready for school. They have to get their lunch boxes together and make sure all their homework is in their folders and their backpacks, and get dressed, and make their beds, and do all those kinds of things. And I usually have to start a load of laundry and start dishes and try to get everything ready so that when I come home at lunchtime I

can do the next phase of whatever housework job there is that needs to happen. So they do that, and then I leave, I basically sit in the car while they get on the bus, and then as soon as they get on the bus I go to work, which is a two-minute commute for me, which is awesome. I work until five o'clock. I usually take my hour lunch break and come home and walk the dog and get the laundry done and do some different household stuff. . . . [W]e usually get home at five, a little after five, and I start dinner, and dinner's at six, and we usually have the same five things every week that we eat. And while I'm doing that they have chores they're supposed to be doing . . . while I'm cooking for an hour and then after dinner we finish up homework. The kids earn the ability to do something with a video game or TV for forty-five minutes if they've done everything so that takes up that time and they do showers, they make their lunches for the next day, and then they each kind of go to bed in succession every half hour. I have one that's going to bed at about seven thirty, and then the other two it's like eight thirty or eight or nine depending on how pleasant they were that day. And then I usually, my husband gets home pretty late from work, so I stay up and hang out and wait for him, and I'm in bed by ten thirty or so. That's my day. It's a busy day. It's a fun day.

For Sam, the home is a well-oiled machine, figured hour by hour, and punctuated with activities designed to optimize both her own happiness (morning prayer) and the happiness of her family (chore and reward systems, morning hugs).

Sam's days are designed to be predictable, efficient, and productive; they have to be, for the weight of her family's well-being is on her shoulders. In her mind, without constant management, family life could easily fall apart:

Well, there's a lot of work that goes into making sure that the family runs smoothly. The things where you have to think out, "OK, next week so and so, the day care's closing early or something so you have to make sure somebody's there to pick up the kid," and just all the planning involves a lot of my brain to do that and it wakes me up in the middle of the night kinda thing. Like, "Oh my gosh, we have to get the cars inspected so I better go ahead and make sure there's a block of time we can schedule that and make sure that appointment's made so that we don't get fined when we get pulled over." It's that kinda stuff that I don't think people see cause it's all going on up here [in my head] in a running list of things I have to remember. That's a big part of my job is just making sure I'm on top of every—they have a test next week so they need probably some extra study time on this, so I need to ask Rob to make sure that he—you know, that kinda thing. The things where you are doin' laundry and stuff like that, yeah, you can see there's a basket of clean clothes there at the end and I think if you really begged I think someone would say, "Wow, thanks for that effort." But I don't honestly feel like that's nearly as difficult as just keeping everything, like all the details of life, straight.

Striving to be the "best mom ever" while rigorously managing the home—planning and charting her way toward joyful family scenes—this is Sam's mode of becoming mamapreneurial.

Sam's exhausting and methodical approach to motherhood crystallizes the extent to which mamapreneurialism constitutes a fourth shift of caring labor. Arlie Hochschild has famously identified mothers' "second shift" of domestic labor and "third shift" of emotional labor, but mamapreneurialism operates as a fourth shift that encompasses the multifaceted and ever-increasing work of family appreciation.[38] This fourth shift intensifies and animates mothers' labors, layering new economic and affective imperatives onto daily family life. As she works to be "the best mom ever," Sam not only governs the domestic realm and her children's behavior but also acts as an insurance agent and efficiency manager in order to lift her family into future happiness. This was clear in her discussion of what feels joyful about mothering.

> They are so funny, so there's nothing better to me than having a glass of wine at the end of the day, and sitting at the dinner table with them, and them just sharing different jokes or ridin' on each other about different things. . . . It's just really funny how smart they are and how creative and how they bounce back and forth. Really it's the observation of my kids, it's not even really the hands-on interaction. It's, like, to see kind of—this isn't obviously the final product—but to see kind of some fruit feels really joyful.

Sam feels joy not in "hands-on interaction" but when she sees "some fruit," that is, when she can verify and "lock down" the impression that her intensive efforts have been productive of concrete happy outcomes.

As in Sam's case, the mamapreneurial fourth shift cuts across her second- and third-shift labors and includes a battery of appreciating activities, which are designed to secure and elevate everyday family scenes as hubs of privatized happiness. Sam, for instance, regularly turns to digital media tools like My Job Chart, an online program that promises to help busy families maintain order while teaching children lessons in financial responsibility. As she detailed, Sam experiments with "many kinds of systems," adopting a new one every year, as "those lists become white noise" and lose their potential to keep her kids engaged and excited about completing chores. Online couponing is also an important technology for Sam. Attuned to the pathologization of extreme couponers, Sam was quick to assure us that she is "not crazy"—"not buying hundreds of things at a time"—while describing the satisfaction she derives from couponing: "I like to see how much I save with coupons just to feel good about myself." While couponing engenders clear evidence of the fruits of her mamapreneurial labors, Sam was in fact most excited about her budgeting work: "I love budgeting. I am crazy about it. I use Quicken to do all my budgeting, and I love it. I love, love, love it. I love making charts and graphs. . . . I love the power of seeing where we are, the challenge of trying to make the budget. We're not awesome at that part, but I love trying. . . . The things I kind of really focus on are my grocery bills, so I can keep a running tally on my calendar of all my expenditures for the month."

These technologies of appreciation are part and parcel of an overall mamapreneurial fourth shift designed to realize Sam's goals for her family. Indeed, the fourth shift shoots through all of Sam's labors, as well-laid-out schedules and balanced budgets certify that "things are going smoothly," that the home has been fully rationalized, and, therefore, that happiness is on the horizon. Put differently, Sam's quest to be the "best mom ever" is conjoined to her effusive love of budgeting, as together they signal Sam's singular path to privatized happiness.

At one level, we can understand Sam's mamapreneurial fourth shift in terms of what Randy Martin calls the "financialization of daily life," in which the home becomes a place where children actively learn financial responsibility through chore systems and allowances, and parents rationalize behaviors by "modeling domesticity along the lines of the modern corporation."[39] According to Martin, mothers like Sam are encouraged to think of themselves as CEOs of their families, expanding the contours of family care to encompass the demands of financialization and privatized risk. While many of the mothers we interviewed assumed primary responsibility for everyday household budgets, bills, bank accounts, and the like, we want to suggest that the mamapreneurial sensibility is much more complex and fraught. For instance, Sam's desire for a highly rationalized, happy family scene regularly slams up against the material realities of her overloaded life:

> I'm finding the hardest part for me is having so many things, so many places where I'm needed at once, and I can only respond to one, but if you have that many things going on, it makes it even harder to choose which one. And it's not even a choice, it's whoever's loudest. I've had this discussion recently with my husband because he was upset. We hadn't really connected for a while, and he had said that he felt like he was at the bottom of my list, and I was trying to explain that there is no list. I don't have a list of things, of priorities. It's whatever hits me in the face next. I really can't suggest that I consciously think, "Oh well, that's my husband, so he can go behind mowing the lawn." No, seriously, that's not what it is. It just happens to be that when I walked through the grass, it was to my knees, so I felt like, "Oh, I better cut the grass while I'm out here." So I think for myself that's the most difficult is just [that] I like to be on top of things. I like to be organized. That's my success. If I have three people needing things at the same time, or even one person and two other household tasks at the same time that I'm thinking of, that's difficult. How do I keep on top of all these things and not make anyone feel like they are not getting their needs met?

Sam's simultaneous denial and celebration of her management strategies—"there is no list," but "I like to be organized"—are indicative of the competing social demands that many mothers navigate as they work to privatize happiness on their own. "Warm" enterprises like love and family are not meant to be "locked" down, and yet, for Sam, the rationalization of domestic life figures as the only way to appreciate her family and ensure its survival.

CAROLINE: MAMAPRENEURIAL FLEXIBILITY

Like Sam, Caroline never really imagined having kids; her plans changed only at the behest of her "very family-oriented" husband, whose family owns a long-running, much-loved small business in Ryeland. Before meeting her husband, Caroline harbored dreams of living a very different life; she has a business degree, which she parlayed into an erstwhile career in corporate banking. She told us, "Until I met my husband, I thought I would end up living in a big city and, you know, doing the corporate thing, that's how I always pictured it. Maybe getting married, maybe not. Didn't really matter. But family really wasn't on my horizon." Expectations slowly shifted over the course of her relationship with her husband: "And, you know, we got married. We waited a while . . . and it just, you know, it really didn't, there wasn't like this decision changing. It just kind of evolved that way, which I think happens to a lot of people. You have these ideas when you're young, but as you get older you realize what you really want in life." In stark contrast to prominent postfeminist discourses about working versus stay-at-home mothers, Caroline does not talk about this situation as an active decision—"there wasn't like this decision"—and she does not readily experience her current family scene as if she were a freely choosing gender agent. Rather, like most workers in the neoliberal economy, Caroline is flexible.

Caroline describes herself as a stay-at-home mom, and she spends most of her days with her two little girls. Unlike many of the women we spoke with, Caroline lives a comfortably middle-class life with her family. They are members of Ryeland's small country club and send their children to private Catholic schools. Her husband's work is seasonal, and during the on-season, his hours are excruciatingly long, so much so that Caroline compared herself to a military wife and reported that it took her ten long years "to get adjusted to it." In the on-season, Caroline prepares and packs up dinner every night so the family can eat together at her husband's workplace: "[it is a] big pain in the ass, but I still do it because it's the only time the kids get to see him, so we go down there and we, you know, just talk about our day or whatever." Though Caroline reported becoming "incredibly depressed" when her husband is gone for the summer, often missing summer holiday celebrations, she quickly interjected that "the trade-off is, you know, Thanksgiving, Christmas, all the other holidays in the winter are not an issue. We can leave, we can go wherever we want, we can basically go away, and it doesn't matter. 'Cause we don't have to worry about a job or responsibilities."

Caroline reported that she has found solace in the extended group of friends she met when her family became involved in the local preschools; however, she is also notably reluctant to turn to the community during the on-season. With her extended family living over two hours away and her husband virtually absent for half the year, Caroline continues to experience periodic bouts of loneliness and doubt. Though other families invite her and the children to be a part of their family gatherings, she says, "I always feel weird, 'cause I know, part of me thinks it's like a sympathy, like 'Oh, we feel so bad for you.' I don't wanna be a sympathy vote! So that is the tough part. . . . It seems to go on forever. Which again, everybody's with their families and going to picnics and it's just the girls and I. That's the hard part." Rather than turning to her community for help, Caroline refocuses on appreciating the family and privatizing happiness, taking family dinner to her husband's workplace and relentlessly scheduling activities with her girls to experience togetherness.

Even during the easier off-season when her husband is home, Caroline shoulders the responsibility for the family enterprise. While she repeatedly praised her husband for being "such a good helper"—he routinely sets out their children's breakfast and packs their lunches—she also told us that she is in charge year-round. "With the kids there's a lot of paperwork," she explained.

> When things come home from school I have to fill out this, or I'm baking cookies for her, or sending in snacks for this person. That kind of stuff. . . . It's better [if I do this work]. If I let him in charge of snack, who knows, he'd send a bag of candy. So, no, it's better that I do that stuff, which is fine. I mean, we're not the traditional, the mom does this and the dad does this. But, I don't know, I like doing stuff like that. I feel like that's a mom thing to do.

Once the kids are put to bed and Caroline can take a brief break from doing the "mom thing," she shifts gears to focus her work on the family business, managing its payroll and maintaining its communications with vendors and customers. This work involves handling the financials for the business, overseeing the company's promotional activities, and constantly monitoring its Facebook page. On a typical day, Caroline works from the time the kids go to bed until midnight.

In this sense, Caroline has adapted to the shifting demands of neoliberal family autonomy, reimagining her capacities and retooling them in the service of her family enterprise. Indeed, Caroline's family life hinges on her mamapreneurial flexibility, that is, her willingness to see and envision her own entrepreneurial self in the collusion of caretaking and helping out the family business. In all, Caroline's labors are geared toward holding the enterprise together and cultivating its capacities for privatized happiness. Caroline is always online, working to become reflexive and optimizing. She reads and shares parenting advice and dialogues with friends and other moms in the mamasphere. Like many moms we spoke to, she identifies herself as very "type A" and "logical," so when her younger daughter turned out to be "a little tornado," "out there," and "moody and emotional," Caroline had to work extra hard to adapt to her daughter's volatile needs and personality.

In the face of her lost career dreams, mamapreneurial labor figures quite paradoxically for Caroline. On one hand, it is an outlet for postfeminist sensibilities of capacity and professional achievement. Caroline spoke to us at length about how she puts her deferred passions and acumen to work on behalf of her husband's small business. Unpaid and unacknowledged, her care work is at odds with postfeminist discourses of capacity, which idealize high-achieving young women.[40] Nonetheless, mothers like Caroline develop their own version of "can-do" capacities and gender empowerment through mamapreneurialism.[41] For example, Caroline told us how fulfilling her accounting work for her husband's business felt, explaining at one point, "I love numbers. I love that stuff. . . . [T]ax season is very thought-provoking but generally just kind of monotonous, but I do like it. It gives me some, like, my brain gets to work a little bit. I do like that." Caroline also expressed pride in the complicated affective and technical work she successfully performed when she discovered that a private, unaffiliated individual had opened a Facebook page for their family's business: "I tried to get this person to give it to me because when I realized that they were answering questions that people were asking, and we didn't know who this was, I was, like, that's not OK. 'Cause who knows what they could have done with that. And it never got bad, but it was just kind of starting to go in that direction, and I was, like, no." Caroline had to work closely with Facebook to get this account pulled, a difficult decision because the page already had five thousand followers. Caroline said that when she finally resolved the issue, "My husband called me the MacGyver of the Internet. It was a proud moment."

On the other hand, becoming mamapreneurial is full of tension and anxiety for Caroline. While she exudes confidence and control in her discussions of helping the family business, she clearly wrestles with other facets of mamapreneurialism, especially the modes of reflexive selfhood it requires. For Caroline, economizing family happiness means constantly rationalizing and calling into question her own practices of women's work. She recalled a conversation with friends:

> I have my group of friends from college. I'm the only one that's a stay-at-home mom. It switched. It was funny when I first graduated, when we first had kids, I was jealous of them. I was like, "Oh, I wish I could be living that," because none of them had kids, and they were still working those wonderful jobs, and they still lived in the same area and got together. I was so jealous of them. But it's kind of turned [out] that they're all working with kids, and I'm a stay-at-home mom. A couple [of] drinks into a conversation, and they're like, "We're so jealous. We wish we could stay at home. You get to do all these wonderful things" and this and that. I said, "No, it's not. It's not as wonderful as you'd think." There are days that I wish that I could just put on a suit, take a briefcase, and go to work. I would wish I had those days sometimes, but I don't. Again I wouldn't change what I have, but I have those days. I said to my one friend who really gets upset about it, because she really doesn't wanna work right now, "You know, to be honest, I look at your stuff, the stuff that you do with your kids, and I'm just as jealous," I said, "because I think you do a better job of, 'OK, I've got from the time I get home from work to the time they go to bed, I have to make these hours count.'" I said I have all day but I don't do, mine is kind of spread out because I'm like, "OK, let's go play outside and blow bubbles." "OK, now momma has to go in," and I have to pay this bill. "OK, now let's do this." Mine's more scattered. Quality time is quality time, but I think that they find that they do more quality in a short amount of time, things. I don't know if that makes any sense. It's kind of an eye-opening conversation we were having. I was like, you know, I'm just as jealous of you as you are of me.

Even though she is a stay-at-home, intensive mother whose life is oriented first and foremost around caring for her girls, Caroline worries that her own efforts are not enough, questioning whether her approach, embedded in the mundane stuff of domestic labor (doing laundry, paying bills, and making snacks), is sufficiently optimized and calculated. While the realities of working moms' lives force them to actively cultivate highly strategic happiness habits to make their hours "count," Caroline sees her less structured mamapreneurial approach as potentially depreciating, so she is constantly checking herself to make sure her daily choices and actions are working to appreciate her family's human capital.

For example, as part of her fourth shift, Caroline checks e-mail and Facebook throughout the day, responding to questions about prices and local events, and managing occasional negative comments that appear on the business's Facebook page. However, she worried that her time online was too often taking her "out of the moment," so she gave up these "daily distractions" for Lent.

> It starts to become a problem 'cause now [e-mail and Facebook are] on my phone, so I just randomly check it. So I gave that up, and I did OK with that. . . . [I]t's like I would go on to check something for the business, and I would just flip over to mine and just see. I have to take that down a notch. But I'm not alone in that. It's kind of like a quick thing that you can kind of remove yourself from the day-to-day grind of "I have to make a sandwich" and "I have to wipe a butt." Well, I can go here and kind of live this . . . OK, see what this person's doing, kind of a distraction. Yeah, I use it. I'd say I'm average. I know people that do it a lot more than I do. . . . I shouldn't really care about this, and it kind of just takes you out of the moment.

For Caroline, mamapreneurial flexibility entails constant self-reflexivity, work that aims to optimize and rationalize her family scene, and her self, for privatized happiness. In chapter 1 we saw the devastating consequences of Caroline's constant self-reflexivity as the perpetual self-monitoring of her own health left her "clinically crazy." As she recalled, "I spent a good six months not doing anything. I couldn't function."

LISA: FAMILIAL RESILIENCE

"That fear, I mean the world is changing so quickly. . . . When we were little, if your car broke down, you could ask somebody for a ride. Now you don't dare. You don't know anybody, so I think my fear is, what is the world going to be like for my sons as they get older and their children? And, I don't know, I worry about where the world is headed in general, and I feel very helpless about that," Lisa, a homeschooling mother of two boys, told us. "I mean, there's nothing that I can do. There are little things that we can, I mean, we are definitely a green household, and that we have control over, but I feel like the political aspect we don't have any control over." A former elementary and middle school teacher who now spends her days with her six-year-old son, Brian, and his four-year-old brother, Everett, Lisa explained, "It's the big global things that I tend to worry about. The smaller things I don't tend to get as worked up about because we just kinda handle stuff as it comes." Her global worries are intense:

> We're fairly conservative. We see things in the world becoming much more liberal, and, you know, I definitely think everybody should be able to make their own decisions. And I think what we have is more and more and more laws that are for the minority rather than the majority, and I'm just very concerned about [that]. OK, I mean, we see things falling apart, and most people, if you ask, Americans say, "Yeah, things are falling apart. When is that, you know, over-the-edge moment going to come?" I don't think it's going to be an all-of-a-sudden, but it's just slowly going downhill. And I look forward . . . not for many, many years, but, you know, having my own grandchildren, and that's something that I want my children to look forward to and not be at a point where it's, you know, the world's getting worse, do we really want children?

Global changes seem to bear down on Lisa, who envisions a "typical American," comfortably middle-class future for her children, a suburban scene filled with grandchildren who live nearby. "Minority" interests and global warming threaten her nuclear family scene and its return on happiness. "There is so little that I worry about that I can actually control at the moment, so I think that lack of control, or not being able to control things, is what I worry about." Unable to make a difference in world politics, she turns her attention to family instead, building a safe haven where her children might flourish despite world ills.

Perhaps more than any of the other mothers we talked to, Lisa closes a circle around her family, generating income, education, and even heat within the confines of the home. She quit her teaching job to stay home with the children and now devotes her days to homeschooling their eldest son, Brian. In the early mornings and late evenings, she writes learning activities for an online homeschooling resource. Her husband, Dan, uses the summer to chop and stack wood for the burner that heats their home in the winter, and he spends long hours on do-it-yourself projects like building a pool at their house. Lisa "hates" Walmart and prefers to shop online when possible, despite having a credit card stolen at one point. Much of the family's social time is dedicated to visiting extended family. Lisa and Dan both grew up in Ryeland and were high school sweethearts, and they spend many days with Lisa's mom—who, she says, is "the end all be all when it comes to mothering"—and her dad, who often takes Brian fishing during flexible homeschooling days. Lisa is active in Mothers of Preschoolers, and she and her family regularly spend afternoons at T-ball or violin practice or swimming together at the YMCA.

For Lisa, becoming mamapreneurial is first and foremost about cultivating familial resilience. She constructs her family scene as a self-contained, self-reliant defensive enterprise, rooted in togetherness and capable of surviving a range of threats associated with advanced neoliberalism, from routinized, underfunded public schools to environmental crises. Lisa responds to a world "slowly going downhill" by building a world of her own.

Familial resilience is, for Lisa, a form of resistance to global capitalism and the forces of precarization that threaten her family and its human capital. Attached to a national fantasy of the white, happy, nuclear family that she knows no longer holds, she blames this shattered fantasy on liberals and a racialized welfare state. Readily accepting "the big global things" she cannot control, she disassociates herself from those "minorities" she perceives to be connected to a corrupt state and the values of a world that is "falling apart." Competition for resources is fierce, and Lisa sees her family as on the losing side of broader trends despite their relative privileges and security, so she takes on more and more responsibility for her family's well-being and constantly tweaks her approach to mothering in order to hang on ever more tightly to the broken promise of a good life for her family.

For example, while Lisa is acutely aware of her powerlessness, she nonetheless enthusiastically directs most of her energy to developing reflexive capacities for conscientious parenting. A self-identified "yeller," she and her husband recently devised a plan to monitor each other's reactions to the kids:

I see how calm and not reactive [my mom was], but consciously making a decision about how she handles a situation. That's where I want to be, and I know that didn't come from day 1, you had a child and "Woohoo! Here I am!" I know it's learned, and I just feel like they are growing up so fast, and I am running out of that time to change, and I really want to change. My husband actually came up with a secret code where if one of us is being too reactive, my kids are both into pirates, and so he came up with, if we say "ARRGGH" that means, "Calm down, we are overreacting," and so every once in a while I hear "ARRGGH," OK, I get the clue. So it's funny then instead of being, "He just judged me" or "She just judged me," you know. It's just a funny way to handle the situation.

For Lisa, time is running out; she feels she must act now to become a "good" mom to her fast-growing kids. She devises lots of strategies for becoming a better mom, instituting a clothespin and coffee-can system for teaching the boys to limit their screen time and enforcing a "no guns" rule in their home. But she is also constantly reassessing these rules. For example, as her children learned about guns from their cousins, she softened the restriction, allowing gunplay, but only under particular circumstances that reflect her family's environmentally conscious lifestyle. And while she limits their screen time, she still wonders how much time she should allow her sons to spend on the computer and frets over what computing skills they need to know. She says, "Those gray areas are difficult. Those are the times that you wish that there were an instruction manual that you could open up and say, 'OK, this is what you are supposed to do.'"

As she weaves together days designed to both keep her family safe and optimize her children's abilities, Lisa is haunted by uncertainty about whether her highly privatized approach to homemaking will engender independent, resilient children who can make their own way in a scary and competitive world. "I fear I'm sheltering my children too much because they are home with me all day. Are they getting enough experiences out in the world?" The children have only slept over at their grandparents' and cousins' houses, and Lisa told us, "I worry about, hmm, am I going to be the cool mom that people want to come over to our house, which is where I'd rather they be anyways, or, you know, am I sheltering my kids too much so that they are going to be so rebellious when they get older?"

In many ways, digital media make Lisa's mamapreneurial resilience possible, as they provide a platform for materializing her highly privatized approach to childrearing and care. Specifically, the mamasphere figures less as a site of connection or community for Lisa and more as a machinic infrastructure for cordoning off and securitizing her home. Most notably, Internet communication technologies allow Lisa to transform the domestic sphere into a private school for her "extremely gifted" son. Lisa and

Dan "went round and round about homeschooling" as Brian approached kindergarten age. Lisa explained that as a teacher, she had been deeply frustrated by the government "red tape" limiting teachers' ability to "let the kids be creative and explore," and so before she had children, she helped develop a small private school in Ryeland dedicated to fostering creativity and curiosity. Despite her reservations about organized schooling, the couple ultimately decided to send Brian to public school. They quickly pulled him out, however, because even his "wonderful teacher" was unable to meet his needs in her large class. "I mean . . . they're told they have to teach to the middle and, you know, kinda hope you get both ends," Lisa explained, "and there was no way he was going to benefit from that." Lisa now works with Brian every day, helping him through a cyberschool curriculum in a way that suits his individual needs. Adopting a "really flexible" schedule, she allows him to advance to upper-level materials as needed and substitutes holistic work, like book reports, for some of the more regimented assignments in the predeveloped curriculum. Everett spends a few hours each week in preschool, but when he is home, Lisa also encourages him to work through the curriculum. She is adamant about her willingness to adapt to her children's educational needs, insisting they will homeschool only as long as it works for the family. Still, if the children do ever go to school, Lisa imagines that it will be to the private school she helped develop, "because they do have a lot more flexibility because they don't have to answer to the state as much as everybody else."

With cyberschool, Lisa feels assured that her kids' education isn't being compromised by standardized approaches. "There's only a little bit that they actually do online," she told us. "We have to record their attendance online everyday and stuff like that . . . but there's not a whole lot of it that's online." The digital curriculum is not experienced as a state demand but rather as an abundant hub of opportunity. For example, Lisa raved about Brian's customized interactions with Brain Pop, " a really cool website" with "tons of information" and "great, very well-organized videos in just about any area of the curriculum that you could think of."

At the same time, homeschooling requires Lisa to hone a flexible approach to paid work. Unwilling to work as a teacher while raising children, she turned to an online clearinghouse for work-at-home moms. Her initial job involved generating content for search-optimized blogs, but she eventually quit, as it became "more and more restrictions and less and less money."

In turn, Lisa found a new work-at-home job creating learning activities for a homeschooling resource. Deeming this job "a great fit," she excitedly reported that the company is planning to develop a book of "tips for parents" from the web content she had helped to produce. Digital media allow Lisa to be the "unavowed glue" for her family, privatizing more and more risks and constantly retooling her labors for a world that is "falling apart."[42]

Still, no matter how resilient her family becomes, worries remain. Lisa recounted how she relies on her husband to handle the bigger economic picture. While she admits to being "pretty good" with money—"I don't overspend. I tend to be a saver rather than a spender. *Frugal* is the kind word; *cheap* would be the word some other people might say"—she defers to her husband when it comes to managing the family finances. However, this became a cause for concern when a close friend's mother was dying of cancer, which made Lisa realize how much she doesn't know about money. She explained, "I was thinking if something happened to David, I don't know if I would know. I mean, I know our bank account numbers . . . which one is which, but we need to go over that stuff in more detail, because I would . . . probably be going right to our financial advisor saying, 'I don't have a clue. Teach me.'"

Because the world is a danger zone, Lisa feels deeply that she must keep blazing trails for her family. It is up to her to constantly create and hold together a sustainable family scene in the face of unknowable global catastrophes. As the world appears to be breaking down around her, Lisa stays focused on the never-ending work of family appreciation and keeping alive the promise of the good life for her own family. For Lisa, familial resilience is the only possible path and political commitment in a competitive world of privatized risk.

JENNY: HAPPINESS MACHINE

Unlike Sam and Caroline, Jenny "always knew" that she "wanted to be a mom." She worked as a nanny through college, earning an associate of arts degree, and moved in with her soon-to-be husband within a week of graduation. Jenny was delighted to become pregnant when she was newly married, and she threw herself happily into the full-time work of mothering her baby boy, as well as her young stepson. By the time she spoke with us, Jenny and her husband had two more young sons. Unlike many of the women we spoke to, Jenny betrayed no regrets about her role. She explained, "I didn't really have the thoughts of, 'Oh, I'm going to lose myself, I'm going to lose my career,' all that stuff. Because I wanted to be a stay-at-home mom, so I guess I never really had those expectations as far as, to have a career, you know what I mean?"

Jenny's comfort in her present maternal role is palpable: she's a relaxed mom, nonplussed by her children's antics and clearly settled in her beliefs about family and childrearing. She has cultivated an ethic of care grounded in conservative Christian values and traditional beliefs about the family. Her kids attend children's church every Sunday and sometimes a class that focuses on Bible verses. She invests deeply in service work, primarily support-ing other families by volunteering as a leader for Mothers of Preschoolers and organizing meal trains for new mothers. And she dreams of adopting a little girl, posting prayers on Facebook that foster children with Down syn-drome might find their "forever families." Clearly, Jenny's life is shaped by family autonomy and her desire to optimize traditional family happiness. Well-kept homes, well-behaved children, and family togetherness all signal security and happiness, and Jenny's ability to maintain this scene is indica-tive of her family's path to the good life.

Consequently, when Jenny's "good life" was shattered by economic in-security, she became mamapreneurial: her first line of defense was flexi-ble fourth-shift labor, enacted "while the kids are either (a) playing or (b) sleeping." As mentioned previously, Jenny did informal in-home day care for a brief time but eventually turned to even more flexible fourth-shift work selling totes and accessories for Thirty-One, because, as she told us, "I wanted to focus on my children when I was home." Most recently, Jenny became a "wrapreneur" for Get Life, a direct-sales company specializing in body-sculpting wraps, as well as nutritional supplements and other health and beauty products aimed toward women. As a Get Life distributor, Jenny spends much of her time on Facebook, enthusiastically selling Get Life products and recruiting other mothers to join her sales team. Founded in 2001 to help struggling families "dream big," Get Life, a multilevel mar-keting company, promises that a "stressed out working mom with a boring job just trying to make ends meet" will find a life of "friendship," "fun," and "freedom" in the Get Life world. Would-be wrapreneurs are thus told that just twenty-five dollars and a willingness to share the promises of Get Life products on their personal social media feeds will launch them into a life free of student and credit card debt and full of quality time with their children. "I've got the life I've always dreamed of," gushes an animated wrapreneur on the Get Life home page. "And you can have it too! To start redreaming your life, join the party today!"[43]

Though her family still feels the effects of losing "everything" just a few years ago, Jenny is relentlessly optimistic. Crucially, this optimism is cultivated through Jenny's online mamapreneurial endeavors with Get Life. In the digital mundane, Jenny becomes a *happiness machine*: she lifts herself and her family into happiness through vigorous online networking and entrepreneurial Get Life performances, peddling hope to her client-friends and posting daily stories of clients' body transformations, her own newfound freedoms as a Get Life distributor, and inspirational memes branded with Get Life logos.

For Jenny, family happiness rests on her Get Life business, as she privatizes happiness by actively constructing a Get Life persona online. The Get Life website is filled with stories of families gaining control over their lives with the help of the company and the optimistic and energized attitudes it engenders. Brandon and Denise Walsh, for example, quit their careers in aerospace engineering and clinical psychology to focus primarily on Get Life. The couple, who have since moved into a new home on six and a half acres with an indoor basketball court, say, "We're in the midst of our story. Thankfully we have the power to change the ending." Denise, who claims that she was a "zombie" in her old job, says, "With Get Life, you're always wanting to become a better person and stay engaged in life." Jenny tells a similar story to her own Facebook network: "As a stay-at-home mom I felt lost and considered myself as someone doing nothing. I woke every morning and took care of my littles and knew that my life was important but wanted more. I was stuck in a rut. I had stopped dreaming, stopped setting goals, and stopped having a fire for life. Every day was the same, and the stress of life pushed at me in every direction." In addition to boosting her family's bottom line and preserving family autonomy, Get Life is, according to Jenny, enabling her to realize her optimal self. Just three months after becoming a distributor, Jenny posted that the company had

> changed my life, my family's life, and our future. Get Life has renewed that fire for life, has us dreaming again, and has us setting goals. And this time not little dreams but BIG Dreams! And you better believe we are ready to "DO SOMETHING"! I love our products, I love our

company, I love the opportunity and I cannot wait to share it with the world. I have said it before and will say it again, this company is unlike any other and it is helping to change lives UPSIDE down! Maybe you have felt lost. Maybe you feel lost now. Maybe you want to gain back your health, maybe you want some extra money, maybe you want a different lifestyle, maybe you want financial freedom.— MAYBE you just want to dream again and DO SOMETHING! Message or text me, friends, let's talk!

Jenny's corporatized online persona exemplifies Sam Binkley's idea of "happiness as enterprise," in which "agency, enterprise, and responsibility for oneself are both the means for achieving and the very content of happiness itself."[44] Jenny claims a deep belief in the Get Life path to family happiness, maintaining that her commitment to the company and her willingness to conquer her fears and assert herself according to its values will bring her family security and freedom. Her "dream," what she's been "working for," is to earn enough income to allow her husband to retire from his physically demanding, time-consuming job as a deliveryman. "Lovin this leap of faith I took," Jenny recently posted on her Facebook page. "Thank you for proving that you can dream big and make it happen!"

However, as Binkley is keen to point out, happiness as enterprise is not only constructivist but also necessarily *destructive*, for the perceived "docility of social dependence, and the negative thoughts that lull us into a state of torpor," must be rendered uninhabitable and unimaginable. In their place is "the vital, enterprising life-spirit that is the wellspring of life's activity, or freedom."[45] Get Life hinges on promising this life-spirit to both its customers and its distributors: customers purportedly find vitality through the company's nutritional supplements and minimizing wraps, while distributors supposedly come alive through their labors for the company. Crucially, this life-spirit comes to stand in for publicly funded social safety nets, as enterprising optimism, rather than a social contract, is what promises adherents the good life. Indeed, Jenny assures us that she believes Get Life can release her family from debt and her husband from long hours by recounting enthusiastically how two of her close friends "got off welfare" after becoming Get Life distributors.

It is important to see that Jenny's becoming mamapreneurial rests on her capacities to parlay social networks—her "warm market"—into both clients and "downstream" distributors for the company. Beyond transforming

Jenny's leisure time into a fourth shift of flexible labor, Get Life transforms her digital nets—her social networks and capital—into highly rationalized, financially driven relationships. Not surprisingly, transforming friendships and the affordances of participatory culture into economic opportunities comes with its own risks. Jenny told us that she has lost several friendships since becoming a Get Life distributor, fielding criticism from those who find the Get Life happiness machine either annoying or troubling. Nonetheless, believing in the company's ability to grant her financial freedom and family autonomy, Jenny has thrown her emotional, social, and financial capital into Get Life. As she recently posted,

> I know some people don't get what I am doing these days with this wrap business. That's ok. But please let me explain: Not only has Get Life helped me gain my health, wellness, and pre-baby body back. BUT over the past 3 MONTHS my income has nearly tripled and this journey has far surpassed my expectations. Guess what, all?! I am just getting started! This is about helping my family become debt free. This is about bringing our little girl home to her forever family. This is about staying home with my kids. This is about my husband retiring from truck driving. AND this is about others' lives being changed and transformed! This is so much more than a wrap. This is about God answering prayers and the prayers of others through this business. It's okay if you don't understand, but you being annoyed isn't going to stop this girl! Feel free to delete me. Love you all but honestly . . . don't knock it til you've tried it! ****What are you doing to make your dreams come true?**** #starttoday #leavealegacy

As featured distributor Megan Baker says on Get Life's website, "if you want to change your life, you have to change your life. You have to let some things go." Of course, what mothers like Jenny need to let go of is not their capacity to labor, nor the sensibility that their labor can insure and help appreciate their families. Rather, women are obliged to affectively release negative, pessimistic attitudes and behaviors—fear of failure, old habits— that cannot be readily optimized or rationalized. Jenny explained, "Before I started with Get Life I had eighteen reasons to fail": "I thought it was a scam. I had little to no sales experience. . . . I doubted my abilities to succeed." But, she continued, "I had four reasons to succeed": her little boys and the daughter she hopes to one day adopt.

Together, these mamapreneurial compositions reveal the cruel promises of privatizing happiness. Though our focus has been on just four women's lives, their labors are exemplary: all of the women we interviewed were becoming mamapreneurial in their own ways in the digital mundane, engaging in fourth-shift practices ranging from participation in online contests to work-at-home endeavors to carefully planned strategies for educating their children at home.

Notably, some women have focused their efforts primarily on enhancing the family's bottom line through engaging the corporate nodes of the mamasphere. For example, in the next chapter, we discuss Elana's dedicated efforts to finance her family's trip to Disney World by winning Disney's "Cutest Baby" contest. For weeks, Elana sent daily e-mail blasts to all of her contacts, imploring them to vote for baby Jared. Meanwhile, Trina, a self-described Pampers "fanatic," visits their site regularly because she can get "little codes [to] . . . win things" and because they offer "hints" for more effective parenting. Trina had only recently dug her family out of an $8,000 debt accumulated after her premature daughter spent weeks in the neonatal intensive care unit; in this harrowing context, online coupons and games afforded an ever-present, reassuring strategy for securitizing an otherwise scary and shaky family scene.

Other mothers approach the economizing of family life through less directly financial, though equally intensive practices of reflexive selfhood. As we saw in chapter 1, Shana reflects constantly on day-to-day mothering life and carefully calibrates her self accordingly. Like Shana, Kim, a stay-at-home mother of three and a former speech therapist, organizes daily activities to enrich her children's minds. She holds daily "calendar time" in their home playroom, which is carefully decorated with children's clocks, calendars, maps, and artwork. Playtime is designed intentionally as learning time, and all hours of the day are dedicated to expanding her kids' minds. For both of these mothers, then, the mundane spaces and temporalities of domestic life are conceptualized as opportunities for appreciating the human capital of the family, for rationalizing a path to privatized happiness.

Still other women, like Jenny, have sought work-at-home and part-time options for enhancing the family income and optimizing their own sense of self. While Brittany's husband is on disability and uses a wheelchair, she has cobbled together various part-time jobs to support her family. Most recently, she became an infant photographer for a local hospital, a job she loves because it unites her orientation toward family with her budding talent for photography. Annie, a mother of two, joined Jenny's Get Life team and recently posted a photo on Facebook with the following caption: "3 Years Ago people would look at this group and see . . . 8 College Dropouts/1 GED/3 Guys in the Military/$375,000 in combined debt/3 families on WIC/1 Guy who was sleeping in his car/Today they see debt free and financially free Presidential and Ambassador Diamonds in Get Life/DON'T LET YOUR PAST HOLD YOU BACK FROM ONE HECK OF AN INCREDIBLE FUTURE!!" Like Jenny, Annie is now working for more "special moments" with her kids. Kendall is a dedicated Beachbody coach, selling weight-loss shakes and supplements, while offering customers online support in the form of inspirational memes and quotes. She looks to Beachbody "celebrities" as role models and communicates with them via Facebook; she recently posted with great pride that Beachbody had requested permission to use the workout pictures she had compiled in their newest infomercial. Kendall, who had just suffered a serious health setback, posted about this invitation, "Pretty amazing stuff. To say that I am excited and honored is an understatement!!!! I will #SurviveandThrive."

Mamapreneurialism is all about making the family "survive and thrive." In so many ways, mamapreneurialism makes advanced neoliberalism livable for mothers; anxiety and uncertainty, lost jobs and abysmal health care, and mounting insecurities all become approachable and attackable through mamapreneurialism's can-do, privatizing sensibility. Determined to do right by their children, mothers take it on themselves to insure their families in a cutthroat world where nothing seems guaranteed, except perhaps for their own love and effort. As digital media multiply opportunities for appreciation, mothers become exceedingly flexible abilities-machines for their families, working all the time to elevate their family scenes above the risks and threats of the precarious ordinary. Yet the digital distribution of the mamapreneurial sensibility also extends the impossibilities of neoliberal family autonomy and its intensified exploitation of women's caring labor. After all, most mamapreneurial labors, while highly profitable for a range of corporate outfits and governmental agencies, do not come with benefits such as health care and participation in social security, resources that would actually work to solidify the family's shaky ground.

Indeed, mamapreneurialism has mothers working harder and harder to appreciate their families, but these privatized efforts will never be adequate social insurance. This is the cruel optimism of mamapreneurialism: as mothers' labors become ever more economizing, privatizing, rationalizing, flexible, and resilient, they optimize the very systems of precarization that threaten their families in the first place.

3 · DIGITAL ENTANGLEMENTS

Staying Happy in the Mamasphere

ELANA

Thirty-something Elana is an intense figure: she speaks rapidly and breathlessly; yearns for meaningful experiences and world travel; harbors deep fears that her son, eight-month-old Jared, might drown or choke; pinches pennies to save for his college tuition; and plans so carefully for her future that her boss jokes she "already has [her] retirement home picked out." Before she had her son, Elana dreamed of being a mother, idealizing her future relationship to her husband and child:

> I knew I was going to love [having children], and I do love it very much, even more so. [But] I guess, you think, "Oh gosh, this is going to be the perfect thing." You're going to have this baby, and then you and your husband are going to come home and have these wonderful bonding moments. And it was completely different from that. Not in a bad way, it's just that . . . the day after we had [the baby, my

husband had to go to work] and he couldn't find a replacement for him working. . . . Even though his boss said, "We'll deal with it," [my husband] wouldn't. And so that made me really sad, because I really thought, "You come with your husband, and this is the most amazing moment, and you all bond together and do all these great things together," and it wasn't like that. I was kind of disappointed with just how the whole process went with just coming home. I definitely knew [I wanted a baby], and I have a great time, but it's even more fulfilling to be a mom and I was expecting that. . . . And I told [my husband] how disappointed I was, and he was like, "Why? I love my son!" And I'm like, "I'm not doubting that, [but] I get up with the baby in the middle of the night if he gets up, in the mornings I feed him, I change him." [My husband] rarely does that. I don't think he's a bad dad. I just think that moms just tend to do that. That's the expectation of the mother. And I don't mind it. But I like help.

The acute sorrow, anger, and hope laced through Elana's account of her early days of motherhood begin with her description of a happy family scene awash in both possibility and nostalgia. This tableau of familial happiness anticipates loyal and loving parents doting over their newborn son and bonding deeply with him. Devastatingly, however, the requirements of the paid workplace, and Elana's husband's lesser investment in the significance of these moments, marred the happy scene and left her longing for an experience that never was. Elana is grappling with a vision of idealized family life and working to hold her family to that image, even though the fit is far from perfect.

According to Elana, the media constantly showcase family happiness. She told us that watching *Full House* as a child, for example, made her yearn for happy family scenes like those in the show: "I know this sounds silly, [but] just the way you see a family bringing [a baby] home, like when Jesse and his, Becky or whatever, brought home her twins and he was so involved." While her description of early motherhood undercuts an idealized image of happy family life, Elana holds on to the family scene, redescribing motherhood as "fulfilling," noting her husband's love for their son, and reassuring herself (and us) that it is normal for mothers to take the lead in family life—and that they do so willingly and happily.

Throughout our interviews, we watched mothers like Elana labor to preserve their family scenes by maintaining their families as happy objects,

Sara Ahmed's term for that which points to and promises happiness in the future.[1] Families promise "the good life," so mothers orient and organize their lives around tending to and stabilizing these scenes. Of course, keeping the family happy in this way always involves carrying a heavy weight. Because happy families are lived in the muck of everyday life (dirty diapers and piles of laundry, screaming children and not-so-helpful husbands), calling these scenes "happy," and experiencing them as such, requires ongoing effort. In the context of neoliberal precarity, however, staying happy comes to demand even more of mothers.

Indeed, Elana organizes her world around the precarity of her family and its promises. The idealized life she yearns for is elusive, but she compensates by constantly working to privatize happiness in the course of her everyday life. In the mornings, she makes sure that Jared is in her room while she gets ready for her full-time job—"to have him with us and watch him and interact with him while we have that morning time with him"—and she prides herself on spending quality time with Jared and making him feel loved. She explained, "He's a very happy baby, and I know he . . . I think he actually understands how much we love him. . . . But to always be there for him is really important. To play with him all the time. To let him experience a lot of new things. That would be successful for me and happy for me." She told us, "I don't ever want to say I don't feel good about being a mother or mothering. But obviously time management's tough. . . . I think the hard thing is I don't have more time during the day with Jared." Her husband's job requires frequent late nights, and so many evenings Elana takes Jared to his workplace so the family can spend more time together. She forgoes the gym in order to have lunch with Jared at his day care and declines regular offers from her in-laws to take him on weekends:

> I don't want that for Jared. I want him to always wake up in our house on Saturday morning. I'll make him pancakes. We can watch cartoons together, play outside. Obviously his grandparents can be there. But I don't want to give my time away. I want to share it. And so to take him to Disney, he's our son. I have to change my life. . . . I haven't been to the gym in months because I would rather visit him right now at lunch. And it's really important to me that I'm always with him and that he's with his family and that we take him and include him in the things we do. My life's changed, we're not going to do certain things we used to do, but that's OK. 'Cause I have him.

Elana believes that her nuclear family needs to be together as much as their world will allow, and she sees it as her job to make room for and securitize happy togetherness.[2]

Elana dotes on her son, choosing to play with him "all the time." But she is also on the Internet "all the time," checking e-mail and CNN, posting photos of Jared on Facebook, hosting Skype sessions with her mom and Jared, and inspecting her online bank account and credit cards to "make sure my husband's not buying anything he shouldn't." She leans heavily on Google to ensure her son's health and happiness: "Of course, if I have a question on something and I have no one to call, I immediately go to the Internet and check," she told us. "I just Google, like, when Jared started eating solids, I really didn't know how many vegetables and fruits to give him per day. I'd go to the main Gerber website or something and obviously use online resources. . . . And they pretty much look consistent with their advice." Additionally, she is "always on Disney's website," planning a year in advance for their family vacation. Indeed, as Elana works to privatize happiness, the Internet teems with happy opportunity, offering connections with family, control over her baby's health and well-being, and occasion to put happy family moments on display.

At the same time, Elana laments the ways that social media pull her and her husband away from family togetherness. Though she loves posting pictures of Jared on Facebook, she once made a sincere effort to quit for a week before getting "sucked back in," and she fends off the Internet's lure by refusing to buy a smartphone or an iPad. In fact, time spent online is a major source of stress in her relationship: "I don't want my Internet to follow me. My husband has Internet on his phone, and I hate it because we're at dinner and he . . . Like, it doesn't matter the score of the game, and come on, we're on a date! Pay attention to me for five minutes." While the couple usually watches TV together in the evening while surfing the web or working on their individual laptops, they instituted a "no-laptop policy" for a special "Friday the 13th movie thriller night" at home. Elana is also wary of the dangers of oversharing on social media, taking care not to post family vacations for fear of exposing her home to theft. In other words, for Elana, digital media ping with happy potential, but they also beckon threateningly, pulling the family away from each other and threading fear through daily life.

Elana lives entangled in the digital mundane, as her life as a mother finds form through ongoing and banal engagements with digital media. In other words, mothers' everyday media lives are best thought of as a series of mundane, ongoing encounters of "affective intensification," or, as Jasbir Puar puts it, "the meeting of technology . . . bodies, matter, molecular movements, and energetic transfers."[3] Zones of digital entanglement are thus potent spaces, quivering with an intensely ordinary power to mobilize, route, and buttress mothers' lives. However, as Elana suggests, because these powers feel dangerous, packed with the imminent potential to short-circuit, mothers feel they must vigilantly manage their energetic flows and transfers.

This chapter explores how mothers come to sustain themselves through various forms of digital entanglement by providing snapshots of mothers' often fraught lives in the mamasphere. As we show, affective circuits of precarized happiness are intimately bound up with the communicative circuits of digital culture. Mothers' lives are "composed and suffered" in banal entanglements of media and everyday life, which simultaneously attenuate and intensify women's work in the nuclear family.[4] Specifically, we elaborate three forms of digital entanglement—charge, commune, and code and recode—to capture how the mamasphere figures as a vital affective infrastructure and comes to engender the resilient happiness required to mother through precarity. Altogether, these snapshots help to register what Kathleen Stewart calls "the pressure points of the compositionality of life" for mothers, where "new structures of attention . . . new sensory registers, and the systematic engineering of affect are begging new political question."[5]

CHARGE

As the previous two chapters showed, contemporary motherhood is an anxious, overloaded scene, as women work to privatize happiness, taking on heavier and heavier material and affective loads in order to appreciate their families. For many mothers, the mamasphere figures as a readily available affective charging station, keeping them fueled with energy and capacity for navigating the challenges of precarized happiness. In a world where things feel fragile and uncertain, always-on flows of inspiration, entertainment, and opportunity environmentalize the potentialities for encounters with happiness. For Addie, the mamasphere is a "major artery"; for Renee, it is her "creative" feed; for Dana, it is a lifeline that brings her back from despair. Mothers' lives take form in these mundane entanglements with digital media: as contingencies get tamed and affects modulated, mothers stay charged for the work of happiness.

Addie's Artery

Addie is attached to her computer. When her husband, Ben, recently took it along on an out-of-town trip for two days, she said, "I was not happy. . . . Oh boy, OK. I'm going to see if I can do this, two days without a computer! I mean, I do have my iPhone, . . . but it was still hard." The computer is Addie's link to the digital world of entertainment, inspiration, knowledge, and control. "I'm online constantly," she declared. "I just feel like it's a major artery for me. I don't know what I would do without the Internet. I really don't. . . . It's a big outlet for me."

Addie and Ben, along with their five-year-old daughter, Ginny, and a new baby who is on the way, enjoy a secure life in Ryeland. Ben has a high-profile position with the local hospital, and Addie works part-time as a school counselor. Their home sits on a plateau on the edge of town, away from the blight that characterizes much of Ryeland. Ginny is one of a few children who attend a new, innovative private school focused on arts-based learning, and the family spends many of their summer days at the local country club. Addie and Ben's home is furthermore characterized by a more equitable division of labor than was described by many of the mothers we spoke to. They both get Ginny ready for school in the mornings, and Ben does much of the grocery shopping, cooking, and yard maintenance. Still, despite her family's security and seeming proximity to "the good life," insecurity looms. "He has more of a mentality that everything is going to work out," Addie said of Ben's approach to parenting. "Mine is the total opposite. Nothing is going to work out unless you're engaged and making it happen."

For Addie, "making it happen" means constantly staying charged with digital media. In a way, Addie is a cyborg, drawing energy from the affective potentialities and intensifications of the digital mundane. While happiness-promising information, advice, and products teem online, Addie seems to revive and stabilize herself in the digital mundane. Indeed, she goes on-line to manage the various "upscaled anxieties" that animate her world.[6] "I'm self-diagnosed obsessive compulsive," she explained. "I organize my neuroses around, like, cleaning. I say my house is a direct reflection of my mental state. So if my house is a mess, I'm generally, like, 'Braaaaaa!'" As soon as Ginny leaves for school every morning, Addie "clean[s] . . . like a maniac," carrying her computer around with her so that she can watch TV online at the same time, "which makes me super happy, and . . . takes away the stress from having to clean."

After Ginny was born, Addie took her fears and worries about parenting to the mamasphere, negotiating new motherhood on her blog and eventually amassing enough followers to be recruited to the BlogHer network.[7] "I have a theory about how to develop a blog and get people to read your site," she said. "As it turns out, [being a new mother] was a very hard time for me, and I didn't have a problem talking about it. I think people generally have hard times with new babies, and they generally don't talk about it. So it was nice to go online and find somebody to talk to about it. I think I just started, and it just sort of snowballed. And most of my friends were bloggers reading all over the place, and we would get together, and it just became more and more community." As a node in the BlogHer network, Addie spent a lot of time reading other blogs, hoping to optimize her work as a mother as well as her own blog, which, in the end, only doubled her anxieties. "I mean, oh my gosh, like, over the top, and that what was so anxiety provoking for me, I was researching all the time," she explained. "I was constantly seeking out advice from mothers and writing about it and it just, it was a mirror of my own anxiety. I was just trying to make sense of my experience and read about how others were doing things." Addie eventually became a recruiter for BlogHer, and though she liked "the perks and the travel," she began to feel all too entangled and decided to quit both blogging and working for BlogHer. "I would be reading three hundred blogs a day, and I totally lost my voice. I didn't have a voice anymore, I had a blogging voice . . . and my work began to come with us everywhere."

Relieved to leave the anxiety of blogging behind, Addie now stays energized with other forms of do-it-yourself media, telling us, "I'm really into house-related decor. I'm hugely into Pinterest and things like that—not parenting related at all. I just love aesthetically beautiful things." For example, Addie had recently been "completely consumed" in making a new headboard for Ginny's bed, and she reported always having "little projects going." These were her "obsessions," which she feels "really happy" working on. Yet Addie has to be careful not to bring her computer to bed: "It can be very energizing for me, and then I can't turn it off." For example, she recounted how recently she was "obsessed" with ordering a particular rug on sale, while Ben pleaded, "COME ON." "It has to change our brain makeup and chemistry . . . direct access to information," Addie suggested. "We planned a trip last month, and, of course, everything was done online. What would we have done before that? Imagine the age of travel agents, having to trust someone else with all of your information. It [digital media] is good for the controlling personality, which I have a bit of."

Renee's Feed

While Addie readily embraces the ever-pulsing networks that fuel her days, Renee is a bit more cautious. A Christian mother of three devoted to a traditional and sustainable family lifestyle, Renee says she "was born to be a mom." When her youngest daughter was born, she stopped working at the preschool she owns. Now she relishes her time at home with her girls; they spend their days doing art projects, cooking, playing outside, and reading, and in the "mad rush" during nap time, she finds time to clean, start dinner, and exercise. Renee thus sees her days with her young children as a brief "season of life," and she organizes things around living it to the fullest. "We don't have cable; we don't go out to eat a lot. We replace a lot of those things with just family time because, you know, you blink and they're in kindergarten, and . . . they're at the mercy of what they learn at school and those kinds of things. It's such a small amount of time that they're at home with us so we tend to wanna pack a lot into that."

Meanwhile, digital media undergird Renee's everyday, promising both daily relief and inspiration. She turns to Facebook while waiting for the laundry to finish, dips into Pinterest while her kids eat lunch, and checks couponing blogs on a daily basis for ideas about maximizing savings. Renee's favorite site is *Couponing to Disney*, a blog that motivates Renee to minimize her grocery budget to save for a trip to Disney World. Facebook fulfills her need for connection: "You're so wrapped up in this little bubble of a world that is your kids and your husband and your house and that kinda thing, so . . . that's part of the appeal for moms. . . . [I]t gives them that connection to the outside world." And though the Blackberry that she and her husband share is not particularly well suited for apps, she turns to a Bible app while she waits to pick her oldest daughter up from school. In those ten minutes in the car, she said, she can "kind of focus [her] mind and . . . pay attention to what it's saying." Hence, throughout the day, digital media stand ready to give Renee a break: "It's kind of an escape even if it's for three minutes with half a cup of coffee, it's a little bit of a break in the middle of the monotony that sometimes can come with mothering."

Above all, Pinterest is Renee's favorite place in the mamasphere, and she uses the site to feed "that creative person that's still inside of me that doesn't have time to be creative."[8] Renee looks for pins to inspire a range of domestic activities:

> Gardening a lot 'cause that's just what we're doing right now, you know, seed starting and those kinds of things. Kids' projects a lot, kids' artwork. Even just things like how to braid my older daughter's hair. . . . Recipes a lot or homemade cleaners and, you know, all sorts of things like that. We've been trying to get away from the chemicals a lot, so I've been . . . looking for the best stain remover or whatever it is. And that's wonderful for that kinda stuff 'cause it's people that have already tried stuff and found stuff that worked for them so it's not, you never know with a website, like, if it's something that's gonna be successful or not.

Pinterest vibrates with possibilities, circulating endless ideas to amplify Renee's family's happiness. It is her trusted happiness exchange—where she goes to "feed" herself as the creative fuel for her family.

Indeed, much of Renee's life as a mom revolves around creative projects inspired by Pinterest, as their execution seems to help Renee at once confirm and materialize her family's path to happiness. For example, when we visited with Renee in her home, she and her husband were putting the finishing touches on elaborate princess bunk beds for her youngest daughter. Renee was clearly proud, telling us how happy it makes her that her daughter loves the bed so much: "She loves it too because of all the cubbies. . . . We put the bookshelf and the kitchen and stuff in there, and then her dress-up clothes and all that. It's been, like, two o'clock in the morning, and you can hear her in there playing, and I'm, like, you don't want to yell at them when they're playing with it but . . ." Year-round, Renee and her kids also do projects related to the seasons, so she turns to Pinterest to find projects that "fit into what we're already doing, instead of just randomly sitting down and looking at it all. 'Cause if I do that, I just won't get up. There's just too much to look at."

In this way, Pinterest is brimming with happy potential, which Renee is keen to harness but also works to contain. As she told us, her experience of digital media is a positive force in her family's life, but she also feels compelled to monitor the intensity of her online connection.

> I'll just cut it out completely and then I'll . . . it's no longer something I'll think too much about. . . . I do find myself getting sucked

into that, and so I do kind of have to maintain that boundary for myself or even set a timer. . . . Now it's more Pinterest, because you get sucked into all the different . . . it's like it feeds my [creative person] because there's, like, fifty different things I wanna look at. . . . I'll be looking around on those things, and then I'll get all these ideas of things I wanna make, and then I'll realize it's eleven o'clock at night, and I need to go to bed. . . . I don't have time to do all that craziness, but I think of all the things. You know, with Mother's Day coming up, we got a lot of good ideas for gifts for the grandparents, some things like that. I kinda try to integrate that into, you know, if we need an art project for the day then we'll pick something off of there, so it's not wasted time completely, whereas Facebook I feel like it's wasted time.

Renee therefore constantly seeks to balance the brimming happy charge of the mamasphere against her "season of life," attuning digital potentialities to the material demands of a devoted mom. Sometimes Renee posts pictures of her family projects to Facebook. Her friends are impressed by these images and often suggest that she should start a blog. Renee can't imagine fitting blogging into her life, though: "I'll make the stuff, and I might take the picture, and then it'll be three months later before I put it on there and everyone's like, 'Oh, you should do a blog.' . . . I don't even have time to put it on from my cell phone to Facebook, which is instant, let alone do a blog." As Renee suggests, too much happy potential can find mothers "sucked in" and actually route them away from the very happiness that digital nodes like Pinterest promise to bring.

Dana's Affective Punches

While the mamasphere figures as a vital "artery" for Addie and creative fuel for Renee, for Dana it is a medium of survival. Dana is a working-poor single mom of three whose life has been marked by bouts of economic and familial insecurity. As we visited, her eight-year-old daughter colored patiently and cuddled up to Dana, while her mom matter-of-factly described the joy she finds in spending time with her children but also the tremendous weight she carries as she works to boost her earning power and manage her daughters' needs.

A full-time student pursuing an associate degree in early childhood education, Dana has pulled together a life for herself and her three kids in the face of domestic abuse and serious economic woes. For her, precarity is more than a structure of feeling; it is a day-to-day material reality. Still, Dana's sensibilities and everyday concerns resonate with those of other mothers, as she frets about her children's safety, whether they're playing with their friends, at their father's house, or on Facebook. "Those are my biggest worries," she concluded. "I mean, financial bills worry me too, but really when it comes down to it at the end of the day, I'm worried more about my children than my bills."

Like other mothers negotiating a world of precarized happiness, Dana parents with "wandering absorptive awareness," vigilantly apprising potential threats to the family's health and happiness.[9] Social media multiply feelings of insecurity, as Dana worries about her children while they are in the nearby park as well as on the computer in their living room. She elaborated, "Not knowing who's really behind those pictures frightens me. You see so many kids and so many people that pretend to be children, and it frightens me. . . . [My eldest daughter] knows that I check her messages regularly. And I don't do it to invade her privacy, but I want to make sure that she's safe."

Dana married at age nineteen, just a few weeks after her first child was born. She and her husband stayed together for thirteen years, but Dana endured infidelity and emotional and physical abuse throughout their relationship. "He's got a lot of physical aggression," she explained. She "had him sobered up," but he recently left her for another woman. Dana "ended up getting shoved, pushed out" of the family home and moving into a women's shelter. Her husband won full custody of their children, and Dana worries constantly about this development. "It's just, it's not getting any better. I would really have figured that with the PFA [protection from abuse order] on us, he would have grown up and realized, hey, this is what I'm doing to my children. Because now it's not even about me. . . . It's how are the children being affected by this." Dana now sees her girls three weekends a month. Consequently, her labors have multiplied and shifted, as she tries to figure out how to manage her children's lives from afar.

Remarkably optimistic, though, Dana described herself as "a fixer" and explained that in court during her custody battle, "I focused on . . . all the kids are doing well in school. . . . [H]ome life is good, we've got this and this for them."[10] Indeed, Dana orients her days as a mother toward the promise of happiness, a future characterized by financial independence and boundless snuggles with her girls, "chitter-chatter noise and laughter just ringing through the apartment." Once she earns her associate degree, she plans to enroll in the University of Phoenix's online education program to obtain her bachelor's and master's degrees so that she can eventually open an affordable day-care program for other struggling women: "Depending on your situation, I may not charge you anything at all. Just supply me with the diapers and the formula for your child. You know, because obviously if you're in a shelter by then, you probably have WIC or welfare. . . . [Running a day care is] the end goal for me."

Her sights set on being able to help other moms as well as herself, Dana thus organizes her days around classes at the local community college, on the one hand, and hours spent on her computer researching projects, completing coursework, and checking Facebook, on the other. Although enmeshed in poverty and lost family dreams, Dana nonetheless hangs on to the promise of happiness in the digital mundane, where everyday exchanges and digital games modulate ordinary affects that emerge in the course of a hard and heavy life. When Dana feels frustrated and overwhelmed, she turns to Facebook as a venting strategy to garner emotional support, and she also uses it as a place to deposit and collect happiness. She posts cryptic messages about run-ins with her ex and other family members: "I do it in the proper way [so] that, you know, only certain people really know what's going on, and if anybody asks questions, then I message them personally and say, 'OK, this is what's going on. This is why I'm venting.'" Old friends and distant family members reach out to her in response to these posts.

> I know that if there's something wrong, they're gonna check. They're gonna check up on me. They're gonna make sure I'm doing OK. When all of this started a year ago, I didn't realize how many friends and family that I actually had, whether related by blood or not. It was just amazing the support I had. . . . And it's even better when I'm posting the happy things. You know, they're all, "We're so happy for you. We're so proud of you." Those are my favorite ones. Because I was never proud of the fact that all I was was a mom. I mean, I loved my children, I loved my job. Love, love being a mom, more than anything in the world. But I didn't feel like certain people were proud of me because I didn't go to school right away.

These comments and messages operate as affective punches: "venting" posts produce feelings of support and "happy things" that affirm Dana, while modulating her anger and discontent. In turn, encouraging messages from friends operate as little zaps of positive energy, propping Dana up and giving her energy to keep going. Altogether, while she turns to her online networks for emotional support and to cultivate a more secure sensibility of self, Dana becomes resilient in the face of precarity. Facebook interactions bolster and push her to keep going, converting profound insecurity into temporary solace.

Moreover, Facebook games have figured as an important way to stay optimistic. In the digital world, Dana can achieve her own version of privatized happiness. "That's my free time," she told us. "That's my 'OK, I've had enough homework, I'm going to play some Castleville.'" The game provides Dana a free space to exercise her creativity and domestic imagination virtually, a privilege she cannot afford in everyday offline life. For example, she shared with us how the games help compensate for limited resources, describing how her lack of funds and the arrival of a new partner derailed her decorating dreams for the apartment's only bathroom.

> It's kind of cool how I can just make my own little world. Decorate it the way I want to. Stan kind of moved in way before I had enough money and time to decorate the apartment the way I wanted to. It did not get my splash of Dana on it. We had it all set up, the girls, our bath, there's only one bathroom, it was gonna be all decked out in, like, a shopping scene. All that stuff that Walmart had. But it was gonna cost us well over a hundred dollars to do it. And then he moved in. He's like, "No, that's way too girly for me." I said, "Ohhhhhh."

Dana's life throws into sharp relief the affordances of the digital mundane's charge. For her, the happiness it computes is no less than a lifeline. But for almost all of the mothers we talked to, the mamasphere swells with happy potential, promising to charge their long, hard days with possibility. The vibrating potentialities of the mamasphere and its regular affective punches prod mothers down happiness's path.

COMMUNE

The charge of the mamasphere is premised on the interactivity and participatory architectures that fuel digital networks. Digital media thus provide new platforms for community that come into being via the free digital labors of mothers.[11] For example, Sasha and Erin, like Addie, turned to social media to navigate their experiences of motherhood in communion with other women and eventually took up blogging as a way to nurture and contribute to these vital online spaces of shared mothering experience.[12] As we show, blogging allows these mothers to embed themselves in bigger worlds and to take on important life projects, but it also layers their lives with new loads and social responsibilities. In this way Sasha and Erin's lives articulate the paradoxes of free labor and the double affordances of such digital entanglements for mothers: new communities yield new intensities that are at once profoundly affirming and exploitative.

Appreciating Sasha

When Sasha's twins were a year old, she set up a BlogSpot account so she could comment on a blog that a friend in her Twins Club had started writing. In her inaugural post, Sasha described reading her friend's work: "I am becoming an addict, like the rest of the world. I decide to be a participant and make a comment, because that is what makes blogs fun." Though she had to create an account to participate, she wrote, "There is a good chance that this will be my only post." Soon, though, Sasha was regularly recounting her own story on her blog, *Sasha and the Hooligans*.

> I just started writing little stories about sort of what was going on with my kids at the time. . . . I wasn't getting a ton of adult interaction, and I found this weird, like, slowly this community of other parent bloggers that had twins that were young, and they were all super helpful, and just to know that you weren't going through that alone. People that have one baby or two babies even a year apart think that they're going through the same thing you're going through, and they're not. It's totally different, and I'm not saying it's easier or harder. I mean, yes, one baby's easier, but having two babies closer together I'm sure is super hard. . . . They don't know that it's not just one plus one equals two. It's sort of exponential. . . . When you have two people that can't hold up their head, it presents its own challenges. These other people got that . . . and then I'd read their stuff and they were like, "Oh, I've done that too," and it got sort of addictive talking, and then it got cathartic, and then I realized that, hey, I'm kind of good at this writing thing.

For Sasha, who described being a mother as "the hardest, best job that anyone could ever have," blogging fulfilled an acute need for emotional release and connection as she trudged through the early days of mothering twins. Typical posts recounted short stories about life with the "hooligans"—

discovering them in the living room with baby wipes flung everywhere and their "little paws" smelling of "fresh springtime lavender, or whatever the hell it is"; negotiating the mall with a "twin mom friend," their four toddlers, and their giant strollers; and wrestling to put sheets on her kids' bunk beds. "I am going to have a nervous breakdown," she wrote. "And if I tell a therapist that I totally lost my shit because I physically could not change the sheets on a bunk bed they will laugh me out of the mental hospital." Eventually, Sasha's humorous and matter-of-fact descriptions connected with other moms, and soon this cathartic hobby evolved into a full-time job that generated income and accolades, as well as new friendships and communities.

In 2006, when the twins were two, Sasha attended her first BlogHer conference on a whim, explaining, "It was, like, I can get out of the house and go to California, and so I did, and it was amazing. I met all these cool people, and I was inspired, and I got jobs." Indeed, the decision to attend the conference changed the course of Sasha's life: "I'm a huge sports freak. I went up to the owner of the website . . . and said, 'Do you need somebody writing about sports?' . . . And so I started writing about sports for BlogHer, that became a paid job, and it just kept evolving. I put ads on my site and made money that way, and then I started writing for other places that paid me, and it just sort of became this thing. This job."[13]

Though *Sasha and the Hooligans* started as a mommy blog, a place to commune and commiserate with other moms of twins, it quickly morphed into a broader enterprise that encompassed a range of other ventures: running and writing her own sites, freelancing for a number of other blogs, undertaking social media outreach projects, and selling "swag." As Sasha put it, "So I sort of have five part-time jobs," but this description perhaps undersells the extent to which blogging has become a career that garners Sasha significant acclaim and reward.[14] She is most proud of the sports blog she cofounded with another blogger from her parents-of-twins community, which, to Sasha's great surprise, was nominated for a Shorty in 2012, pitted against Bill Simmons's *Grantland* and other "big-league . . . sports sites." Sasha rubs elbows with sports celebrities, hosts swanky corporate-sponsored parties for her friends, and travels to speak at conferences. She is always expanding her networks, and her world of domestic caretaking is now layered with the energetic and exciting world of professional blogging. "It's just incredible that this all came out of screwing around on my computer originally," she explained.

Though Sasha struggles to maintain boundaries between her public persona and her personal life, and constantly regulates how much she writes about her kids (as they get older, she says, she is less comfortable telling "their stories"), professional blogging has figured as a sustaining technology in her life as a mother. She talked to us about how good it feels to have her digital work recognized, something that doesn't happen as much when it comes to her affective labors as a mom:

> There's something about having an audience that likes what you do. [At home] you get the "I love you, mommy," and every once in a while, you get, "Hey, you're the best mom in the whole wide world," but, you know, you usually get stuff like "[I want] chocolate." . . . But [online] . . . people are like, "I loved it when you wrote this thing," or "It was so funny when you said this," or "Oh, you're so talented." You know, I mean people in that realm actually say nice things to you about what you do, whereas, in regular life, that shit doesn't happen very much. It's just, you know, people don't come home and be like . . . "Hey, you vacuumed super good today." Even if you really worked, you know, you really worked. Like, I did seven loads of laundry yesterday and nobody said anything . . . but you write something, and you work really hard, and people will say nice things to you. I feel very validated in that world. I feel appreciated.

For Sasha, blogging opened up doors to new business ventures and community, while also compensating for banal gender hurts with affective punches of validation and appreciation.

At the same time, though, blogging seems to exacerbate these hurts. Like most of the moms we encountered, Sasha continues to shoulder most of the burdens of domestic life, even as blogging has evolved into a demanding full-time job. She told us, "I work from home, so it's helpful, but . . . when they're sick there's never a question of who is gonna be in charge, who is gonna take them to the doctor. That's my job." She sometimes works fourteen-hour days and stresses a lot about how to keep working when her twins are home round-the-clock for summer vacation.

Moreover, the maintenance of Sasha's microcelebrity demands new constant forms of affective labor.[15] For example, in her work with corporate sites like Babble, Sasha's compensation is contingent on how much traffic she can drive. She absorbs all the risk: it is up to her to cultivate and promote her online persona in ways that will capture and channel eyeballs for advertisers. Thus, Sasha spends much of her online life engaging in the "feeling games" of performing authenticity, while also trying to quantify and rationalize her influence.[16] According to Sasha, what distinguishes her online persona is her comical approach, so she strives to keep her content "upbeat" and "funny." However, the work to maintain this authentic persona is unrelenting and demanding, and it reaches into all corners of her everyday life. She elaborated:

> It's hard to be out there all the time, you know what I mean. It's hard to, if you, I don't feel like I can, I don't feel like I'm allowed to step away from the Internet for more than a day or two. There are expectations of what you should do. . . . It's hard to, it's hard to be consistent, it's hard to be smart and funny all the time. It's hard not to complain when bad things are happening or [to] use it as a weapon sometimes. And sometimes I do, but I try not to. It's hard to be interesting all the time 'cause you know you're not. I'm not always interesting, and I don't always have something to say, but I have to.

Accordingly, the community Sasha sought in her early days of caring for twins has morphed in many ways. Now Sasha finds herself generating carefully calibrated content designed for the tracking, capture, and valorization of community. While these new forms of community work are profoundly energizing and affirming, they also complicate Sasha's life as a mother; she finds herself harnessed to her screens, compelled to perform and constantly modulate for corporate enterprises that ultimately promise few material benefits in return. Sasha is caught up, in other words, in the affective circuits of communicative capitalism, which, as Jodi Dean argues, increasingly relies on "communication for communication's sake," the perpetual, never-ending circulation of online content that renders communication exploitable.[17]

Erin's Life Project

Like Sasha, Erin is a stay-at-home mom and the author of her own blog, *Green Mama*.[18] She turned online for community and found real sustenance in blogging. "It relaxes me and refreshes me to have a place to have an educated voice," she says. Passionate about environmental sustainability, as well as traditional family life and Christian ministry, Erin is an ardent information gatherer who pursues motherhood as an all-consuming project. She not only homeschools, but also mills her own flour for home-baked bread and carefully develops a personal family plan for talking to her kids about Santa without perpetuating Christmas's rampant consumerism. In our interview she summed up her personal ethos this way:

> I try to create a home of peace. I want my children to feel that home is the most peaceful and safe place on Earth, so they always want to come home. I also do the same thing with the food and products I serve or use. I want them to love my food so much that when they try other foods they choose the real thing. For example, I want them to think a hamburger is a burger made with free-range bison so that when they eventually have a McDonald's burger they are disgusted. Coming from a broken home, I make every effort to love their father first and with all my heart, as well as create valuable time and memories as a family. We have weekly family game nights and other traditions we enjoy. As well as regular date nights with my husband.

Deeply moored in the domestic scene, Erin has a vision of motherhood that is heavy and expansive. She sees contemporary culture as "obsessed with greed" and wrecked by divorce as well as absentee parents who leave their children in day care or alone at home "to do whatever they please." "We are spending money faster than we make it and working ourselves into the ground at the expense of our children," she says. "Our children need two parents that love each other and are committed to their well-being and success. Our generation cares too much about ourselves and not enough about the welfare of those around us." Erin sees the everyday work of women as the solution to systemic breakdown, saying, "I do see hope in daily life. I see women working hard to support one another and move forward." She regards supporting the efforts of other mothers as a vital part of her own gender work.

Green Mama enables Erin to materialize her weighty vision of motherhood. She describes the blog as "an outlet to share my journey as a wife with others. To encourage them in their marriages and home life, and, interestingly enough, I often find it encouraging to myself." Erin writes during much-needed downtime, when her kids are sleeping at night and during nap times; the blog nourishes her, allowing her to tend to her community of mothers, while replenishing the energy depleted in the course of caring for children and negotiating conflicting and urgent advice about how to mother well.

It is important to see that *Green Mama* is part of a holistic and broader life project. Erin dreams of writing a book and regularly offers workshops to moms' groups about babywearing, cloth diapering, and cooking. After her second son was born, she started Mama Codes, an online supplier of green and natural parenting products like cloth diapers, baby carriers, and breast-feeding accessories. Her goal was to coordinate a national network of Green Mommy consultants who would run workshops and sell her products, and, for a short time, Mama Codes existed as a brick-and-mortar location, which its website described as "a local learning center and retail store . . . that is passionate about creating a community of moms supporting one another to experience the healthiest life possible for their families and each other."

Initially, writing *Green Mama* helped Erin combat the disempowerment she felt as a new mother:

> I felt compelled to teach other moms because as a new mom I deeply struggled with feeling like I needed to do things the way current American culture tells me to: let baby cry it out, formula feed, baby food, even though every fiber of my being felt that was not right for me. As I began to research I found a great divide between the two camps, the "crunchy granola" moms and the "typical" American mom, and I didn't feel like I fit either camp. I wanted to provide a place where moms felt they could come and get information and support and feel empowered to decide what is best for their family on their own without guilt put on by either part.

Now *Green Mama* is a powerful ethopolitical project that helps Erin and her readers forge their own way as mothers.[19] As she writes to combat the mommy-wars mentality and to value mothers' caring labors, Erin believes deeply in green living; she labors to validate the experiences and choices of mothers: "As passionate as I am about green living and raising children naturally, I am even more passionate about empowering moms to be the best moms they can be without making them feel guilty about the choices they make. I want moms to leave my blog feeling empowered by the decisions they make." She carefully monitors her tone on the blog to encourage other mothers and to avoid judgment. "I don't want to be just another place where I share my opinion and tell everyone to do things my way. I also don't want to come across as the perfect Suzy Homemaker, making moms feel inadequate. I of course share my opinions but then encourage moms to go and form their own" with careful research.

Committed to "Old World family values," Erin appears less interested in the affordances of microcelebrity that feed Sasha. While *Green Mama* has over two thousand Facebook followers, Erin doesn't tweet or Instagram as a professional blogger. She has not attended blogging conferences, and *Green Mama* has just a few independent sponsors. Nonetheless, the blog buoys Erin by providing an outlet for helping other mothers (and helping her) to live a slow, sustainable, child-centered lifestyle while also staying educated and connected. Though Erin would love to bolster the family's bottom line, the blog is not oriented toward economic gain. Rather, she considers this her individualized life project, a creative contribution to holding together a world that appears to be crumbling and rotting around her.[20] Being a celebrity is "not my goal," she explained. "I more want to bring about change within the American culture." Indeed, though her blogging pursuits and now-defunct small business are not economically productive, they do allow Erin to feel that she is working to "bring about change." For example, she enthusiastically relayed to us her recent experience meeting with the local chamber of commerce before opening Mama Codes. "I deeply struggled with what to do with [my infant son]. I still haven't ever left him except with my husband, and he had to work. The more I thought and prayed about it, I realized that this was a perfect example of what I am trying to do." She chose a baby carrier that matched her business outfit and took him to the meeting, where "everyone thought he was the sweetest thing." She concluded, "Do most businesswomen bring their babies with them to work? No, but that is what I am trying to do, help bring moms back home with their little ones without sacrificing the ability to contribute to society and their family income."

Of course, blogging while the kids are sleeping also allows Erin "to contribute to society," as the release of her words into the mamasphere is meant to serve a greater purpose by empowering and educating mothers. Still, she feels immense guilt about the time she spends at the computer and always works to temper its pull. "I have had to step back from my blogging as I enter into a busy season of life and have had to try to decrease my computer time. I have to work hard to not allow the use of my computer to invade my life as a mother," she explained. But the pull is strong, for blogging is a crucial space of self-expression: "A year ago I was blogging almost every day and loved it, but then it began to feel like work, so I had to step back from the frequency a little bit. Now I blog much less frequently, but every few weeks I feel a press to write on a specific topic, and the press does not leave until I write."

For both Sasha and Erin, then, the "press to write" is an affective "pressure point." Indeed, communicative capitalism runs on the free labor of digital participants such as these women, whose contributions figure as new horizons of capitalist accumulation and systems of valorization.[21] However, not only is this free labor readily exploitable; it is also living labor, undertaken in the spirit of community and aimed at sustaining women's lives.[22] Through these digital entanglements, the exploitation of women's labor is extended, both online and off, and mothers stay caught up in the work of privatizing happiness in communion with other moms.

CODE AND RECODE

As mothers work to privatize happiness, the mamasphere transforms everyday family life into a computational field of digital potentiality—from its ever-beckoning charge to its promises of communion and community. In the mamasphere, platforms for remediating the muck, hurts, and insecurities of mothering through precarity are ubiquitous, as participation easily takes the form of coding and recoding happiness. Indeed, the proliferation of digital cameras, technologies of curation, and social media converts the present into a terrain of potential happiness that can be actively mined and cultivated through mundane digital acts of snapping and sharing. For example, as Carly's and Caroline's experiences posting family photos to Facebook suggest, happy moments are lurking everywhere, ready to be captured, coded, and recoded as such.

Carly's "Promise of a Fun Summer"

Amid the tumult of lost jobs and dreams (as discussed in the book's introduction), Carly decided to spend a summer with her kids making "good" memories. For this work-at-home mother of three, digital media are an important way to stay connected to family and a larger community of mothers. Twice a year, Carly sends her mother-in-law, who lives several states away, a memory card full of photos to display in her digital frame, and she posts photos of her kids on Facebook as a way of giving back to her social media community. "I feel digital media is great for moms and helps to bind us closer together in sharing our own family stories," she told us.

"I don't want to feel like a stalker and only read about other people's lives without sharing some of my own. Plus, my kids are so funny, and I love the things that they come up with. It's therapy sometimes to read and see those things. I like to make people laugh."

Feeling that her time at home with her daughters was fleeting, as she would soon return to work outside of the home and the girls would be in school full-time, Carly searched online for fun, low-cost activities to fill their days. Carly documented the summer in "Promise of a Fun Summer," a series of Facebook albums that she captioned, "I have made a promise to myself to make it a memorable summer for my little ones (without breaking the budget). Here is a pictorial of our summer!" The albums are filled with daily snapshots of fun family times: eating popsicles, going to the zoo, collecting pinecones, visiting the amusement park. Eventually, Carly created a photo album using Snapfish, and she is delighted that she now has "a gorgeous coffee-table book from our summer."

For Carly and other mothers, family photos are an important signifier of family autonomy: they help to cordon off the family as a separate sphere while elevating it as the embodiment of a "good life." As Judith Williamson writes, "the representation of the family as an autonomous emotional unit cuts across class and power relations to imply that we all share the same experience. It provides a common sexual and economic goal: images of family life hold out pleasure and leisure as the fulfillment of desires, which, if not thus contained, could cause social chaos."[23] Family photos seemingly engender the family's integration, displaying its unity and togetherness, and thereby its happiness. Mothers, of course, have long been encouraged to document and materialize family happiness through family photography and album making, as labors productive of what Todd Goodsell and Liann Seiter call "family capital": "When a woman constructs and preserves a family narrative that aligns with what she perceives to be the dominant family type of her society, she tries to give her children credentials that they come from a socially validated family, build their competence in doing that particular type of family, and guide them to develop dispositions to replicate such a family in their own lives."[24] As Susan Sontag famously argued, "through photographs, each family constructs a portrait-chronicle of itself—a portable kit of images that bears witness to its connectedness."[25]

Though Carly is excited about her "gorgeous coffee-table book," it seems the enactment of the "Promise of a Fun Summer" on Facebook is perhaps more important than its end result or the capital it accrues. That is, the act of recording the fun moments and uploading them to a specially designated digital location is what elevated them from fleeting moments to noteworthy, happy ones of family autonomy. Through creating and curating digital images, Carly classifies everyday precarious life as happy; "making memories" is literalized in the creation of albums. In this way, Carly codes the present, not simply capturing happiness out of the continuous plane of caretaking, but materializing it through the computational act of creating digital records.

Long before the advent of Facebook walls and Pinterest boards, Don Slater suggested in 1995 that physical pinboards and photo walls were perhaps an apt metaphor for digital photography. While traditional photo albums are representational narratives that "seem to bolt a constructed identity into the natural flow of time," pinboards and walls are "ways of acting out and embodying a relationship in the present."[26] Snapping a photo and uploading it to her Facebook album shaped the present moment for Carly, pulling it out of the ongoing flow of everyday life and pinning it as a promise of happiness. "The image," Slater says, "is the way we present ourselves in the heat of the moment rather than the way we represent that moment as an object of reflection."[27] Mothers' work as family archivists has thus moved from producing a reflective narrative of the family's unity to continuously presenting the family as a way to live in and experience the present. Indeed, this is a critical shift for family photos, as Carly's Facebook albums don't look back and reflect on fun summers past but instead scan the present for signs of happiness while also looking forward to the promise of future fun. Moreover, Carly's fun photos, uploaded to her album in the "heat of the moment," are not a strategy for reflecting *on* that moment but a way of presenting the present. In times characterized by profound insecurity, the digital presentation of family life therefore seems to "pin down" family happiness.[28] Here family does not so much come to know itself through reflection on a photographic narrative but instead experiences life in the present moment, through coding its happiness.

Mamaspheric Snark

The mamasphere is fueled by the codings of mothers like Carly, which abound and multiply alongside even more reified images of family happiness housed by happiness exchanges like Pinterest. It is important to see, however, that these happy codings are also always already available for recoding. For example, author Sara Given's Tumblr blog *It's Like They*

Know Us invites readers to "relax on your pristine white couch and enjoy these realistic depictions of happiness." On her blog and on Facebook and Twitter, Given, who recently published *Parenting Is Easy: You're Probably Just Doing It Wrong*, posts stock photos of happy families with clever captions. "Just remember," reads one of her sarcastic Facebook status updates, "if someone else's life looks perfect in every way it probably is and you should really be trying harder." In one particularly apt post, a stock image of a white pregnant woman looking at her laptop reads, "Oh, good, it says here that my symptom is either a completely normal part of pregnancy OR everyone is going to die. #clearedthatrightup." Another photo on *It's Like They Know Us* depicts a well-dressed, smiling white couple pushing a stroller on a sidewalk with boats in the background. Given captions the picture, "At first we were nervous, but it turns out that having a baby is nothing but capricious yachting adventures and oversized sunglasses! Who wants mimosaaaaas?! #GetTheBabyAMimosaaaaaaa!" In another a photo of a family of five in matching union-suit pajamas gathered merrily around their Christmas tree is captioned, "Greg was skeptical at first, but now he just loves his festive butt-flap pajamas! He never takes them off, not even for work. He's either full of the holiday spirit, or he's had a psychotic break. Either way, Merry Christmas!" The friendly snark that circulates through *It's Like They Know Us* scoffs at airbrushed visions of flawless families basking in togetherness, and the Facebook page's 43,240 followers add to the fun in the comments. For the yachting image described above, for example, one reader commented, "They actually both died from sleep deprivation, and the baby is Weekend-at-Bernie's-ing them, pulling their strings from inside the stroller." These are recodings: as readers layer sarcasm and humor over whitewashed images, they remediate demands of perfected happiness, honing their own resilient and privatized ones.

This sort of snark thrives in the mamasphere, providing relief from ever-present pressures. The *Reasons My Son Is Crying* Tumblr blog gathers reader-submitted photos of crying children, wryly labeled with their reasons for crying: "He asked when he would be a baby again. I told him 'never.'" "His hoodie wouldn't zip up any further." "She dropped a receipt we got from the gas station." "He doesn't want to go (even though we repeatedly told him we're not going anywhere)." A baby lying on a shoebox and crying is captioned, "He could not get down." A toddler waist-deep in a toilet and sobbing is labeled, "She doesn't want to come out." Here miserable family moments are recoded as funny. Rather than offering solutions to messy

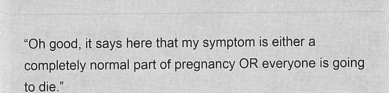

"Oh good, it says here that my symptom is either a completely normal part of pregnancy OR everyone is going to die."

#Cleared that right up

299 notes   ⋯ ⟲ ♡

FIGURE 3.1. Sara Givens's Tumblr blog, *It's Like They Know Us*, recodes the whitewashed images of perfect family happiness shown in stock images with captions conveying the anger, frustration, or terror that might lie behind them.

I broke this cheese in half.

APRIL 2, 2013 (8:19 PM)   12766 NOTES

FIGURE 3.2. Greg Pembroke's Tumblr blog, *Reasons My Son Is Crying*, reframes images of family misery with droll captions that highlight the absurdity of life with children.

and unmanageable encounters with children, these sites both embrace the chaos and offer distance through sardonic commentary. They tweak images of family happiness to apprehend the misery lurking just beneath the surface, reframing familial frustration with droll narratives that call to attention the absurdity and uncontrollability of life with small children.

For example, the Honest Toddler Twitter feed (tagline: "Not potty trained. Not trying.") tweets pedestrian observations from the point of view of an "honest toddler," a shrewd enfant terrible. In tweets such as, "Her words said 'Goodnight' but her tone said 'Don't try me'"; "Just discovered something even better than sharing: having"; and "If you make me breakfast I'll tell you where your debit card is. Hint—not your wallet," @HonestToddler imagines toddlers as clever little devils who easily deflect their mothers' attempts to shape them into good citizens. The mother behind Honest Toddler, Bunmi Latidan, who has also published *The Honest Toddler: A Child's Guide to Parenting* and *Toddlers Are A**Holes: It's Not Your Fault*, started tweeting as a way to cope with life with her toddler. She told CNN, "At one point or another you realize, there is no one way to [raise children], it's going to be messy, we can pretend all we want with our Instagrams and Facebook photos that it's all going great. But it's a struggle, so we do have to support each other and give each other a little bit of slack."[29]

By recoding the digital injunction to be a happy family, these clever and fun sites circulate authentic and even resistive modes of maternal support. Yet we can also think of these recodings as affective punches for weathering the paradoxes and impossibilities of mothering through precarity. They hone a flexible form of happiness, reminding mothers that life is, of course, not always happy, while providing a "tiny affective nugget" where happiness nonetheless accrues.[30] In this way, recodings certainly resist dominant ideologies of the "new momism," but they still tether mothers to their mounting loads and labors by providing the affective fuel needed to keep moving through them.[31]

Caroline and Ally's Valentine's Day Box

In the digital mundane, mothers find themselves caught up in these circuits of coding and recoding in the context of their everyday lives. For example, stay-at-home mom Caroline enthusiastically shared how she had effectively pushed back against feelings of anxiety and inadequacy that constantly threatened to overrun her life as a highly self-reflexive stay-at-home mom:

> I actually read a really interesting story on Facebook about how, in the age of Facebook and Pinterest and Etsy and all these things, mothers are feeling very inferior, because they're seeing all these wonderful things that go on. . . . Their kids are well adjusted and happy, and . . . people are getting kind of a skewed view of what they should be doing. . . . It was a funny article, and it was like, "I'm not making flower-scented soap roses. My kids are lucky that they get a sandwich in their lunch." . . . I reposted it, and I got a lot of people saying, "Thank you for posting this"; "I so needed this because I always feel inferior to [other] moms, and I have moms that feel inferior to me."

The sole stay-at-home mom among her college friends, all of whom have moved on to corporate jobs, Caroline recalled experiencing the sense of disconnect and jealousy that arises when mothers compare lives. Envious of their "wonderful jobs," Caroline found, "a couple of drinks into a conversation" with them, that they keenly desired what they perceived to be her carefree life filled with meaningful moments with the kids. "I'm well aware that my kids don't care if their birthday parties are perfect," Caroline shared. "They'd rather chill out and read a book." Describing "snuggl[ing] in bed and read[ing] books" with her girls the night before our interview, Caroline told us, "We could have done some fabulous project to post on Facebook, but we just sat and read a book. And I kind of wonder, you know, some people that post things, if they just do it for 'Look what I'm doing.' It's not just 'My kids and I did this together, this was a great experience.' It doesn't ever look like a kids' project." Here Caroline's "unproductive" time with the girls is recoded as a critical moment for relationship building, while the more perfect images that surround her life are reimagined as inauthentic.

Tellingly, Caroline told us about a recent Facebook post she shared with her networks.

> Ally's Valentine's Day box: I just let her go. "Here's your stuff, and do what you wanna do." The thing was so ugly and gaudy. I mean, there were [silk] flowers and gemstones, and that was my post. I said I had to let Ally take control, which was hard for me to do, because I wanted it to be, you know, two-toned and make it look nice and . . . I just let her go, and that was the thing I said, "There's times as a mom

you just have to let go." And I said everybody's gonna know that she did this box, and that I had nothing to do with it. But it was funny, and that's the response that I got was, "Good for you for letting her be creative and do what she wants to do."

For Caroline, her Facebook post recoded a stressful, anxious scene (her daughter's "ugly and gaudy" Valentine's Day box) as a happy one. The feedback Caroline received was profoundly affirming: it not only confirmed Caroline's approach to caring for her daughter but also helped Caroline to privatize her happiness.

Through these codings and recodings, mothers like Carly and Caroline modulate their volatile affective lives, taming anxieties and computing a form of privatized happiness that is all theirs. To be sure, within the affective infrastructure of the mamasphere, all moments carry the potential to become "precious" moments, because they can be noted, captioned, narrated, shared, coded, or recoded as happy.

RESILIENT HAPPINESS

On her chic and modern blog, *Finding Joy* (tagline: "Beautiful. Connected. Life"), blogger and mother of seven Rachel Marie Martin introduces herself as a "seeker of joy. Lover of the little things." Martin's husband is currently in remission from cancer, and one son suffers from celiac disease. Confronted with these challenges, Martin dedicates her blog "to seeking joy in life, specifically in motherhood." *Finding Joy* carries with it a fundamental tension, for while she pitches her blog as a "spot to breathe in a busy and crowded online world full of should do this and should do that's," her work is haunted by the sense that "finding joy" is also a form of emotional labor, or, as she puts it, a "constant journey." Martin attempts to reconcile this tension in this way:

> I lived for years seeking happiness but was without joy. I kept think-ing if I could get this or that or change this or get rid of that then I would be happy. I realized, by the grace of God, that chasing happi-ness was [a] lesson in futility. Happiness seemed to be based on life's circumstances while joy was based more on the heart. So, in the years following my husband's cancer diagnosis I began to pray and seek joy. What I found was that the sweetest moments in life, the real joy, often is found in the little simple things.[32]

Martin's blog is rich in its grappling with the affective contradictions of mothering through precarity: that is, with the sense that family life *should be happy*, that it is *not always happy*, and that it is the job of mothers to find a way around this predicament. For example, in her post "Why Vacuuming Should Always Be Beautiful," a response to the December 14, 2012, shooting at Sandy Hook Elementary School in Newtown, Connecticut, when twenty first graders were killed, Martin implores mothers to "choose something, a daily task—laundry, dishes, folding clothes, picking up—and make it a benchmark, a reminder, for you to remember the preciousness of the life that you have in front of your face." In response to the precarious ordinary, where mass shootings inject terror into the white privilege of nuclear family life, mothers must work emotionally to identify the happy in their lives; as she notes, "We don't know our days. . . . Those parents [in Newtown] would give anything for a room cluttered with a pile of stuff and an eager little one there to help sort through the pieces and here I was grumbling." Martin questions, "When did I lose the beauty in this normal, even though the normal like today was frustrating? When did the gift of having children in my home get lost and I instead just wanted every little thing perfect and tight and without mess?"[33]

With her notion of joy, Martin is urging a form of resilient happiness premised less on fantasies of the good life through consumption and more on constant affective modulation. This resilience requires vigilant attention: a capacity for seeking out and insisting on the promise of happiness, "finding joy" in the nooks and crannies of what often feels like an unhappy everyday, and constantly tuning one's affects and capacities to the promise of precarious happiness.

Martin wants mothers to see that real family happiness lurks in the mundane "pockets" of ordinary life, and that it is up to mothers to notice and appropriately code these pockets for happiness. According to Stewart, a pocket is "a space [that] opens up," where it seems that some*thing* is going to happen.[34] We might imagine everyday life as moving along inconsequentially until pockets open up, creating sensibilities and potentialities where lives could go this way or that. A pocket is a situation or, as Lauren Berlant puts it, "a state of things in which *something* that will perhaps matter is unfolding amid the usual activity of life. It is a state of animated and animating suspension that forces itself on consciousness, that produces a sense of the emergence of something in the present that may become an event."[35] Indeed, Martin's resilient happiness rests on a particular mode

finding joy

FINDING JOY   LITTLETHINGSMATTER   MOTHERHOOD   PARENTING   PERSPECTIVE   Q

why vacuuming should always be beautiful.

I've had this post mulling in my head for weeks. It was one of those where the words would play out beautifully in my head, and then every time I would sit down to write the words would come out as a jumbled mess. Then Friday happened, that absolute horror in Connecticut, and I found myself in Target with tears rolling down my face grasping to understand evil and crying for the parents and families whose lives were robbed of normal. So now, I finally write. And those words? About life – and normal. –rachel

I was grumbling.

Not your normal grumble, but rather that under the breath discontent grumble that can be easy to adopt when one isn't careful. My older boys' room looked like it had never been cleaned before. I am completely *not joking sadly* serious. Toys mixed together with papers with peels of a clementine that should never have been there with pens and markers and clothes and dirty socks and books and anything else you could imagine. It was all there – percolating into this gigantic mess that took me four hours to straighten and deal with. Leftovers from weeks where the cleaning was just on the surface leaving behind residue and the obvious example that looking at stuff on the surface doesn't really solve

FIGURE 3.3. In her blog, *Finding Joy*, Rachel Marie Martin promotes a resilient happiness based on hypervigilant attention to the joy that might be found in the mundane muck of caring labor. "Why Vacuuming Should Always Be Beautiful" urges mothers to see the joy in everyday life by remembering the fragility of family togetherness.

of perception, one that is anxiously anticipating and interpreting the contingencies of the present. As Brad Evans and Julian Reid argue, "resilience then teaches us to live in a terrifying yet normal state of affairs that suspends us in petrified awe. . . . [E]very aesthetic moment reveals a potential for something potent to emerge. . . . So we become enlightened by the realization of our infinite endangerment."[36] For Martin, vacuuming gets reenvisioned as an "aesthetic moment" of enlightenment, cherished and opened up as a pocket for happiness (and actively shut down as a space for anger, frustration, and failure). Martin implores, "Don't let the mundane moments in life rob you from the beauty of normal that surrounds you. Remind yourself to look for the beauty, the gems that are tucked within the fabric of the everyday normal. Force yourself to wake up, to see, to remember, and to be thankful for the blessings that fill your life."[37] Accordingly, everyday labors like vacuuming must be coded as happy, as mothers must stand ready to capture the happy as some*thing* in their lives.

More than any other mother, Elana seems to experience her life as a series of pockets that must be constantly coded as some*thing* happy. Indeed, Elana works exhaustively to tame unknowable contingencies. She worries "24–7" about her son and refuses to allow her husband to bathe him, fearing he might drown. She told us, "With the binky, what if the nipple falls off the bink, breaks off? . . . What if he chokes in the middle of the night on his pacifier? I'm one of those anal moms. . . . I told a friend of mine [about the pacifier], and I have someone else I need to call about this. . . . I am just always worrying. . . . I'm sure it's never happened, or else the binky company would be sued all the time, but, um, I don't know." Fears like this expand and intensify Elana's work as a mother—she never gets a break from bathing Jared, and she wakes constantly in the middle of the night to ensure his pacifier has not become an instrument of death. In the thick of these churning anxieties, as well as ongoing frustrations connected to both her marriage and her labor situation, Elana attunes and adjusts by constantly plugging into the mamasphere to code and compute her quest for family happiness. For example, when we interviewed Elana, she was spending much of her time enthusiastically planning for a family vacation to Disney World over a year in advance. She hoped to subsidize this trip by winning a "Cutest Baby" contest sponsored by Disney and was sending daily messages to her social media friends reminding them to vote for Jared.

Elana concentrates on the navigation and detection of pockets, staying attuned to the various potentialities of the expansive, tumultuous present. These pockets provoke uncertainty and reflection and often call for intervention, so Elana turns constantly outward to the digital mundane. Consequently, life becomes one big rescue effort fueled by her resilient happiness. Indeed, her work as a mother is primarily about impossible forms of affective coordination, that is, lining up her family with its broken promises.

Put differently, Elana inhabits what Berlant calls an "impasse": "a stretch of time in which one moves around with a sense that the world is at once intensely present and enigmatic, such that the activity of living demands both a wandering absorptive awareness and a hypervigilance that collects material that might help to clarify things, maintain one's sea legs, and coordinate the standard melodramatic crises with those processes that have not yet found their genre of event."[38] For Berlant, living in the impasse is akin to living in the cul-de-sac, where "one keeps moving, but one moves paradoxically, in the *same space*."[39] We can think of Elana's work of navigating precarized happiness in this way, as a sort of "holding station that doesn't hold securely but opens out into anxiety, that dog-paddling around a space whose contours remain obscure."[40] Mothers are constantly working to maintain their "sea legs" through honing in on happiness, as the impasse "marks a delay that demands activity."[41] Mother and author Shauna Niequist urges readers, "Just paddle, because that's what gives you what you need to stay afloat. Paddle, because forward motion allows you to steer, to turn, to head into a wave, or away from one. Paddling is what puts you in charge of the situation, instead of being at the mercy of the waves, waiting for stability that will never come."[42] This "dog-paddling around" is another way to think of maternal resilience: it's about one's capacity to stay afloat, to keep moving toward happiness, even as one wears down and out, even as happiness's horizons recede.

In the impasse, waves of precarity regularly slam into fantasies of the good life: while motherhood is supposed to (and occasionally does) feel happy, it is also surges with anxiety and uncertainty and the sense that things could fall apart in an instant. Yet it seems that living in the impasse is both at odds with and in careful alignment with family happiness. As the family has gotten "stuck" on happiness, it becomes difficult to inhabit the impasse where happiness is precarious, and yet the promise of happiness still intensifies, taking on new weight and potentiality as some*thing* to be cultivated and materialized by mothers. Paradoxically, happiness is at once deeply precarious and immanently present; it is this paradox that compels vacuuming to be beautiful and mothers like Elana to "just paddle."

As advanced neoliberalism destabilizes every family's life, mothers like Elana find themselves "dog-paddling around" happiness entangled within digital media. The mamasphere charges mothers' everydays with opportunities and connections, reconstituting overloaded lives as outwardly brimming with potentialities. Consequently, mothers get caught up in new affective circuits, as the participatory conduits of digital culture beckon them with affective punches, promises of community, and platforms for coding and recoding. The mamasphere thus provides a powerful affective infrastructure for mothering through precarity, engendering the ongoing affective modulation and resilient happiness required to keep paddling.

4 · INDIVIDUALIZED SOLIDARITIES
Privatizing Happiness Together

RENEE

Renee describes herself as a happily married, "intentional" mother to her three daughters. These days Renee works primarily in the home, raising her girls: "an eight-year-old going on forty-eight," a "very spirited almost five-year-old who loves mud as much as her older sister loves pink things," and "this little pumpkin . . . [the] baby of the family," who is "a wild thing." Over the course of an hour and a half, Renee detailed her approach to parenting and experiences with motherhood as the "wild thing" ran around us—darting from her bedroom to the living room and back, stopping every once in a while to hug her mom. Like many of the women we interviewed, Renee is Christian, socially conservative, and white working class. Bible and marriage study are a regular part of her everyday life, and Disney World is the ideal family vacation destination.

Renee is deeply committed to practicing and promoting a sustainable lifestyle—canning, making her own bread and yogurt, gardening, and buying local meats and eggs. She explained, "I think it's kinda common that people of our generation are . . . being a little bit more sustainable on their own instead of just depending on everybody else. We try not to go to Walmart a lot. . . . [W]e try to support local businesses and just kind of teach our girls that there's more to it than just ordering something off Amazon. There's a name and a face and all those kinds of things." These sustainable practices are important facets of Renee's intentional approach to raising her girls so they become strong, independent, self-reliant women who embody Christian values of compassion and caring for others. Ultimately, Renee hopes to model a guiding set of values, while creating the freedom and space for her girls to be themselves.

Renee was one of the least anxious mothers we encountered. Self-assured and content, she seemed to approach motherhood with a mix of ease and conviction. More than any other mother we encountered, Renee embodied the promises of ethopolitical mothering discussed in chapter 1, in which mothers are "empowered" to cultivate a family lifestyle rooted in their own personal morals and values. Indeed, Renee experiences family government as a validating and aesthetic project of self-making and family making. For example, Renee detailed how her intentional approach is woven throughout her everyday activities in her discussion of bread making:

> We, just as a society, have such a "I want it my way, right now, right away" kinda thing, and we try to teach our children that, you know, it's more about service to others and what you can give back and not what you're always getting. There are a lot of times where it would probably be easier to go out and buy a loaf of bread, but I'm teaching them math by measuring. And it's a creative activity because they're getting their hands dirty. And I'm teaching them patience because they have to wait for it to rise, and all those kinds of things. And we're teaching nutrition because there's not chemicals in it. And there's so many valuable tools that, I don't even know that my grandmother necessarily talked about any of that stuff with me, but I picked [them] up through that situation, so we just try to be intentional with our parenting and try to introduce those concepts to them through our everyday life.

Renee's intertwined commitments to faith and sustainability provide a "gauge" for her parenting; they represent a personal ethic that unites her myriad labors as a mom.

Things hadn't always gone so smoothly, though; not long before we spoke, Renee had experienced a painful divorce prompted by multiple infidelities on the part of her ex. In despair, Renee turned to her local Mothers of Preschoolers (MOPS) group for support, finding the strength and resources to see both herself and her girls through what was a heartbreaking and scary time:

> I started at MOPS when my second child was a baby, and that was mostly out of necessity because as a single mom . . . I just felt it was so necessary to be with other moms who could kind of help me in that stage of mothering. . . . I mean, they would bring me meals. They would stop over and just pick my kids up and take them to the zoo, or, you know, whatever I needed. Because I walked through that, I feel like now that I'm in a different place, I want to be able to offer that to other moms and support other moms. So I'm on the steering team, the leadership team that kind of guides that whole program. . . . That's been very rewarding to be able to give back 'cause it's definitely a program that helped me when I needed it.

Nowadays Renee embraces her newfound nuclear stability, relishing her work as a mother, making an elaborate "princess bed" for her youngest daughter, perusing Pinterest for new craft and gardening ideas, and supporting other moms through her extensive work with MOPS. Renee always wanted to be a mom, and caring work is at the core of her identity. At age twenty-one, inspired by her passion and knack for nurturing children, she opened her own childcare business, which is now run primarily by Renee's employees so that she can focus her energies on her own family. Renee's peace of mind is palpable and connected to her involvement with MOPS. Her stories suggest that, despite the highly privatized and overloaded character of contemporary mothering, as explored in previous chapters, mothers may indeed find crucial forms of solace and support in the proliferation of mothering communities, both online and off.

Grounded in Emily's extensive participant observation with MOPS and immersion in the mamasphere, this chapter explores the more collective forms of living that animate mothers' lives. Here we dig into two mothering communities—MOPS, a grassroots, international Christian network devoted to mentoring mothers like Renee, and the online community that has formed around Momastery, a blog and website developed by writer Glennon Doyle Melton—to excavate the solidarities they afford to mothers.

More specifically, we elaborate these collective modes of mothering as *individualized solidarities*, where the ultimate aim of collectivity is privatizing happiness, that is, stabilizing and valorizing individualized nuclear families. Mothers feel and act in solidarity with each other, providing significant forms of material and affective support in hopes of keeping one another attached to nuclear family life despite its mounting impossibilities.

As we show, these communities and the individualized solidarities they engender operate as *resiliency nets*, catching mothers as other social safety nets around them fray. Whether through material supports—delivering meals in trying times or raising funds for families in crisis—or affective punches that incite mothers to stay optimistic about their families, mothering communities bounce mothers back from daily hardships, big and small, enabling them to inhabit the social insecurities and fragilities that make up their everydays. In effect, these are nets for becoming resilient under conditions of material and affective insecurity. Ultimately, then, individualized solidarities are cruel: through collectivity and community, mothers come to stay stuck to unworkable family scenes and tethered to the horizons of neoliberal precarity.

MOTHERING COMMUNITIES

In 2007 Emily finished her doctoral work, had her first baby, and moved from Michigan to Georgia in the space of three short weeks. Faced with a colicky baby and a new life as a stay-at-home mom, she found herself on unsure ground: her days, filled with care work dictated by her infant's needs, were far removed from her recent life as a graduate student on fellowship. Frustrated and wallowing in both boredom and perpetual labor, Emily turned to the Internet in search of ways to make sense of her new life, and she found an expansive array of communities available to mothers of young children. In short order, Emily joined Gwinnett Area Mommies (a local branch of the Mommies Network), La Leche League, and a number of infant activities, such as Gymboree's baby classes, designed to both enrich babies' lives and connect new mothers. Gwinnett Area Mommies met online and off, hosting a vibrant message board where moms sought advice, offered emotional support, and set up informal playdates, outings, and "moms' nights out." Mothering communities were an important part of Emily's year as a stay-at-home mom—a meeting place for new friends, a time to get out of the house during stretched-out days, an opportunity to spend time with adults, and a space to get advice about her nap-refusing baby.

After returning to her hometown, Hugo, Emily found herself less entrenched in new mothering communities. Still, she circulated in groups of mothers who found great sustenance in these networks, and it was clear that mothering communities played an important role in Hugo. The mamasphere was also exploding during this time. A Facebook group supplemented the Gwinnett Area Mommies' message board, and blogs and websites began to offer the same kind of support and advice that Emily had found through La Leche League and the Mommies Network. Consequently, when we set out to hear mothers' everyday stories, Emily became a part of mothering communities online and off. She joined a MOPS chapter in Hugo, going to twice-monthly two-hour meetings at Hope Church, a 45,000-square-foot institution that houses a coffee shop, a children's wing with themed rooms and brightly colored murals, and several large meeting rooms. At MOPS Emily was assigned to the "Yellow Table," along with Jenny; Calley; Annie and her sister, Donna; and three other women. Over the course of a school year, Emily and the Yellow Table participated in MOPS activities with about fifty other women organized into small groups, and also organized playdates and other activities outside of the large-group meetings. Then pregnant with her third baby, Emily put her second son into the on-site day care during MOPS meetings, and she spent time with the women in their homes, at the zoo, and on the playground. Here she came to know their dreams, their families, and their frustrations with everyday life.

Emily also became a regular visitor to the mamasphere, checking in daily on a host of "mommy blogs" and websites, including Momastery. A recovering alcoholic and survivor of bulimia nervosa, Glennon offers an "authentic" take on the hard, "brutiful" stuff of motherhood that has garnered her an active and loyal following among mothers. Glennon's microcelebrity is premised on her pointed, often heart-wrenching critiques of "the mommy myth" and her active embracing of her own failures as a mother.[1] Positioned against dominant mothering media and culture, Glennon presents Momastery as a place for acceptance, peace, and recharging: "It's a place to take a deep breath. It's a place to drop out and tune in. It's a place to stop striving, stop competing, stop suspecting, stop hiding. To hear and tell truth."[2]

In 2013 Emily traveled about ninety minutes away from Hugo to see Glennon at a book signing in a local bookstore. There she joined forty other women in a room on the second floor, eating Twizzlers, drinking bottled water, and chatting idly while they waited for Glennon, who bounded in about twenty minutes late, wearing a white dress with pockets and black-and-white-striped platform heels. Picking up the microphone, she exclaimed, "You're all real! I love you all! You're not teeny tiny Facebook avatars! I know you're all out there, over the magical interwebs, but I love seeing you in real life." Over the next hour, she talked intimately with the audience. Funny and charismatic, Glennon effuses deep love for her children while bemoaning the stressful labors of caring for them. During the book signing, for example, she described her response to her grade-schooler's request that she stop working and stay home: "Oh, you think that when I leave, it's work. No, it's when I'm home that I work. Going on a book tour equals hotels, room service, and not watching Dora all day." She details her own fallibility while inviting others to join her in helping women in need.

Indeed, Glennon is immensely empathetic about the work women do and the frustrations they face. As she told the crowd, at every book signing a few women wait at the end of the line ("on purpose") and then tell her, "I don't know who you are, but I just wanted to get out of the house!" "I love this," Glennon said, "that I am someone who gets women out of the house." But more than being an excuse for other women to leave behind their domestic duties for a few hours, Glennon operates as the leader of a far-flung community of women who offer each other both affective and material support. She positions herself as a "listener" and a "treasure chest of women's stories." Faced with any of life's problems—divorce, day-to-day frustrations like nightly bedtime battles, the death of a child—Glennon can "flip" to other women's stories in "the jukebox in my head" to think through how to face those issues. At the end of her talk, Glennon asked the audience to fill out index cards detailing their stories so that she could read and hold on to them for her community. For Glennon, supporting women—listening to their stories, lightening their loads—is a way to change the world. She told the group, "If you fill women up, they just burst and explode and help everyone around them."

Mothering communities like MOPS and Momastery are a crucial facet of contemporary motherhood, and their proliferation in recent decades can be traced back to the early stages of neoliberalism and the ethopoliticization of mothering discussed in chapter 1. Amid growing distrust of dominant medical discourses and mainstream consumer culture, mothers are actively encouraged to develop their own regimes of family government in concert with other moms. While family autonomy has effectively cordoned off the family, leaving mothers alone to anchor social and moral life, the gradual rise of neoliberalism has had the somewhat paradoxical effect of reconstituting the privatized terrain of mothering as a highly collective endeavor to be practiced in community with other mothers. Mothers clearly garner vital forms of support through participation in mothering communities, both online and off. These spaces socialize the work of mothering, combating feelings of isolation and inadequacy.

Women have been extended membership in a variety of mothering communities. While these communities differ in terms of their cultural politics, they are all held together by situated maternal knowledges, values, and meanings germane to family government. For example, La Leche League was founded in Chicago in 1956 in response to a national decline in breast-feeding in order to "help mothers worldwide to breastfeed through mother-to-mother support, encouragement, information, and education, and to promote a better understanding of breastfeeding as an important element in the healthy development of the baby and mother."[3] The group published its first edition of *The Womanly Art of Breastfeeding* in 1958 (currently in its eighth edition), and in 1965 began circulating its magazine *Leaven*, devoted to breast-feeding and organizational news and updates. Addie Eavenson founded *Mothering* magazine in 1976 to celebrate the endangered "art of mothering" and to "provide through its pages a meeting place for an exchange among caring people who feel that children are the most vital aspect of their lives."[4]

Just a few years earlier, in 1973, MOPS was founded as a Christian ministry devoted to empowering women in their labors as mothers.[5] Mothering communities like MOPS are rooted in particular times and places, and thus contingent on geography and transportation as well as family schedules and situations. However, in the mamasphere opportunities for mothering in community become diffuse and multiply, especially through the energetic and expansive networks of mommy blogs. Through these practices women create new sensibilities and narratives of mothering that, in many ways, challenge those of the traditional patriarchal institution of motherhood. But they also constitute modes of solidarity highly germane to mothers' overloaded lives, engendering vital affective infrastructures for inhabiting precarity.

According to Nikolas Rose, neoliberal societies hinge on "government through community," as, "in the institution of community, a sector is brought into existence whose vectors and forces can be mobilized, enrolled, deployed in novel programmes and techniques which encourage and harness active practices of self-management and identity construction, of personal ethics and collective allegiances."[6] In contrast to traditional notions, the community engendered by neoliberalism is "a moral field binding persons into durable relations. It is a space of *emotional relationships* through which *individual identities* are constructed through their bonds to *micro-cultures* of values and meanings."[7] Accordingly, neoliberalism governs *through* community and the "active practices of self-management and identity construction" that communities afford; as the limited social supports of the welfare state are dismantled, "personal ethics and collective allegiances" become an increasingly vital medium of governing "at a distance" and of providing for privatized social welfare.[8] In the case of most mothering communities, their "moral field" is delineated by family autonomy: while different communities are animated by different "micro-cultures of values and meanings," they remain oriented toward stabilizing and enhancing the autonomous private sphere of family and the increasingly hard work mothers must do to hold it together.

While mothering communities like those that have formed around *Mothering* and Momastery often appear countercultural, they are in no way about disrupting the grammars and scripts of family autonomy. For example, *Mothering* was founded to provide a forum for mothers to collectively reflect on alternative practices of mother love—vegan diets, home births, homeschooling, and vaccination exemptions—in a consumer-based world that generally denigrated and devalued traditional mothers. Members are encouraged to submit articles based on their own experiences and current research, as well as creative works including poems and art. However, despite the alternative family lifestyle it promotes, *Mothering* is still powerfully oriented toward family autonomy. In the introduction to its "How to Survive Parenthood" guide, for example, mothers are reminded, "These are difficult times. Giving children the freedom to grow in health and happiness, developing and expressing their deepest and truest selves, is a difficult task for a parent. As parents we are responsible for the future of humankind. We can nurture love, trust, and wholesome intelligence, or we can interfere with a child's natural development, and produce a generation of frustrated individuals. . . . We must continue to make every effort to protect and encourage our children's natural development, though we lack the support we need in this increasingly unnatural world."[9] "The future of humankind" rests on the private sphere of family: it is up to mothers to nurture the development of healthy personalities and fully realized "truest selves" and thereby to save the endangered scenes of family life and ensure happy futures.

Regardless of their ideological stripes, mothering communities are most often about keeping mothers attuned to their family scenes and enhancing their individuated women's work. Mothers share resources and knowledge and support one another through their interminable and frustrating labors, to be sure, but they also build communities germane to family life and the government of mothers. Mothering communities may cohere around different lifestyle approaches to the art of parenting (i.e., breast-feeding, "natural" mothering, Christian living), but they share an orientation: family autonomy and its promise of happiness.[10]

These communities thus articulate a fundamental paradox: they are built on particular "micro-cultures" of shared beliefs and values but are animated by a more universal "moral field" of family autonomy. Mothering communities often traverse this paradox by insisting that membership is open to all and that open judgment of other mothers' lifestyle choices and/ or familial situations is not part of the code. Early on, *Mothering*, for example, assured readers potentially concerned about its focus on alternative parenting practices that the goal of the magazine "is not to promote one style, method, technique, philosophy, or idea over another, to set standards, to judge, to criticize, or to oppose" but rather to offer "life-supportive" perspectives.[11] Today both MOPS and Momastery similarly insist that their Christian-inspired spaces are places where "everyone is in." The MOPS website proclaims, "We've all been placed in this time and place in history, as the tribe of women who are raising the world. And the beauty of it is that we don't all have to agree with one another but everyone is in and we all need each other."[12] Momastery, on the other hand, presents itself as a raucous yet respectful community of Monkees:

> We call ourselves Monkees because we're like monks, in that we put our faith in something beyond ourselves, we find value in quiet, and we practice living peacefully in community—here on the internet

and beyond. We're unlike monks in that we curse and watch trash tv and become annoyed quite easily. So we settled on Monkees. We are the Monkees. The first rule of Monkeedom is that everyone is invited. If you want to be a Monkee, you are a Monkee. Everybody's In, baby. The second rule of Monkeedom is that you never have to agree with me. Or anyone else here. You do have to practice disagreeing with respect and love.[13]

In all of these cases, mothers negotiate the ethopoliticization of maternal subjectivity, pushing back against the "mommy-war" mentality. United around the project of family autonomy and the responsibilities it puts on mothers, many mothering communities seem to embrace, in theory at least, all mothers, regardless of the particularities of their paths.

Mothering communities are often built on new maternalist sensibilities, where motherhood is regarded as an important civic act and imbued with moral authority.[14] For example, MOPS and Momastery envision their communities of mothers as vital collectivities helping to change, stabilize, and heal the world through shared practices of mutual and self-care. The former "believes moms are world influencers," and its website states, "We also believe that incubating hearts and giving just-because-hugs can change the course of history. That's why we connect moms all over the world to a community of women, in their own neighborhoods, who meet together to laugh, cry and embrace the journey of motherhood. MOPS groups are rallying women to be more honest, to feel more equipped and to find our identity by journeying alongside one another. . . . We are moms, and we believe that better moms make a better world."[15] Momastery's "third rule" positions mothers similarly: "The third rule of Momastery is that we are not just mothers, we are Mothers, with a capital M. A Mother with a capital M knows that the children under her roof are not her only children. A Mother knows that All God's children are her children and all God's mamas are her sisters. Here we remind each other that we are ALL family."[16] In mothering communities, caring for the self and other mothers has global implications; mothers are to embrace their role, for "better moms make a better world." Recall the crucial role MOPS played in Renee's life. When her marriage fell apart and she found herself alone trying to raise a daughter and a newborn, MOPS provided both emotional and material support. When Renee lost hold on her "good life," mothers stepped in, providing food and childcare, as well as mentoring and friendship. For

Renee, "that support system, especially when the kids are little, can be a lifeline to other moms."

It is important to see, however, that despite their world-influential imaginaries, these new maternalist sensibilities engender deeply individualized modes of solidarity, as *mothers come together to privatize happiness*. Through participation in mothering communities, mothers expand the scope of their care to include providing social support to other moms, while at the same time garnering much-needed reinforcement for their own fragile selves and shaky scenes. Animated by the mounting demands of neoliberal family autonomy, mothering communities ultimately help individual mothers stay attached to and invested in their growing loads and social responsibilities. Enacting privatization as a promising mode of collectivity, these modes of solidarity keep mothers—in their labors, affects, dreams, and possibilities—collectively oriented toward the precarized family and privatizing happiness.

Mothering communities like MOPS and Momastery are thus very different from the feminist consciousness-raising groups of the 1970s. While countercultural communities like *Mothering* certainly emerged within the broader feminist movement and its critiques of patriarchal systems of control over women's lives and health, their sensibilities were much more attuned to the burgeoning neoliberal culture of identity and lifestyle politics premised on recognition rather than redistribution.[17] As Kara Van Cleaf notes, consciousness-raising and its insistence that the personal was political was, after all, a method: "Through sharing personal stories, women found commonalities and connected their experiences to systems of oppression."[18] As we will see, contemporary mothering communities and the sharing of everyday family life are not about social, much less structural, transformation; rather, they are about providing "relief from the political": that is, shoring up maternal and familial resilience through recognition, shared family governance, and the circulation of collective affect.[19]

RESILIENCY NETS

The MOPS meetings are aimed toward providing a peaceful respite and gathering place for overloaded moms. At the Hugo MOPS, mothers used a bank of computers to check their children into the childcare wing and then gathered in small, organized groups around tables carefully decorated with color-coded tablecloths and homemade, themed centerpieces. At the first meeting, Emily found beautifully packaged teas and candy at each seat, with a reminder to "take some time for yourself," and the mothers were given supplies to craft themed name tags to use at every meeting. Every MOPS meeting was buffered by an abundant spread of breakfast casseroles, coffee cakes, fruit, veggies, and brownies, all of which were prepared by the small groups on a rotating basis. The intensely feminized focus on hospitality and the attendant attention to the decor, food, and gifts are intended to communicate that MOPS cares about mothers and, more importantly, will *care for them*.

As such, caring for moms in this context means alleviating the everyday stresses engendered by care work itself, as well as recognizing the economic stresses experienced by contemporary families. At each meeting participants contributed castoffs—such as old holiday decorations, coupons, books, and children's toys—to a "free table" where other mothers could help themselves, and the women invited one another to participate in their own direct-sales enterprises, attending parties to buy cosmetics, handbags, natural supplements, and more from one another. Members were always ready to lend a helping hand to families facing a job loss or health crisis, and they contributed small donations to provide relief for various nuclear family issues, including long-distance travel to obtain health care for children and high adoption fees.

In this sense, the care of mothers is embedded in the MOPS structure. Each meeting began with one of the local leaders offering a group prayer, thanking God for the opportunity for fellowship, praying for members who were sick or otherwise struggling, and seeking protection over members' families. The local leadership team included a hospitality coordinator and a care coordinator, who organized, respectively, food for the meetings and the sending of greeting cards to all members for birthdays, illnesses, and new babies. The programming, which we detail below, was intended to fill the mothers up with inspiration and strategies for making home life easier. Some meetings were explicitly designed to be a soft landing place for harried, overwhelmed moms. For example, the Hugo group's last meeting of the year was organized as a "spa day," during which the women made and tried out bath products at tables decorated to mimic a spa. Designed to pamper women, these homemade products centered on the mothers' experiences, recognizing their stress and desire for respite and recharging.

Table groups regularly celebrated their members, offering cards and cake on birthdays and hosting baby showers for one another. In the spring

Emily hosted a playdate and surprise baby shower for Jenny at her house, with all of the women bringing homemade food and gifts for Jenny, then pregnant with her third son. Jenny, facing serious economic instability and surprised by this third baby, was grateful for the gifts, which offered some small relief in light of the impending need to stock the nursery and clothe the baby. Renee found the same experience in small discussion groups at her MOPS meetings, designed for "really coming alongside the other moms and just living life with them and supporting them and loving them."

Emily herself experienced these supports firsthand. At a meeting in November, the Yellow Table surprised her with a small baby shower. Jenny brought a cake to share, and each of the women gave Emily cards with small gifts to welcome her third baby. Emily was moved by this gesture, carried out by a group of women she had known for just a few months. The small gifts, and, more importantly, the focus on Emily's experience, provided temporary respite from her long days of variously caring for her two small children, her husband, her house, and her students. Later, when the baby was born, the Yellow Table organized a meal train, providing lavish and well-rounded homemade meals to her family for an entire week. By taking on the material load of feeding another family for the night, each of the women at the Yellow Table made Emily feel cared for and made her expanding family feel a little more possible, and even desirable, during the trying days with a newborn.

It is critical to see that the support that MOPS offered Emily and other mothers transgressed ethopolitical boundaries, uniting the women in a project of mutual care that was rooted less in lifestyle-consumer politics and more in shared affective orientations. Emily lives on the boundaries of MOPS's ethopolitical terrain, inhabiting a lifestyle as a feminist working mom that at times grated against MOPS's conservative family values, highly feminized domestic scenes, and Christian ministry. Indeed, mommy-wars discourse would position Emily in opposition to the women at MOPS, but although Emily did sometimes squirm at the group's heteronormative assumptions and affinity for patriarchal norms, MOPS offered welcome support. Jenny said, "I love MOPS. I really do. MOPS is like, apart from my kids it's my second passion right now, just in the season of life that I'm in. I love getting to meet other moms, I love helping other moms, I love building that relationship with them. I love knowing that you're not the only one going through something, or going through certain things. Being a mom of a preschooler is a lot of work, so it's nice to have that support." It *is* nice to have that support, for what is most important about mothering communities is not the lifestyle they propose but the individualized solidarities they engender. Together, through often mundane practices of community, mothers weave together caring nets that make them feel supported, nurtured, and recognized and that keep them tied to family and community. These nets catch women in the throes of everyday precarity, holding them up through trying times and reconstituting them when their mother loads break them down.

Indeed, mothering communities, both online and off, enable mothers *to provide each other* with vital, privatized nets. Glennon perfectly crystallized this idea in her post "I Have No Idea What to Title This. I'm Not Even Sure You Should READ It. Nets. We'll Call It NETS." In the post Glennon recounted a dialogue with her therapist in which they reflected on what she learned after breaking down onstage at a large public event at her alma mater:

> I learned that people need help. And the people who need the most help are the ones too lost to ask for it.
>
> YES. GLENNON. YOU LEARNED THE IMPORTANCE OF A NET.
>
> What?
>
> PEOPLE NEED A NET. SCHOOLS, CHURCHES, NEIGHBORHOODS— EVERY INSTITUTION NEEDS NETS. NETS ARE GROUPS OF PEOPLE WHO WATCH OUT CLOSELY FOR EACH OTHER. WHO NOTICE WHEN SOMEONE NEEDS HELP. WHO HAVE THE SKILLS TO REALLY HELP WHEN REAL HELP IS NEEDED.
>
> Yes.
>
> YES. YOUR LIFE HAS TAUGHT YOU THAT NETS ARE NEEDED, AND THAT IN THIS COUNTRY WE DON'T HAVE ENOUGH OF THEM. AND THAT EVEN IN FAMILIES WHERE THERE IS A LOT OF LOVE, THERE STILL NEEDS TO BE A NET.
>
> Yes. Yes. That's why I loved the mental hospital. And my third grade classroom. And it's why I love my Sunday school class now. Because those places are Nothing But Net.
>
> GLENNON, THAT'S YOUR LIFE'S WORK. YOU ARE CREATING A NET.[20]

Nets are spaces and practices that provide "real help." They are material and affective infrastructures for making life feel livable and for helping mothers stay afloat. Glennon offers a net through her blog and social media accounts, circulating stories of family frustration and redemption and inspirational memes like "We Can Do Hard Things" and "Love Wins." The words are meant to cushion the trials of daily family life, and women respond enthusiastically to the support they feel in these nets.

Glennon's nonprofit, Together Rising, claims to have emerged from the care circulating through Momastery. On the blog

> a whole community of women began to tell their truth and work hard to understand one another. People who were very different, but who had the common goal of understanding and loving each other better. Quite unexpectedly, they felt so deeply connected it filled them up. And once they filled up, they began to spill out and overflow. So they reached out to a couple of hurting women who needed help. . . . When they added up all of their little offerings of time, money, and talent, together they could make amazing things happen. Things they never could have done alone. This created a deep sense of belonging to one another. Together Rising is the natural outpouring generated by these women's small efforts. It's a helping, healing revolution.[21]

Together Rising materializes Glennon's net through small donations directed toward families with emergent needs and two larger projects, Love Flash Mobs and Holiday Hands. In 2014 Together Rising's small gifts included "$100 gift cards for 50 single moms on Valentine's Day" and funding for a number of families struggling under the weight of underemployment and serious health issues.[22] These donations are designed to catch families on the verge of falling into disrepair and despair, offering them help with getting through the next cycle of bills, and hope in the form of small kindnesses like gift cards.

Holiday Hands is a clearinghouse connecting people who "have a little extra" to people who are struggling. Every November the clearinghouse lists a variety of small requests—requesters ask for both emergency funds (for heating bills, Christmas presents, car repairs, a month of groceries, and so on) and emotional support (greeting cards for sick children, gift cards for an evening out for struggling mothers, inspirational books, etc.). Holiday Hands insists that the nature of the request is not important: "We don't need to judge whether someone's particular need is worthy. It doesn't matter. . . . We are just meeting that particular need in an effort to meet the REAL need. Which is: 'TELL ME I'M NOT ALONE. PROVE TO ME THAT LOVE WINS.'"[23]

Together Rising has also hosted five Love Flash Mobs, online fund-raisers aimed at satisfying specific needs through donations that are capped at twenty-five dollars. The first Love Flash Mob sent a mother dying of cancer on her first vacation with her eight children and her husband. Other Love Flash Mobs bought wheelchair-accessible vans for mothers with health issues; provided companion dogs for children with diabetes, autism, and Down syndrome; raised funds to house a teen mom and her infant son in a group home; and collected money to help four mothers with cancer. In short, the flash mobs buttress families rocked by the brutal realities of privatized risk and welfare. But Together Rising insists that, beyond their material needs, these families want to know they are supported by a community: "We offered these families what they needed—and then we learned that what we really needed was to believe that we live in a world where LOVE WINS and WHERE STRANGERS BELONG TO EACH OTHER. And the way we make that true is that we MAKE THAT TRUE."[24]

Communities like MOPS and Momastery are resiliency nets: they provide mothers with material and affective resources for privatizing happiness. But they are also affective communities of belonging that, despite "everybody's-in" mentalities, cohere around the project of family autonomy and its promises of happiness. Built on long-standing systems of privilege and advantage, they assume shared orientations toward nuclear family life and the forms of social, cultural, affective, and economic capital that underwrite and make possible privatized happiness.

For example, the community of Monkees that make up the net of Together Rising has been stitched together under Glennon's microcelebrity. This celebrity emerges from her blog, which is infused with the stuff of nuclear family life. Glennon describes her childhood as "relatively magical," and her struggles with bulimia and drug addiction were fought on distinctly middle-class territory, occurring despite her happily married, loving parents (Bubba and Tish) and taking place in the sorority houses of James Madison University.[25] Glennon peppers her blog and social media feeds with silly photos of her three children and husband in their suburban home in Naples, Florida, and describes frequent escapes to the nearby beach. And Glennon began her blog with musings about life as a stay-at-home mom with a minivan and a bad shopping habit.

Despite its middle-class milieu, Momastery's cultural politics are complicated. While Together Rising is decidedly aimed at helping families to maintain their autonomy, it works in small ways to be inclusive across classes; for example, limiting Love Flash Mob donations to twenty-five dollars apiece and inviting nonmonetary donations like supportive letters to those in need during its Holiday Hands campaigns. The vast array of comments on both the Momastery blog and its Facebook page also betrays a readership that traverses class lines. Since the death of Michael Brown in Ferguson, Missouri, Glennon has been broaching racial politics more directly. On August 14, 2014, she posted on her Facebook page, "So, listen—I don't know enough about #Ferguson or white privilege or how much a part of the problem I am yet. I'm learning, though, because ignorance is overly convenient and lazy and dangerous and inexcusable, really." She then asked her Facebook readers for reading material to learn more about these issues. The post generated 884 shares and 259 comments, both positive and negative. On May 27, 2015, in response to Freddie Gray's death in Baltimore and the ensuing riots, she recommended Michelle Alexander's *The New Jim Crow* on her Facebook page. And in October 2015 Glennon posted "Why I'm Prejudiced and So Are You" on the blog, writing, "Listen. We can be good, kind, justice loving, anti-racist people in our hearts and minds—but if we're living here—we're still canaries raised in a racist mine." At the end of this post, she recommended Beverly Daniel Tatum's *Why Are All the Black Kids Sitting Together in the Cafeteria?* Of course, these educational posts, directed toward antiracist ends, are aimed toward a primarily white audience who needs to be educated on these issues.

While Glennon is quite clearly working to use her blog as a platform for addressing and ameliorating existing inequalities, her net nonetheless coheres around her celebrity, which took off when the blog went viral and she wrote the best-selling book *Carry On Warrior: The Power of Embracing Your Messy, Beautiful Life*. Though she resisted celebrity, she was well equipped to navigate it, fitting in easily with the white, suburban norms of popular culture in her appearances on the *Today Show* and in various interviews. Over 300,000 people have "liked" Glennon on Facebook, and her blog posts are regularly shared over ten thousand times (and often more). As a singular node in a highly corporatized broader network of networks, the Momastery net hinges on the cultural and social capital embedded in Glennon's celebrity, capital built on the foundation of her status as a white, middle-class, gender-conforming mom.

Put a bit differently, Glennon's digital net takes shape as an "intimate public." According to Lauren Berlant, members of an intimate public "*already* share a worldview and emotional knowledge that they have derived from a broadly common historical experience." "A certain circularity structures an intimate public," Berlant explains; "its consumer participants are perceived to be marked by a commonly lived history; its narratives and things are deemed expressive of that history while also shaping its conventions of belonging; and, expressing the sensational, embodied experience of living as a certain kind of being in the world, it promises also to provide a better experience of social belonging."[26] Indeed, as we will see, Momastery "flourishes as a porous, affective scene of identification among strangers," offering its Monkees a "complex of consolation, confirmation, discipline, and discussion" about how to mother through precarity, while providing much-needed "relief" from the politics of precarity.[27]

Consider Glennon's intimate public in relationship to Dana's dream to open a day care for struggling mothers, which we discussed in chapter 3. Dana, who is working-poor and endured her ex-husband's physical and emotional abuse for years, is—like Glennon—incredibly proud of her three children and takes delight in them. She spends her days in community college, hoping to one day earn a master's degree online from the University of Phoenix and open her own day-care center. She'd like to provide free childcare to other mothers who have suffered abuse, but, for now, she struggles to support herself. Her past efforts to earn a living through work-at-home enterprises failed in large part because of her lack of social capital, and her dream of building a net for struggling moms like herself seems unlikely to materialize.

In this sense, the individualized solidarities and privatized nets of mothering communities like Momastery hinge on forms of affective community that, in practice, get cordoned off from the struggles, needs, and dreams of poor, marginalized mothers like Dana who are not imagined to live in material proximity to family happiness. In the intimate publics of mothering communities, women wrestle through particular sensibilities and experiences of precarity—"brutiful" labors, broken marriages, unanticipated job losses, and health scares—but mothers like Dana, who are living very different realities, are not necessarily likely to find themselves "in."

The MOPS meetings are places where women come into community to learn how to be "better moms" who, as we have shown, orient themselves toward happy, autonomous families in the face of mounting demands and daily hardships. An ambitious and organized mother of three, Sam attributed to the MOPS community her own self-discovery and development:

> They really emphasized mentoring mothers, not just . . . how to potty train and stuff like that, which is important too, to give you some direction, but to help you figure out who you were, which is part of my goals for my kids. So we would do things like personality assessments, and [they would] challenge us in terms of how are we leaders in our community. . . . I was the leader for this particular MOPS group, for most of the seven or six or eight years, I don't know, I did a different leadership role. And it helped me grow tremendously. . . . There were things that I never understood about myself that I finally figured out in the midst of mothering thanks to those . . . people that were there who could help me figure this stuff out and the tools they provided. So that's what I loved about it. I felt like that was invaluable. I wish every mother could get that lecture so they can find themselves before their kids grow up. . . . I just think that's a great gift.

For Sam, MOPS was a place to meet friends in a small, tightly knit town at a time when she primarily stayed at home with her new baby; at the same time, it was an opportunity to work on her own self. From potty training to leadership, MOPS offered Sam strategies and opportunities for doing better work on herself and for her kids, learning and practicing those strategies within a net of new friendships and mutual care.

Individualized solidarities and their privatized nets both enable and cohere around participatory governing. That is, rather than just being a gathering space for mothers of young children, MOPS is organized as a community for developing mothers' capacities for family autonomy. The organization promises that each meeting will offer mentorship, "leadership development," "honest conversation," and "relevant teaching." At a typical meeting, the women listen to a speaker for about forty-five minutes and then discuss the presentation at their tables. In Emily's year at MOPS, the group watched a cooking demonstration encouraging them to cook with their children, listened to the church pastor detail the dangers of gossip, learned how to make T-shirt scarves (a craft found on Pinterest), listened to a personal testimony from a local mother whose husband had molested their children, and learned about the five "love languages," a concept developed by Baptist pastor and author Gary Chapman to help people understand differing strategies (affirmation, gifts, physical touch, quality time, and service) for helping their families and friends to feel loved. During the presentations, mothers completed worksheets that provided space for note taking and structured reflection, and they engaged in guided small-group discussions reacting to the lectures, relaying their own struggles with family happiness and offering each other tips for better family life.

For instance, the cooking demonstration sparked a long conversation about creating and maintaining family traditions—a practice centered on elevating family autonomy and generating nostalgia for routinized happy moments. The testimony about child molestation generated a list of strategies for talking with children about "good touching" and "bad touching," and the love-languages lecture gave women space to discuss their frustrations with toddlers' temper tantrums and to think through best practices for aligning their methods of displaying love with their toddlers' unique needs. Understood as a cry for love, tantrums became an opportunity to try out new love languages on kids, a manageable problem that could be solved with the simple application of new techniques. While lecturers provided fodder for discussion, mothers helped to govern one another, listening to the minutiae of care work and discussing techniques for making it easier and optimizing its impact.

Beyond monthly local meetings, MOPS International offers publications and conferences designed to enhance mothers' collective efforts at family appreciation and self-appreciation. MOMcon, the MOPS International Leadership Conference, provides space for mothers to join together to learn and reflect on techniques for family government and self-care, while cultivating their own capacities for leadership and mentoring other mothers. Workshops have included "Celebrate the Season," designed to help moms enjoy the "season" of raising young children; "Intentional Families: Fostering a 'Family Culture,'" with strategies to "re-calibrate your inner compass"; "Only What Matters: The Life-Giving Pursuit of Clutterfree Living"; "Growing Up Social: Raising Relational Kids in a Screen-Driven World"; and "Celebrating Authentic Mom Relationships." The schedule also includes morning workouts, MOPS brainstorming sessions, and special programs for military moms and teen moms.

Importantly, MOPS members are offered numerous opportunities to become leaders in the participatory governance structure. "Table leaders" organize the small groups, leading discussions and organizing small-group activities outside of the regular meetings. The large group includes an area coordinator, a secretary, and a treasurer, and interested women are invited to organize large-group activities and offer workshops or lectures. The MOPS leadership team meets regularly, brainstorming ideas for programming and drawing on MOPS International publications to boost the group's feeling of community and mom-to-mom mentorship. Jenny, who we discussed at length in the previous chapter, was Emily's table leader; she had become involved in MOPS when her oldest was a baby. Jenny saw numerous opportunities for creative leadership in the organization, and she found the work of "helping other moms" to be quite gratifying. She explained that she had been working closely with leaders in other local MOPS groups to brainstorm ideas for more inspirational speakers and potential connections with other area organizations such as local support groups for abused mothers and their children. She also described the MOPS International leadership team, noting that they include "field leaders and they're there to help start MOPS groups and help, not facilitate but help the other groups in different areas, or different ideas, and things like that." Clearly, for Jenny, MOPS was a place to not only find friendship and advice but also to improve and work on her own capacities by becoming a community leader and organizer.

The promises of participatory governance are appealing to mothers trying to hold on to the promises of family happiness, for they reinscribe those promises and offer a support system for realizing them. Indeed, while Emily struggled with the highly gendered and conservative nature of MOPS—she found the pastor's warnings about gossip to be especially condescending as the male patriarch admonished this group of women about being "mean girls"—she was also grateful for the situated and practical advice from other mothers. Participatory governing offers mothers a sense of stability and validation, as well as much-needed feelings of relief, particularly as they find themselves ensconced in their family scenes and traversing the paradoxes of precarized happiness. Mothering communities show moms that they are not alone and offer tested tips for staying pointed toward happiness.

Renee's description of her family life exemplifies the MOPS promise, for she embodies a clear, intentional approach to family government and the ways in which other mothers' support can help moms realize their potential. Indeed, many of the mothers we spoke with were, like Renee and Sam, grateful for the participatory government they found at MOPS meetings. Calley, who was also a member of Emily's small group, said, "I really enjoy it purely from the aspect of the stuff that I, like, when it comes to just the practical parenting stuff. I've felt so much more normal just hearing what other people have to say and the things they've dealt with. Because so many of us had at least one child the same age, that was really beneficial to me, and most everybody has a boy. So that has just really been helpful to me."

Furthermore, the mamasphere distributes opportunities for participatory governing into the nooks and crannies of everyday life. Online, mothers can easily post questions and comments germane to family government, seeking out best practices and offering solace, understanding, and emotional support to other struggling mothers. Glennon's community of Monkees, for example, operates in large part as a forum for participatory governing, as she presents and circulates parenting advice culled from her own experiences as well as from the "jukebox" of other Monkees' experiences in her head. One post shares a letter Glennon read to her son before his first day of third grade. Part of this letter reads:

> Chase—We do not care if you are the smartest or fastest or coolest or funniest. There will be lots of contests at school, and we don't care if you win a single one of them. We don't care if you get straight As. We don't care if the girls think you're cute or whether you're picked first or last for kickball at recess. We don't care if you are your teacher's favorite or not. We don't care if you have the best clothes or most Pokemon cards or coolest gadgets. We just don't care. We don't send you to school to become the best at anything at all. We already love you as much as we possibly could. You do not have to earn our love or pride and you can't lose it. That's done. We send you to school to practice being brave and kind.[28]

Crucially, Glennon's post is not meant to be simply consumed and reflected on; rather, she offers it up in the spirit of participatory governing to help other moms in a culture of bullying and violence. The end of the note explains:

> ***Each year people ask my permission to substitute their child's name for Chase's and read this letter together the night before school

begins. YES. Others ask if they might change the word God to their family's name for love and read it that way. OF COURSE. This letter belongs to all of us. I'd be honored if you took it and made it work for your family. Heck, tell 'em you wrote it. I'm always picking up pre-made grocery buffet food, throwing it into a casserole dish, placing it triumphantly on the table and then stepping back and smiling as humbly as possible in the wake of such triumph. Same/Same. Love, G.[29]

Ultimately, though, participatory governing and the "everyone's-in" promises of MOPS and Momastery hinge not simply on "collective intelligence"—the collective and egalitarian production of knowledge through networks—but also, and more fundamentally, on *collective affect*, as individualized solidarities cohere around shared dispositions and investments in nuclear family life.[30] Indeed, what seems to matter most to mothers, perhaps even more than material supports or particular technologies, is the sharing of ordinary affects that participatory governing enables. As they discuss everyday struggles of family life and offer one another strategies for managing that life, mothers also pass around their feelings, creating affective communities of belonging. At MOPS, small-group discussions about preventing child molestation opened up space for collective fears; likewise, conversations about creating traditions opened into emotional discussions about husbands' absences and crushing experiences with miscarriage and childhood illnesses. The moms at MOPS, therefore, offered one another opportunities to present their intimate and sometimes shameful feelings, and, perhaps more importantly, affirmed that these feelings were shared—that all moms experience paralyzing fears, exploding frustrations, and heartbreaking sadness. The group confirmed that happy family life is not always happy and thus, paradoxically, affirmed that even unhappy families can be moving in the right direction.

Similarly, like all mamaspheric nodes, Momastery is fueled by the generation and distribution of collective affect. For example, the blog gained national prominence with "Don't Carpe Diem," which was featured on the *Huffington Post* and went viral in 2013. In this post Glennon resists a particular mode of family government, talking back to entreaties for mothers to relish the brief time they will be parenting young children. She writes, "This CARPE DIEM message makes me paranoid and panicky . . . that if I'm not in a constant state of intense gratitude and ecstasy, I'm doing something wrong."[31] The post elaborates on how suffocating and unsupportive this kind of government is, likening it to onlookers imploring mountain climbers to enjoy every second of their climb. Glennon steps in with new strategies for family happiness, acknowledging that mothers slog through "chronos time," which is "staring down the clock till bedtime time," and suggesting that they take note of "Kairos time. Kairos is God's time. It's time outside of time. . . . It's those magical moments in which time stands still. I have a few of those moments each day. And I cherish them."[32] For Glennon, these are the moments when she notices the bounty in her life, her grocery cart full of food, her daughter's beauty, the presence of her family in her life. "If I had a couple Kairos moments during the day," Glennon writes, "I call it a success. Carpe a couple of Kairoses a day. Good enough for me."[33]

As suggested by the viral spread of Glennon's post, mothers turn to the participatory governing of the mamasphere not only for advice but also for emotional comfort and the sense of belonging its intimate public affords. Momastery posts provide affective punches that help mothers stay on the path of happiness in the face of frustration, anger, and perhaps even unhappiness. The responses are telling. One commenter thanked Glennon for this "bravely honest" post, noting that she had recently lost her job, "many friends and my sense of self" and was struggling through parenting. "Everyone tells me the same, enjoy every moment! But most of the time, I work, work work and not a day off, not an evening out. . . . I love my family, but the loneliness is killing me. . . . Your blog post helped" (Tanya, January 25, 2015).[34] Another Monkee reported that she had recently written a blog articulating the same sentiment: "After I posted it, I was immediately riddled with self-doubt. WHAT IF I'm the ONLY one that feels this way? . . . But then the comments eventually came . . . two of them leading me here. So thankful that you have written these words. I feel normal. For once. Well, maybe not normal. But at least part of a really cool club" (Jordan, March 5, 2014). Other responses included:

> This is my favorite blog post of all time. Literally. I read this a few years ago and have shared it with friends and cherished it ever since. Sometimes when I have a rough day I will refer to this post because it has such a great message, especially when you're in the throes of raising young kiddos. (Gina, September 25, 2014)

> Always come back to this post . . . it keeps me centered. Thank you! (Beth, January 31, 2014)

I think raising children is a lot like labor. It was freaking painful and a lot of hard work, but when we walk away, or at least a few months later, we no longer really remember the pain. We take away the moments of bliss or as you call them the kairos times. Those are the moments as we get older and our children grow up that stick around. Because yes all that hard work, made those moments so much sweeter. (Leiya, December 20, 2013)

Thank you! I am a new mama and I am overwhelmed by the feelings of exhaustion, guilt, self doubt mixed with delight, love and devotion. This is so validating! (Nikki, November 20, 2013)

On the one hand, collective affect is what pulls mothers to community and underwrites their individualized solidarities. As mothers enter into intimate publics seeking to "close gaps" between their overloaded precarious lives and the gender scripts of family autonomy that are supposed to bring stability and certainty, collective affect is constituted by the shared ordinary feelings of everyday family life and their desperate search for happy circuits.[35] On the other hand, collective affect is what gets produced through the individualized solidarities and interactive workings of participatory governing. Affective punches meet mothers' daily experiences and seal their membership in "a really cool club": a community of women who understand and feel one another's struggles. Through this cycling of collective affect, mothers sustain collective investments in family life, keeping one another oriented toward the family in spite of its broken promises. At the same time, they produce affective communities of belonging, separating themselves from those mothers who are not able to stay on happiness's path.

CRUEL SOLIDARITIES: EMBRACING PRECARITY

Through participatory governing and its distribution of collective affect, mothers construct affective infrastructures, attuning themselves to the precarity of family. Individualized solidarities become cruel solidarities, in this sense, to the extent that they keep mothers cycling through nuclear family scenes and their broken promises. Individualized solidarities route ordinary affects that emerge from the impossibility of mothers' loads back into the promise of happiness while constituting the shared work of privatizing happiness as a vital, life-affirming mode of collectivity and community.

It is important to see that, more and more, the individualized solidarities of mothering communities are affective infrastructures for becoming resilient, that is, collectivities cohering around bracing for and embracing precarity. Both MOPS and Momastery promise to help mothers hone their collective affects and capacities for resilient happiness, providing technologies, platforms, and affective punches for weathering precarization. For example, MOPS chose "Be You, Bravely" for its yearly theme for 2015. Symbolized by a feather to signify risking heights and flights, this theme is meant to help mothers learn together to "risk bravely"—to identify and take "healthy risks" and thereby "choose the extraordinary." A large component of "Be You, Bravely" is "The Brave Collective," which MOPS's blog, *Hello, Dearest: This Is Motherhood*, describes as a "table movement" where mothers organize to share meals and become brave together. According to the site, "it is in sharing a meal that hearts are nourished and soul-sisters are born." The site goes on to explain:

> The Brave Collective is a rallying cry to live in proximity, to widen our circles and be brave together. Maybe your Collective is about being brave enough to invite people over, or maybe it is about making new friends. Perhaps you need to talk about the things God is whispering in your ear and invite others to do the same. Bravery comes in as many varieties as there are humans to give it life. There is bravery to live more fully. To do less and be more. To face an avoided obstacle. To reconcile. To hold valiantly to hope. To give voice to those who are diminished. To wear proudly a version of ourselves previously hidden. To be kind to ourselves. To listen to our own heart.[36]

Like other MOPS activities, the Brave Collective is a highly structured venture, and hosts are provided with detailed guidelines and parameters. They are to adhere to "basic Brave Collective aesthetics," which include meeting at a table covered in butcher paper decorated with feathers and utilizing glass accessories such as bottles and candleholders. They also are urged to follow the "Brave Collective Conversation Guide." Conversations start with mothers finding their "brave"—choosing "one brave thing stirring in their souls" to focus on in the upcoming months. The site explains, "The first meeting of The Brave Collective is about new beginnings, about being vulnerable and about a step, however small, toward the future." In future gatherings around the table, mothers work to collectively "unpack" their braves, encouraging each other through the hard parts of learning to

FIGURE 4.1. Mothers of Preschoolers' theme for 2014–2015, "Be You, Bravely," symbolized by a feather to signify risking heights and flights, encourages mothers to thrive through risk by supporting one another as they work to become brave.

risk bravely: for example, according to the "Conversation Guide," mothers must "encourage one another to keep going or to start over if someone realizes their brave wasn't the right one for this season of their life." Along the way mothers are also to celebrate "the journey you are on together and the commitment you have made to show up in each other's lives."[37]

Supporting and cheering each other on in these "brave" activities creates an infrastructure for resilient happiness. As MOPS suggests to mothers, they must learn to privatize happiness in the context of constant obstacles, diminished hopes and dreams, and permanent insecurities, and to thrive through risk by finding their "brave" and thereby becoming resilient. As Brad Evans and Julian Reid argue, resilience reorients social life toward survival, staying afloat, adapting.

> Rather than enabling the development of peoples and individuals so that they can aspire to secure themselves from whatever they find threatening and dangerous in worldly living, the liberal discourse of resilience functions to convince peoples and individuals of the risks and dangers of the belief in the possibility of security. . . . To be resilient, the subject must disavow any belief in the possibility to secure itself and accept instead an understanding of life as a permanent

process of continual adaption to threats and dangers which are said to be outside its control. . . . The resilient subject is not a political subject who on its own terms conceives of changing the world, its structure and conditions of possibility. The resilient subject is required to accept the dangerousness of the world it lives in as a condition for partaking of that world and accept the necessity of the injunction to change itself in correspondence with threats now presupposed as endemic and unavoidable. . . . Building resilient subjects involves the deliberate disabling of the political habits, tendencies and capacities of peoples and replacing them with adaptive ones.[38]

The MOPS "Be You, Bravely" campaign assumes the inherent dangers of the world and readily admits the human inability to control them. It provides a "table movement" for navigating and inhabiting this world where security is impossible, teaching mothers to live with, accept, and embrace life's riskiness through finding their own "healthy" "brave" and sticking to it, even when things are hard, all the while always being ready to let go. Here MOPS mothers are "world influential" not because they can actively build a better world but because a better world is imagined to hinge on their resilient happiness.

The "Be You, Bravely" campaign and its focus on risking healthily and bravely seeks to govern mothers' paths toward becoming resilient in order to tame and temper precarity. Through precisely decorated tables and carefully guided conversations, mothers can learn to live with danger and even to thrive. Momastery, on the other hand, is also an affective infrastructure for resilient happiness but is more about helping mothers to open themselves up to precarity: to feel it and acknowledge it, so as to keep on moving through it.

Glennon's microcelebrity and the intimate public it engenders take shape around collective affects that adhere to sticky buzzwords like *brutiful* and *happyish*, as she readily admits to failure and insecurity. Glennon creates solidarity around mothers' capacities for accepting and surviving contemporary nuclear family life; in fact, she sees her own work as the leader of the Monkees as first and foremost about witnessing the fragility and pain that shoots through mothers' lives and providing a space for it to live and breathe and be recognized. She writes to her readers, "I want to be your witness. I love you and I want to fix your pain but I can't do that and I shouldn't do that because like joy, pain is holy and it should not be snatched away from people. I won't do that to you. I won't be a pain snatcher. But I will witness for you. I will let my heart break open for you—that is the greatest honor of my work."[39]

For example, in a post entitled "5 Ways to Secure Your Happyish Ever After," Glennon writes, "If you've 'fallen out of love' and so you are disillusioned about marriage—join the club. All the married people in the whole world are in the club." In fact, "being disillusioned is good," explains Glennon.

> It means you've stopped believing a lie. The lie is that marriage is like it is in the movies and that everyone else is having hot love affairs while you are cleaning up smelly socks and trying to get someone to actually listen to you instead of pretending to listen to you. The truth is that cleaning up socks and trying to get someone to really listen to you is marriage. It's less sweep you off your feet and more sweep the kitchen four times a day. Like everything good in life—it's 98% back-breaking work and 2% moments that make that work worthwhile. So—just get ready to sweat."[40]

Glennon goes on to offer up her own confused and painful sex life with her husband as a means to double down on the importance of family:

> No one talks about this, which is a shame. I've been married for eleven years and my husband and I are still trying to figure out how to make sex enjoyable for both of us. Right now sex is a source of all kinds of confusion and resentment and shame and pain for us. But we don't think this means that there's anything "wrong" with us or our marriage. We just assume that our confusion means that we're normal people who've been paying attention to the world's mixed, dangerous sex messages forever and so we have some unlearning to do. When our kids were young—we knew we were stuck when it came to sex—but we couldn't find an extra hour or dollar to spend figuring it out. Now that the kids are older, we spend hours a week in therapy muddling through this stuff. It's annoying and painful and expensive and necessary. Mating comes naturally, but healthy sex lives don't. They take work.[41]

Ultimately, all this painful, hard, and expensive intimate work is worth it, because, as Glennon explains, "Marriage is still the best chance we have to become evolved, loving people . . . Lasting, True Love is not about being swept off your feet. Sometimes love is just sweeping the kitchen and being grateful that there is a kitchen and a partner who is contractually obligated to share it with you forever."[42] Happiness here is not the fantasy of a picture-perfect nuclear world but rather a deeply precarious privilege to be held onto through resilient happiness. As Glennon puts it, "Happy Ever After is not a thing. You have to start over everyday."[43] In other words, mothers are to accept their unhappiness and brace for, and embrace, the hard work of "happyish."

Women's responses to this post crystallize Momastery's affective infrastructure for resilient happiness, for a happiness composed of confronting and accepting the "happyish." Mothers described how Glennon's honesty made them feel "less alone," especially in regard to sex in marriage. One women responded, "I so wish I would have known this at the beginning of my marriage. We spent so many years struggling, not knowing how to talk about sex, and just feeling broken. I love your honesty and openness! It's amazing how just knowing we aren't alone can make things better" (Becca, October 14, 2014).[44] Another poster reflected on how she "wanted guarantees" for her family but has since come to accept that " 'Never' and 'Always' are dangerous, dangerous words":

> I wanted guarantees, G, and even when I got them from my husband, I was suspicious, because, duh, that's not how life works. I had to mostly let that worry go in order for my marriage to work. I had to let go of my fear of failure. I had to accept that there might come a day when my marriage might end, and I had to find the confidence to say that if that day ever comes, I will be okay. Strangely enough, accepting all of those things has made my marriage better and stronger (but not perfect! Jeezus, not perfect—not by a long shot). Choosing to stay because I want to be there is so much better than choosing to stay because I'm afraid of the alternative. Last thing: I'm glad you mentioned sex, G. I have a hard time talking about it, and even a hard time reading about it (silly, right?) Why aren't women talking about this more? Why aren't I? Sex was never an issue in my marriage until very recently, and it threw me for a loop. We are working hard to get back on track, and when I hear a whisper in my mind that says "What if we never get back on track again?" I push the thought away, because perhaps the only thing I've learned in the 10 years that I've been with my husband is that absolutes like "Never" and "Always" are dangerous, dangerous words. (Andrea, January 9, 2014)

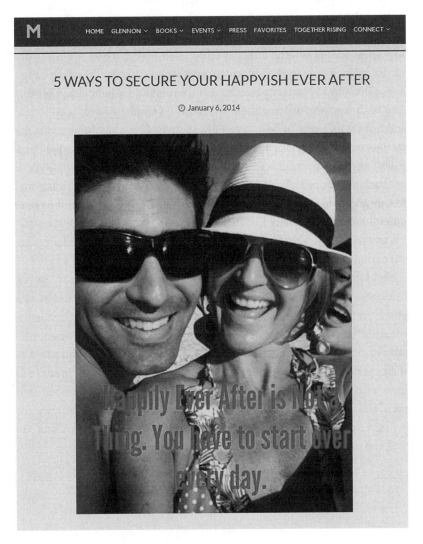

FIGURE 4.2. Glennon Doyle Melton positions her website, Momastery, as a space to recognize the everyday troubles of nuclear family life. The post "5 Ways to Secure Your Happyish Ever After" portrays marriage as a deeply precarious privilege to be held onto through resilient happiness.

In sharing her own "insecure intimacies," Glennon enables mothers to reflect on and thereby embrace the fragilities and volatilities of contemporary nuclear life, providing them with crucial affective punches and resources for weathering fraying family scenes and promises.[45]

We might think of Glennon as an "affect alien": someone who readily, and subversively, admits to the gaps between heteronormative nuclear family happiness scripts and the ordinary affects that make up everyday intimate life for women.[46] In these performances of feeling that are "alien" to happiness, Glennon engenders powerful and meaningful individualized solidarities with women, assuring them that their own unhappiness is collective and not theirs alone to bear. Crucially, though, Glennon always saves the family scene, coming back to happiness through doubling down on the "happyish" and the "brutiful." This collective cycling through unhappiness to get back to "happyish" validates and affirms mothers' lives, providing fuel to stay afloat, to keep on moving through their family scenes, and to keep on embracing their precarity. This cycling also shuts down their own status as affect aliens, ensuring mothers through individualized solidarity that alienation is just part of the path.

In Momastery's affective infrastructures for embracing precarity, the politicization of maternal subjectivity engendered by the rise of ethopolitics gives way to the depoliticization that Evans and Reid suggest that resilience requires.[47] It is through embracing precarity, not necessarily a particular lifestyle or personal ethic, that mothers come to inhabit and stay attached to their overloaded scenes and the horizons of neoliberal precarity. What feels most promising, life giving, and even resistant in these individualized solidarities is also what is most oppressive and cruel: embracing precarity means giving up on the potentialities for alternative worlds that "affect aliens" reveal and the shared affective infrastructures that might take us there.

SOCIALIZING HAPPINESS
(OR, WHY WE WROTE AN UNHAPPY BOOK)

NANCY

Nancy is a new mother who works full-time as an administrative assistant at a local educational institution. When we spoke, she was trying to survive the grueling emotional and physical terrain of caring for an infant. As our interview began, Emily briefly introduced our project and reassured a nervous Nancy. "I have three little boys," Emily explained, "a four-and-a-half-year-old, a two-year-old, and a three-, almost four-month-old, so I get it, don't worry." Our first question asked Nancy to simply "walk us through your day" and "introduce us to your family." Nancy replied,

> This is our first child, so this is all new to us, but, I mean, it was something that my husband and I talked about, children, and were wanting to start a family, so this was part of our plan. He is ten months old now, and my husband has a brother and he is a teacher, so he deals with high school students. And I come from a family of three. We

both come from parents that are still together so that's kind of our family background. So our day-to-day is getting up. Fortunately, he's really helpful, and he's usually home. He doesn't travel or anything. In the morning it's both of us, which makes it nice. I'm fortunate that way, and it's just kind of make sure we're up early enough to have a little bit of time before we bring him to day care. He goes to day care up here, which is a huge benefit. I was fully against the whole day-care thing, period. I was like, "Oh, we'll have kids, I'll stay home," you know, and I went to college and I wanted to have a career. I thought, "Oh, I'll just stay home for a little bit and then go back to work." Not an option, just financially basically. Which is fine 'cause I love my job, but my mom stayed at home when we were younger. She went back to school when we were probably, my youngest sister was, I don't know, maybe [in] fourth or fifth grade, and my dad worked out of our basement. Jeff, my husband, went to day care. Both of his parents worked, and he's a teacher, so he's like, "Day care's great. It's such a good experience for them." [I was] like, "No, our kids are not going to day care. No way." But, like I said, that was not an option, so he goes to day care up here, which is nice. I really love the day care. I'm really happy with it, and it's nice because while he was little I would go up at lunchtime, which made it a little easier. He's the age now where I need to quit doing that, but that's made it easy. I get to see him at lunchtime. And then we go home, have dinner, probably keep him up later than we should just because we're like, "Oh, we're gone all day. We need to play with him and interact with him." We're starting to hit the age where he's starting to have, like, problems going to bed and sleeping through the night. We're like, "Oh, we probably keep him up late." So that's kind of our new struggle right now, but it's funny 'cause some days I'm like, "Oh, this isn't so bad. We've got it. We have time. We're organized." For getting through the days it's kind of nice to be with my coworkers, and then other days I'm like, "I cannot do this. This is not working. We're falling apart. . . . We don't have clean clothes." So it's kind of a day-to-day up-and-down kind of thing. But it's overall working pretty well.

These words spilled out through tears. Teeming with insecurity and over-wrought with responsibility, Nancy could not "walk us through [her] day" without relentlessly interrogating her own affects and capacities as a mother:

"I need to quit" (going to meet him at lunch); "we probably keep him up late"; "We've got it. . . . We're falling apart."

Our time with Nancy weighed heavily on us. Of course, mothers are anxious and distraught, especially in the throes of new motherhood. But more than any other mother we spoke to, Nancy clearly articulated the cruelties of precarized family happiness, as well as the intense, affective work required to inhabit its infrastructures. Nancy and the other mothers inspired—or perhaps required—us to write a decidedly unhappy book, one that focuses on the "prismatic" political-economic, cultural, and affective structures undergirding mothers' lives.[1] After all, our interviews themselves were usually unhappy—overrun with anxieties, fears, threats, job losses, health scares, and mundane impossibilities—despite the intense love and certain pleasures mothers found in caring for their children and families.

Throughout our writing, then, we wrestled with what to do with the undeniable pull that mothers feel for their families, especially their children. Call it joy or mother love; it doesn't matter. It exists, it's powerful, and it's something that's sometimes happy, even tremendously pleasurable. It undoubtedly has to do with that vital reproductive power that Adrienne Rich identified at the core of the mothering experience, a power that, she argued, must always be contained by the patriarchal institution of motherhood.[2] Ultimately, we decided to leave that powerful pull unquestioned as an unshakable affective force that emerges from the precariousness and potentiality of motherhood itself and that compels mothers to live their overloaded everydays. We wanted our book to show how this indisputable force is nonetheless historical and subject to assemblages of power (not simply patriarchy): it gets channeled, worked over, and exploited in myriad ways.

We wanted the experience of reading this book to throw into relief the contingencies and compositionality of mothering through precarity and thereby to provoke detachment from the infrastructures of privatized happiness. Put a little differently, in capturing how hard, heavy, and seemingly hopeless things are for mothers, we also hoped to bring to life their fragility and the immanent potentialities for socializing happiness.

PRESSURE POINTS

Specifically, Nancy called attention to the affective "pressure points" of mothering through precarity.[3] She deeply wanted to stay home with her son during his early years, like so many other mothers are urged to do in the name of good, neoliberal gender citizenship.[4] Nancy had also inherited a powerful happiness script from her own mother, which compelled her to feel that staying home and avoiding day care was the "good" thing to do. She told us, "I just remember the way we were raised. . . . [M]y mom was always doing this with us or doing that with us, and I didn't go to day care, and I did fine in school. I didn't need all of that, and I just think growing up that way that you automatically assume, 'Oh, that's how I'm gonna do things.' . . . Even as we started to talk about kids, my experience was, this is what my mom did, so every time I would think about something it was with that frame of reference." Nancy's happiness "frame of reference" is traditional nuclear life: two parents, mom at home, "doing this" and "doing that." In Nancy's mind, this is a clear and simple path for living a good life. However, material realities—including, most significantly, her husband's impending layoff from his position as a public school teacher—require mamapreneurial flexibility and a more resilient approach to happiness. And so Nancy was quick to assure us, even through tears, that she really did "love" both her job and the day care. After all, leaving her job and staying home was ultimately "not an option."

Nancy's option for family happiness is painfully out of alignment with her happiness "frame of reference." Instead of living a simple, good life, Nancy inhabits a family scene of constant "added stress" and "chaos":

I feel like we're running around like crazy people at home, because the laundry's not done. "Wait, I don't have any socks to wear today! Great. What am I gonna do?" I just feel like, I honestly feel like, it's just all that added stress. And not that Jeff is like, "That's your job. You have to do the laundry," but he's got things he's doing, and I know if he's taking care of the lawn then that's something I don't have to worry about. I'll take care of the laundry. That'll be done. I just feel like we're not home, and like we're just, like, always in this state of like chaos.

Nancy reported being surprised and disappointed by how out of control her life felt, explaining, "I guess I just thought that I would be able to have a little more control over things. Like, have my day structured the way I intended it to be, and be able to make dinner, and there are days [that] I'm like, 'Oh, we haven't even eaten yet!'" Indeed, Nancy feels grateful for her crockpot and the abundant archives of crockpot recipes available online: "a good solution to not eating at nine o'clock at night or not eating crap every night."

Nancy seems to move through her chaotic days with a strong sensibility that things might be easier, or at least that she would feel less guilty, overwhelmed, and exhausted, if she could just follow her inherited happiness script.[5] In Nancy's mind, by staying home, she wouldn't be constantly thrown for loops by the challenges of childrearing and domestic government.

> Now he's waking up at night and not going back to sleep, which I knew at some point he would do purposely: not go back to sleep. I was like, "Oh, sure, I know it's going to be tough, but when it happens, we're gonna be strict about it and put him back to bed and let him cry it out." And then I didn't realize we were already at that point. I'm like, "Oh, he's teething," or "He's hungry," totally oblivious that this is actually happening, and I think I feel guilty. If I was home during the day it wouldn't bother me as much. But I'm gone all day, and he's with someone else all day, and this is our only time at night. We have to be together, so if he's crying, I'm like, "Oh, I have to make sure he's OK." So I think that is something that . . . would be different if I were home. Although I'm sure it would be hard regardless.

Nancy knows that mothering is "hard regardless." Yet she takes personal responsibility for her perceived failures at mother love (e.g., not noting new developmental phases, not being "strict" with sleeping regimens), reading them less in terms of a fixed ideology and more in terms of a privatized happiness script that she herself must learn to rewrite and follow in the face of precarity for her family. This adaptation is hard for Nancy, though, as the constant clash of inherited happiness scripts with the realities of everyday family life makes mothering an intense and volatile affair that requires ongoing modes of reflexive affective labor.

Indeed, Nancy seems to have to work intensely to "close gaps" between powerful ordinary affects—"I cannot do this. This is not working. We're falling apart"—and the promise of happiness—"But it's overall working pretty well." As Sara Ahmed explains in her discussion of the unhappy bride on her wedding day,

> the capacity to "save the day" depends on the bride being able to make herself be affected in the right way or at least being able to persuade others that she is being affected in the right way. When it can be said that "the bride looked happy," then the expectation of happiness has

become the happiness of expectation. To correct our feelings is to become disaffected from a former affection: the bride makes herself happy by stopping herself being miserable. Of course we learn from this example that it is possible not to inhabit fully one's own happiness, or even to be alienated from one's happiness, if the former affection remains lively, or if one is made uneasy by the labor of making yourself feel a certain way. Uneasiness might persist in the very feeling of being happy, as a feeling of unease *with* the happiness you are in.[6]

Throughout our conversation Nancy was clearly working hard to "save the day" and to appear to be happy, cycling through the affective circuits that route her fraught and unsettling ordinary affects back to happiness. But she was also bubbling up with a deep uneasiness. Though she eventually settled into the interview, her words and stories, like those of so many of the mothers we spent time with, were always tinged with an intensity and volatility that felt to us deeply entwined with happiness-saving work.

Put differently, despite her conservative gender beliefs and deep investments in traditional nuclear family life, Nancy seemed to be teetering on the edge of becoming an "affect alien."[7] According to Ahmed, affect aliens kill the joy of the family, refusing to inhabit its happy affective infrastructures. So many of the mothers we encountered appeared to be similarly teetering, poised to jump ship. And yet they always ended up "saving the day." This constant cycling back to happiness is, of course, not surprising. As the previous chapters have shown, mothers possess immense resources in the digital mundane for stabilizing the promise of happiness in precarious times—from the pulsing potential of the mamasphere to the individualized solidarities of mothering communities. As they wrestle with affective alienation, mothers therefore come to stay stuck to family happiness, even while advanced neoliberalism perpetually breaks and precarizes its promises. Of course, the viscosity of family happiness comes in part from the immense love and responsibility that mothers feel for their children, even through the mundane, often unhappy, muck of everyday family life. A daily life of "chaos," "added stress," anxiety, and unease is perhaps a small price to pay for imagined lifetimes and generations of proximity to happiness.

At the conclusion of *The Promise of Happiness*, Ahmed wonders what possibilities might open up if happiness were no longer "weighed down as a sign of the good—of the virtuous subject or of the good life."[8] As Ahmed suggests (and Nancy's words reveal), "happiness becomes an exclusion of possibility, and thus a good defense against crisis, as if the decisions about the future are already made."[9] Though Nancy continuously encounters the crisis of unease bubbling up in her ordinary affects, she need not—and cannot—tackle it head-on. For happiness makes (and has always already made) good decisions for her. In this way, happiness shuts down possibilities for alternative sensibilities of who and what Nancy might become by always routing her bad, unhappy affects—affects that stem from broken promises—back to these promises, as if they are still viable. In this way, mothers like Nancy are overloaded by happiness, by its insistence on family autonomy as a good and virtuous life, even as precarity, in so many ways, renders this life increasingly unworkable and impossible.

Ahmed suggests that affect aliens show us possibilities for new worlds. Nuclear mothers like Nancy work very hard to defend and stay attached to this world, however, thanks to the cruel optimisms of resilience that sustain mothering through precarity. As their lives get progressively loaded up with responsibility and impossibility, mothers continually attune and rewrite their scripts to sustain and stabilize their family scenes and keep alive their promise of happiness. Constantly routed away from affective alienation by friends, family, community, and the mamasphere, mothers continue to pursue the good life even as neoliberal precarity undercuts and unravels it. Consequently, mothers live lives full of stress, anxiety, and unease, where just staying stuck, keeping afloat, and maintaining one's "sea legs" figure as profoundly affirming and gratifying in themselves.[10] Through affective resilience, mothers push back against alien affects, staying tightly, though tenuously, tethered to their families.

But what if Nancy did jump ship? What if her ordinary affects found new infrastructures? What if, instead of embracing precarity through resilient happiness, she embraced the potentialities embedded in her alien affect? As Nancy's life attests, instead of reaping stable and material benefits from nuclear life, mothers today are asked to live lives of perpetual labor and anxiety and are offered cruel optimisms and solidarities that keep them stuck to the impossible scenes of mothering through precarity. We are wondering: in a context of widespread dispossession and shriveling public resources, what do mothers like Nancy have to lose by jumping ship? Certainly not long-term wealth, health, peace of mind, or time. All they seem to have left to lose is their heavy happiness scripts.

Mothers appear to be yearning for different worlds, yet, as our book shows, they are often unable to sense or think them thanks to the entrenched grammars of family autonomy, which load up happiness, and mothers' lives, with more and more weight. Indeed, alternatives would require feeling and moving beyond family autonomy and the idea of a social world held together by autonomous, individualized domestic spheres. The "good" family of family autonomy is cordoned off from civil society, the market, and the state, though, of course, lives are never made or experienced so neatly.[11] Even before the onset of neoliberalism's enterprise society, the "good" family did not ostensibly rely on public social supports but rather benefited from invisible systems of institutionalized racism and naturalized gender regimes. After all, the family's promises of intimacy and happiness were, and still are, imagined to hinge on its independence and self-reliance.[12] From these promises to the ever-churning mamasphere, family autonomy constantly impinges on mothers' affective infrastructures and thus on their sensibilities of what might be possible, of what worlds they may want to live in. Family autonomy is the blueprint on which mothers' affective infrastructures have been, and continue to be, constructed and reconstructed. It is the master script on which mothers' privatized happiness scripts continue to be rewritten and adapted. As such, family autonomy is a chokehold on alternative possibilities.

As we have shown, mothers are "free" and "empowered" to develop their own approaches to family government, just never outside the contours of their own homes and families. In turn, their lives and labors get progressively loaded up with more and more social responsibility in the name of ever more privatized freedoms. For example, in her writing on the privatization of education and childhood, Megan Erickson argues, "'Family' continues to be a sentimental concept imagined as a refuge from the wild and awful world or autocratic workplaces, but its project has become protecting and preparing offspring for the cutthroat global economy."[13] "Childhood is now a . . . desperate challenge full of lotteries and high stakes," Erickson suggests. "All the anxious messaging around children as fun, smart, savvy, adventurous assets is a response to the intensifying economic stratification that leaves parents desperate to give their children an edge. Parents' energies are absorbed by their children's needs and schedules with a totality that is monolithic and exhausting. . . . [A]s socioeconomic stratification intensifies, there is less room for mistakes than ever."[14] Thanks to family autonomy, families have little choice but to respond to scarcity, competition, and insecurity with the ongoing and always already impossible privatization of risks.

Alternative futures become unimaginable as mothers hone their affects and capacities for familial resilience. As women's everyday lives attest, the exploitative and unreasonable gender demands of family autonomy are increasingly felt—they register in alien affects—but the only option seems to be to work harder and become mamapreneurial: to learn and do more, to save and stabilize the fraying scenes, to constantly readjust, retool, and retune: that is, to privatize more and more happiness.

This chokehold on mothers' affective lives runs deep and wide, especially when it comes to the new modes of solidarity that might engender alternatives to family autonomy. Even in their collective modes of privatizing happiness, nuclear mothers are necessarily separated from each other. Despite the proliferation of individualized solidarities, as well as mothers' ongoing personal struggles to push back against "mommy-war" mentalities, mothers often remain trapped inside their own, asphyxiating happiness horizons.[15] Moreover, as mothering media churn in and out of overloaded lives, demanding more and more self-reflexivity and communication, mothers regularly create communities with other mothers that tend to entrench even more the demands of family autonomy, by making its impossibilities livable and life affirming. These are cruel solidarities, in which solace, support, and community double down on family autonomy by helping mothers stay attached to its promises and keep moving through its affective infrastructures, even in the face of its mounting demands and quiet brutalities.

At every turn, family autonomy insists that other routes and different worlds are not possible for nuclear mothers. Even as they reach out for help, often in desperation, to their communities, mothers are primed to recoil from communal approaches to social organization that might lighten their happiness loads. From within the affective infrastructures of family autonomy, these paths are not viable options: they signal dependence, a lack of intimacy and virtue; the promise of happiness insists that the "good" family circulates through private lives cordoned off from the rampant and unknowable dangers lurking beyond the family circle.

The mothers whose voices make up this book are by and large oriented toward heteronormative, white, middle-class, nuclear life, so it is not surprising that they don't see possibilities beyond family autonomy, even as they teeter on the edge of becoming affect aliens. But even from a broader critical perspective, the chokehold of family autonomy on our collective political imagination seems hard to break. In critical-cultural work on mothers and families, are we *really* ever thinking beyond family autonomy? While research on black families and by black feminists calls into question the power of family autonomy, prominent work on motherhood routinely fails to challenge its logic and assumed virtue.[16] Take, for example, Shari L. Thurer's *The Myths of Motherhood*, which offers a long history of images and ideals about motherhood in order to "make mothers' internal lives acceptable to them, to undo some of the *angst* among mothers (and mothering persons) at large."[17] Thurer hopes to make mothers' alien affects less alien, and though she concludes that revealing "the myths of motherhood" should open space for a new "family climate" wherein "the well-being of *all* children is a transcendent public priority," the thrust of the book is aimed at freeing mothers "to create their own philosophy of child rearing."[18] Similarly, Sharon Hays unpacks "the ideology of intensive mothering" to undercut pervasive gender norms that keep nuclear mothers tied to unpaid domestic labors, but the book does not challenge family autonomy.[19] Indeed, much feminist work on nuclear motherhood, like Momastery and so much of the mamasphere, disrupts representations of mothering without calling family autonomy into question.[20]

In political life as well, we debate which policies should or should not be enacted on behalf of happy families—maternity and paternity leaves, daycare subsidies, marriage equality, and so on—but it is hard to imagine political horizons that promise new social arrangements outside the grammars of family autonomy. In this sense, family autonomy is a flexible, liberal rationality that does not necessarily foreclose new visions of the happy family (e.g., marriage equality) or of "outside" public supports the family needs for its "inside" private happiness. For example, as Naomi Mezey and Cornelia Pillard argue, while the online mothering community MomsRising has an aggressive and progressive political agenda for moms, it still doubles down on family autonomy, promoting a new maternalist sensibility where the load is still on mothers.[21]

We want to suggest that moving beyond family autonomy ultimately requires more than critiquing dominant ideologies or writing better liberal policies to "free" and/or support mothers. It requires new sensibilities of what might make for a livable life and new configurations of care and collectivity. Despite the challenges of thinking beyond family autonomy and its chokehold on our cultural and political imaginations, mothers' own practices seem to be implicitly pointing in this direction. Indeed, at the level of mothers' everyday material lives, neoliberal precarity begs the question of continuing investments in it.

As suggested by the privatized nets of mothering communities—for example, Momastery and its Together Rising initiative—fewer and fewer nuclear families experience the material privileges of family autonomy. Many mothers are barely hanging on and are in need of direct "outside" interventions—for car repairs, heating bills, groceries, or kids' presents— from the Holiday Hands of Glennon's Monkees. Together Rising makes these struggles visible and implores Monkees to help one another, to "remind each other that We Belong To Each Other."[22] Families are also envisioning new structures for embedding collectivity in everyday life. The rise of cohousing—where families, often headed by single mothers, enter into intentional communities, maintaining private residencies but sharing common spaces and governance—suggests a transformed vision of family autonomy rooted in autonomous family *collectives* rather than autonomous family *units*. A deeply felt desire for collectivity is clear, and mothers are forging new possibilities.

It is critical to see, however, that neoliberalism's world of privatized risk and happiness accommodates revised approaches to family autonomy and new happiness scripts. Permutations of the nuclear option can proliferate, so long as they remain privatized and weighed down by happiness: that is, so long as they help to distinguish between those "virtuous" subjects on the path to a good life and those who are not capable of forging their own paths. As Lisa Duggan predicted, the neoliberal state has come to welcome marriage equality, helping to cordon off virtuous homonormative citizens invested in family autonomy from unvirtuous or queer affect aliens.[23] Likewise, the cohousing movement relies on common orientations to the good life and shared visions for nuclear family living in community. These communities are cohered by the cultural and social capital, as well as access to economic capital, of those "virtuous" citizens who are welcome in consensus-driven lifestyle communities. The neoliberal state relies on a combination of traditional family autonomy, counseling mothers to stay home and volunteer as part of the privatized social safety net, *and* new configurations of family autonomy that help mothers, and families generally, privatize happiness in the face of precarization.[24] However, as an aggressive criminalizing machine, the neoliberal state is eager to lock up (and lock out of happiness) those who are alien to its enterprising society.[25] Family autonomy, in all its forms, thus helps to render disposable those deemed unworthy of happiness, and so families are keen to pioneer new nuclear options, elevating their own family scenes above the situations of those who cannot privatize the happiness of their family.

Indeed, family autonomy breeds affective communities around shared investments in nuclear family life, and mothers are happy to see themselves in common with each other, so long as they are imagined to share this happiness horizon. However, these affective communities are historically rooted in white supremacy and capitalist exploitation, and, as we have suggested, they continue to betray deeply quotidian racialized and classed attachments and investments.[26] Ostensibly color-blind, these communities cohere around the entrenched whiteness of family autonomy and its exclusion of poor families, who are imagined to be too dependent on the state to adhere to the demands of family autonomy. Holiday Hands, for example, provides for families with emergency needs but does not extend itself to help families facing persistent poverty. Nor does it imagine upsetting fixed policies and structures that reward autonomous family units, from tax relief for mortgage interest to social benefits associated with marriage. And, perhaps most importantly, Holiday Hands is always centered on the project of family autonomy, bouncing families temporarily disabled by hard times back into happy self-reliance. Mothers' resiliency nets thus allow mothers to imagine themselves as part of larger communities that are irrefutably *not* associated with citizens who refuse the promise of family happiness, or are otherwise deemed to be failing to strive and survive.

Really moving beyond family autonomy, then, requires not only new configurations of nuclear families and/or new sorts of nets but also, and crucially, new sensibilities of belonging, new affective infrastructures. As Erickson puts it, "the care of children must become an economically and emotionally collective experience."[27] Upsetting family autonomy means opening up to affect aliens and extending collective resources to those who have been shunted to the edges of contemporary neoliberal life. It means erasing the boundaries between the virtuous and the disposable, shedding attachments to visions of a good life weighed down by privatized family happiness.

Affective infrastructures are immensely powerful. Like material infrastructures (e.g., roads, bridges, broadband Internet), affective infrastructures connect everyday lives to power and to other lives. Infrastructures define how folks can connect, travel, build, and live together. Infrastructures enable and constrain; they make certain social worlds possible while foreclosing others. They can fray, tear, break, and collapse, but they can also be built and rebuilt. Affective infrastructures thus define the possibilities for social life. They unify and solidify, separate and divide. They provide road maps for identification, belonging, and solidarity, and, in doing so, they cut folks off from those who travel different streets. Affective infrastructures keep us stuck in scenes that don't work, tethered to the mundane brutalities of our present conjuncture, but they are also potential pathways to new, more livable forms of living.

As our work shows, mothers don't seem to like the affective infrastructures they inhabit very much, but they still stay caught up in them, hanging on to and defending the heavy and privatized happiness of family autonomy. Still, despite autonomy's stranglehold on political imaginations and mothers' sensibilities of belonging, we want to suggest that perhaps new affective infrastructures could be in the pipeline, primed for construction. It is the promise of family happiness that makes family autonomy so powerful, and, as strong as this affective infrastructure is, and as tightly as mothers are tethered to it, it is also immensely fragile and unstable thanks to precarity's punishing and privatizing tides. As Nancy and so many mothers seem to know, at least at the level of their ordinary affects, the nuclear family "is not working." Collectively, both online and off, they are pioneering ways to navigate these tides, yet the routes they are compelled to travel feel broken and in desperate need of repair. Consequently, they are anxious, uneasy, exhausted, and constantly on alert; they rely on one another for material support and emotional solace, only to find themselves still "dog-paddling around," alone within happiness's receding horizons.[28]

We want to end on the suggestion that crossing the line between embracing precarity and embracing possibility might not be so hard, especially for mothers. After all, mothers live on the edge of affective alienation, and as they dog-paddle around, overloaded and overrun, might they also be moved to embrace other possibilities for family? Instead of embracing precarity in the name of a heavy, broken-down privatized happiness, might they come to embrace the possibility of the affect alien? Might the immense material and affective support mothers find in their cruel solidarities reveal not only the power of family autonomy but also the limits of its power over our collective imagination? Might we be ready for a world built on new infrastructures, for a world built on the promises of socialized happiness?

Ahmed wants us to consider what possibilities might open up if mothers like Nancy stopped defending happiness's inherited duties and scripts: "If we do not assume that happiness is what we must defend, if we start questioning the happiness we are defending, then we can ask other questions about life, about what we want from life, or what we want life to become. Possibilities have to be recognized as possibilities to become possible."[29] Ahmed suggests that *happenstance*, for example, might be a more vital, less asphyxiating approach to happiness that holds open new possibilities.[30] As she explains, "happiness" derives etymologically in part from "hap," meaning "chance" or "fortune." Happenstance, unlike happiness, is not weighed down by the shoulds and musts of family autonomy, by promises of good lives and virtue. Rather, a happenstance orientation means accepting that both good and bad things will necessarily happen. Here "the condition of possibility for happiness includes other possibilities."[31] As Ahmed continues, "if we think of happiness as a possibility that does not exhaust what is possible, if we lighten the load of happiness, then we can open things up. When happiness is no longer presumed to be a good thing, as what we aim for, or as what we should aim for, then we can witness happiness as a possibility that acquires significance by seeing a possibility alongside others."[32] Amid neoliberal precarity, mothers are in many ways already adopting a happenstance orientation, as they readily accept that good and bad things will happen to their families.

Rather than taking happenstance as an orientation of possibility, however, mothers tend to refuse the "hap" happily and instead hone a resilient happiness that embraces precarity and its ever more privatized scripts. They live everyday life as a series of "pockets," where at any moment a space or situation might "open up" where it feels like some*thing* that matters is going to happen.[33] For mothers, the most mundane pockets are usually the most consequential. Pockets push and pull mothers to and from the humming potential of the digital mundane, which promises mediation and intervention. As we have seen, mothers' resilient happiness is honed in the ubiquitous affordances of the mamasphere, where resources for privatizing happiness are always at the ready to help mothers retool for and retune themselves to precarity.

Thus, socializing happiness requires not only feeling and moving beyond family autonomy but also developing a new sensibility of resilience, that is, of power and potentiality in the face of precarity. As Ahmed suggests, lightening the loads of happiness also requires a certain critical and experiential distance from the deeply entrenched sensibilities of capacity and belonging that move folks in and through the world. Ahmed writes that "to learn about possibility thus involves a certain estrangement from the present. Other things can happen when the familiar recedes."[34] If affect is, as Melissa Gregg and Gregory Seigworth suggest, an "in-between-ness" where potentialities "to affect and be affected" are constantly modulating and cohering, then possibilities for making new worlds require alienation from familiar scenes and the affective infrastructures that animate and sustain them.[35]

In unfolding the compositionality of mothers' everyday lives in the digital mundane—and the affective infrastructures that make this form of life livable, and thus meaningful—we have tried to open up space for feeling alienated from mothering through precarity. Through mothers' own voices and narratives, we have tried to make everyday familial scenes strange by exposing the invisible, energetic force fields that keep mothers moving through and attaching to these scenes, even as they constantly find themselves on the verge of detachment. Critically, we have decoupled mothers' immense love for their children from the stickiness of family autonomy and the cruel optimisms of resilience to suggest that that indisputable love and force they feel might be routed differently. Indeed, it could follow alternative paths that would open up new entanglements and open onto new worlds.

Ultimately, advanced neoliberalism's powerful yet broken affective infrastructures put pressing questions on the table. As we desperately search for a world beyond neoliberal precarity, how might we—whether as mothers, Marxists, lovers, dreamers, antiracists, feminists, queers, or revolutionaries of any kind—participate in building new infrastructures for socializing happiness? How can we wrestle our imaginations away from the cruel optimisms that precarity seems to demand and let go of our "sea legs," abandoning ship to swim somewhere else together? More specifically, though, what does this snapshot of "how the world can be said to be working" for

some mothers teach us about the immanent potentialities for new structures of collective caretaking?[36] In wearing out mothers' bodies and spirits,
is advanced neoliberalism also wearing down their capacities for continued
gender exploitation, as well as for family appreciation and its world of generalized competition? Might we be ready, finally, to see the home and the
family not as a private sphere—providing refuge from the public and "relief
from the political"—but as a radical site of struggle for being in common
where we might really realize—materially and affectively, economically
and emotionally—that, as Glennon puts it, "we belong to each other"?[37]

PACKETS AND POCKETS

In February 2013 Julie was in Albuquerque, New Mexico, visiting her dad and stepmother, while her husband, Joe, attended an academic conference. She spent most of her days toggling between teaching her father how to use his new smartphone and reading Tiziana Terranova's *Network Culture: Politics for the Information Age*. Emily was back home, dabbling in affect theory. Inspired by our recent explorations of Sara Ahmed's *The Promise of Happiness* and Lauren Berlant's *Cruel Optimism*, Emily picked up *Ordinary Affects* by Kathleen Stewart and found her way to Stewart's meditation on Berlant's book, a short piece called "Pockets."

At the time, we were searching for something that felt right, something that felt adequate to capture the lives of the twenty-nine mothers we had just finished spending time with, whose mundane media lives are the subject of this book. More specifically, Julie was trying to get "outside" unhelpful debates about the new powers of digital media (i.e., participatory culture vs. surveillance culture), while Emily was trying to push beyond the literature on postfeminism and mediated motherhood. We had tried these on, and they didn't fit.

Julie called Emily, excited. "PACKETS!," she said. Terranova's description of the Internet as undergirded and made possible by the constant movement of packets felt right somehow—it helped us to understand the ontological turbulence of the digital media world that we were studying. "If packet switching is the condition of possibility for digital networks," Julie mused, "maybe it's the movement of packets underneath and through everyday lives that matters." Emily replied enthusiastically, "POCKETS!" With her piercing yet pensive depiction of pockets as restless cavities of potentiality in the plane of everyday life, Stewart honed in on the feelings that bubbled through our interviews. "Maybe pockets," Emily ventured, "are what make particular movements of packets come to matter." There we had it: a theory of digital media and everyday life that finally felt adequate. And even though we have mostly dropped the language of packets and pockets from the book, our husbands still rib: "Packets and pockets. Packets and pockets. Packets and pockets. Everything's packets and pockets."

While *Mothering through Precarity* is very much about the ways mundane digital media come to matter in the course of mothers' ordinary lives, "packets and pockets" is more than a theoretical insight or ethnographic approach we developed over the course of research. It is also a metaphor for our partnership. Indeed, this book came to fruition through a series of fortuitous collisions, as our lives, ideas, and orientations to research sometimes clashed and sometimes harmonized. These spontaneous and unpredictable collisions sparked new assemblages of thinking and being, generating intellectual energy and deepening our partnership. Our process of researching and writing thus ultimately came to feel like an energetic meeting of packets and pockets, an extended encounter that made our scholarship, like life, feel full of potential.

Mothering through Precarity took form in collisions of divergent ways of knowing, thinking, and writing social worlds. Emily is an ethnographer. She is comfortable living in the weeds of everyday life—in the contradictions and complexities of "the ordinary"—and she wrestles to bring theoretical form to her thinking. Julie, in contrast, prefers more manicured intellectual landscapes. She is "a theory head" drawn to abstract systems of thought and conceptual structures, so she struggles when things get too messy. When it comes to writing, Emily starts in the middle and writes into ideas. Julie yearns for direction; she is comfortable when she knows where things are headed. Emily is an extrovert. She talks in order to think. Julie is an introvert. For her, talking is annoying, and ideas must gel quietly. Emily's life is very full; free time is sparse. She has three young boys and a husband, a substantial commute to her teaching job, and lots of family nearby. Her days are layered with many activities and swamped with responsibility. Julie's life is more open; she has Joe (and a dog and two cats) to care for on a daily basis, and her shared position with Joe lessens her teaching load. While Julie's time is filled with students and community work, it expands and contracts easily for the needs of the day.

Carol J. Singley and Susan Elizabeth Sweeney write in their essay, "In League with Each Other: The Theory and Practice of Feminist Collaboration," that "collaborators must face differences in moods, methods, schedules, and energies."[1] Indeed. Navigating such differences regularly tests one's patience and confidence, but we cushioned the impacts of our collisions by radically embracing and accepting our differences. We stayed open and ready for unexpected convergences between our lives and our thinking, wrestling for months—years!—with our ideas in the interstices of teaching and the other demands of our everyday lives. "Packets and pockets" moments came unexpectedly, but when they happened and things clicked into place, they felt at once mundane and monumental. In excited texting while Emily rocked her youngest to sleep, in the exchange of web links that seemed to encapsulate our ideas and confirm we were onto something, and in intense conversations where we hashed out our arguments by harnessing the tensions between our worlds, we developed a deeply productive and affirming marriage of minds. As Singley and Sweeney write, "collaboration allows us to elaborate our ideas, liberate ourselves, and turn our labor into pleasure. It integrates the intellectual, emotional, and social aspects of our lives. . . . How can we convey the excitement of a shared idea that one person originates but that, once developed, belongs to both? Or the moment when our interaction generates an energy that neither of us provides alone? Or the almost guilty feeling that we are accomplishing so much while having so much fun?"[2]

Together we learned to move in new ways between theoretical innovation and grounded cultural analysis of women's lives, something that could not have happened without the ongoing collisions of our own lives as women. As a feminist pursuit, our partnership has meant listening to one another, adjusting and attuning, and living in the impasses of multiple ways of knowing and being. While our partnership most obviously resists the long-standing obsession with individually produced work in the academy, it also, in its own very small ways, has encountered potentialities for new modes of being in common. Our ongoing collisions engendered a kind of melding of our family lives, a familiarity between kids and adults that continues to bolster all of our days, heavy with writing, teaching, and caring for family and community. Holding together these tensions and traversing the boundaries between scholarship, families, teaching, and community, we've experienced how the intimacy of feminist partnership and scholarly collaboration can offer some salve in the face of the heaping burdens of life and labor in advanced neoliberalism as we continue to struggle for new worlds.

INTRODUCTION. THE DIGITAL MUNDANE

1 Throughout the book, names of people and places, as well as informant biographical and narrative details, have been altered to preserve anonymity.

2 In her history of "the myths of motherhood," Shari L. Thurer writes, "The vulnerability of children makes us fervently want to be our best selves, to embody tender nurturance and sweet concern. . . . [H]ow our children turn out has become the final judgment on our lives." *Myths of Motherhood*, xiii.

3 See, for example, Douglas and Michaels, *Mommy Myth*; and Hays, *Cultural Contradictions of Motherhood*.

4 Cooper, *Cut Adrift*, 23. Cooper argues that mothering today figures as a security project. Specifically, for middle-class families in particular, this security project is about "holding on" as women deal with job losses, debt, and increasing levels of financial insecurity.

5 The project builds on research Julie conducted in graduate school with her advisor, Dr. Laurie Ouellette, on Dr. Phil's multimedia self-help empire. See Ouellette and Wilson, "Women's Work."

6 Ang, "Ethnography and Radical Contextualism," 250. In addition to Ang's work, we also have in mind that of Janice Radway. For methodological discussions, see Ang, "Ethnography and Radical Contextualism," and Radway, "Hegemony of 'Specificity.'"

7 We interviewed three mothers who blog. Two of these women are discussed in chapter 3, the chapter that focuses most heavily on digital media, in the section entitled "Commune." Otherwise, all of the mothers in this study hail from either the Hugo or Ryeland areas.

8 Bird, *Audience in Everyday Life*.

9 Couldry, *Why Voice Matters*, 13.

10 Bird, "Are We All Producers?"

11 On "nonmedia people," see Couldry, "Playing for Celebrity."

12 Our work aligns with Valerie Walkerdine's sensibility: "what is important to me," she writes, "is to be able to talk not about subcultures or resistance, or an audience

making its continually resistant readings, but about the ordinary working people, who have been coping and surviving, who are formed at the intersection of these competing claims to truth, who are subjects formed in the complexities of everyday practices." *Daddy's Girl*, 13.

13 A Google search for "mommy wars" returns over three million results; the discourse is so rampant that parodies are easy to find. In a Similac ad in 2015 ("The Mother 'Hood"), working moms, breast-feeding moms, "hippie" moms, hipster moms, and stay-at-home dads converge on a playground, preparing for a brawl, before they all come together to rescue a baby in a stroller rolling down a hill ("The Mother 'Hood Official Video," August 4, 2015, https://www.youtube.com/watch?v=Me9yrREXOj4). In a similar vein, in 2015 "mommy blogger" Deva Dalporto produced "Bad Mom," a parody of Taylor Swift's video for "Bad Blood" ("Bad Mom—Taylor Swift—Bad Blood ft. Kendrick Lamar Parody," August 4, 2015, https://www.youtube.com/watch?v=_kRk53UfahU).

14 Rose, *Powers of Freedom*, 179.

15 See, for example, Douglas and Michaels, *Mommy Myth*, and Walters and Harrison, "Not Ready to Make Nice."

16 Nick Couldry often calls for a decentered media approach. See, for example, *Listening beyond the Echoes*.

17 Gregg, "Mundane Voice," 369.

18 Gregg, "Mundane Voice," 368.

19 Gregg, "Mundane Voice," 364–65.

20 Stewart, *Ordinary Affects*, 2–3.

21 Stewart, *Ordinary Affects*, 2–3.

22 Stewart, "Interview with the Author."

23 Stewart, *Ordinary Affects*, 5.

24 Williams, *Marxism and Literature*.

25 Grossberg, "Affect's Future," 318.

26 Lauren Berlant, "Time Out."

27 Of course, we might attribute this particular reticence to television's status as a "bad object," but we suspect there is more going on here.

28 Massumi, *Parables for the Virtual*, as quoted in Puar, "'I Would Rather Be,'" 61.

29 See Hillis, Paasonen, and Petit, *Networked Affect*.

30 Dean, *Blog Theory*, 95.

31 Papacharissi, *Affective Publics*, 29.

32 See Mark Andrejevic's works, such as *iSpy: Surveillance and Power in the Interactive Era* and *Infoglut: How Too Much Information Is Changing the Way We Think and Know*.

33 Mejias, *Off the Network*, 10.

34 As has long been the case, white nuclear mothers, as the alleged primary consumers of domestic goods, are big business for advertisers. As Lynn Spigel shows in *Make Room for TV: Television and the Family Ideal in Postwar America*, the early television industry worked vigorously to shape women's reception by constituting television viewing as integral to women's work as housewives.

Advertisers went so far as to provide instruction to female viewers about how strategic television viewing would enhance their productivity as homemakers, while even making housework pleasurable. In *The Daily You: How the New Advertising Is Defining Your Identity and Your Worth* Joseph Turow documents how today marketing giants like Procter and Gamble work with data-exchange firms to track and record mothers' online activities, access and penetrate their networks, and present them with keenly customized content and advertising. Increasingly, these companies are partnering with well-linked mommy bloggers, paying them small fees in exchange for product reviews or mentions in parenting posts.

35 Mejias, *Off the Network*, 25.

36 Terranova, *Network Culture*, 67.

37 Hansen, *Feed-Forward*, 2.

38 Hansen, *Feed-Forward*, 226.

39 Hansen, *Feed-Forward*, 3.

40 Lorey, *State of Insecurity*, 10–15.

41 Lorey, *State of Insecurity*, 18–22.

42 Lorey, *State of Insecurity*, 2.

43 Lorey, *State of Insecurity*, 1.

44 Binkley, *Happiness as Enterprise*, 151–71.

45 Silva, *Coming Up Short*, 21. Our work is indebted to Silva's, especially the link she draws between neoliberalism's privatization of risk and the mood economy, that is, the privatization of happiness. She explains, "Just as neoliberalism teaches young people that they are solely responsible for their economic fortunes, the mood economy renders them responsible for their *emotional* fates."

46 Sara Ahmed in *The Promise of Happiness* suggests that the family is a "happy object," an object that points to and promises happiness—belonging, virtue, a good life. However, advanced neoliberalism precarizes this promise, so mothers organize their lives around its securitization.

47 Mothers' responses to neoliberalism and insecurity have been beautifully documented in two recent ethnographies. *Cut Adrift: Families in Insecure Times*, by Marianne Cooper, looks at how families of different socioeconomic backgrounds come to "do security" differently in insecure times. Relatedly, *Motherload: Making It All Better in Insecure Times*, by Ana Villalobos, shows how mothers respond to insecurity by investing in the mother-child relationship.

48 Duggan, *Twilight of Equality*, 15–19.

49 Glenn, "Social Constructions of Mothering," 3.

50 Cooper, *Cut Adrift*, 23.

51 Hansen, *Feed-Forward*, 6.

52 Hansen, *Feed-Forward*, 17.

53 Hansen, *Feed-Forward*, 6–7.

54 Berlant, *Cruel Optimism*.

55 Evans and Reid, *Resilient Life*, 13.

56 Berlant, *Cruel Optimism*, 4.

57 Rich, *Of Woman Born.*

58 Institute for Precarious Consciousness, "We Are All Very Anxious."

59 Institute for Precarious Consciousness, "We Are All Very Anxious."

CHAPTER 1. MOTHER LOADS

1 On intensive mothering, see Hays, *Cultural Contradictions of Motherhood.*

2 See Villalobos, *Motherload.*

3 In *Motherload* Villalobos calls for a "nonpathological understanding of intensive mothering" (6), which, she argues, figures as mothers' "security solution" for living in the "risk society" (9).

4 Williams, *Marxism and Literature,* 128–35.

5 Douglas and Michaels, *Mommy Myth,* 4.

6 Douglas and Michaels, *Mommy Myth,* 4.

7 Villalobos suggests that "intensive mothering is not as much child-centered as it is 'mother-child-centered.'" *Motherload,* 11. In risk society, she argues, mothers find a sense of security in their relationship with their children.

8 Brown, *States of Injury,* 144–45.

9 Brown, *States of Injury,* 147.

10 Brown, *States of Injury,* 147.

11 Brown, *States of Injury,* 149–50.

12 On connections between white wealth and the organization of family, see Collins, "All in the Family."

13 Black family life is often imagined to stand in stark contrast to the ideal of family autonomy; through "domestic networks," responsibility for childrearing is managed and spread across a range of households and caregivers in response to economic and social forces. See Stack, *All Our Kin.* Black mothers, especially single black mothers, have been vilified and sometimes criminalized for these arrangements, as they signal dependency and mark a "culture of poverty." See Stabile, *White Victims, Black Villains.* While research shows that mothers have been rewriting what family autonomy looks like in response to broader political-economic forces for decades, its racialized dimensions continue to shape mothers' sensibilities; see Stacey, *Brave New Families;* Beck and Beck-Gernsheim, *Individualization.*

14 See Foucault, "Governmentality" and "Ethics."

15 Dean, "Foucault, Government," 222.

16 On maternal anxiety, see, for example, Warner, *Perfect Madness.*

17 Rose, *Governing the Soul,* 129.

18 See Apple, *Perfect Motherhood.*

19 Rose, *Governing the Soul,* 132.

20 Ezzo and Bucknam, *On Becoming Babywise.*

21 Plant, *Mom,* 7.

22 See Plant, *Mom,* 86–117.

23 See Apple, *Perfect Motherhood;* and Ehrenreich and English, *For Her Own Good,* 76–108.

24 Antimaternalism also emerged within the broader biopolitical project of mental hygiene. As Theresa Richardson shows, the "mental hygiene paradigm originated with the premise that society could be perfected through the socialization of children; happy, healthy children were argued to be the society's best assurance of a rational and productive adult population." *Century of the Child*, 2. Mental hygiene was thus a regime that targeted the vitality of the population at large by seeking to regulate the individual psychologies and emotional states of children. As Viviana Zelizer argues in *Pricing the Priceless Child*, as children were increasingly seen as useless from an economic perspective, their value was imagined to reside in their emotional status and well-being. Parenting brochures insisted that for the "real inner happiness" of a healthy personality to blossom, the early years of a child's life were key. Children's Bureau, "Healthy Personality," 2. Personality "was not considered a product of a child's given nature and his own dogged effort" but rather of "elaborate nurture that must begin promptly." Hulbert, *Raising America*, 107. Children came to be seen as both vulnerable and emotionally complex, as possessing "a real mental life, full of hopes, ambitions, doubts, misgivings, joys, sorrows, and strivings that are being gratified or thwarted much the same at three years of age as they are at thirty." D. A. Thom, "Child Management," Children's Bureau: 1925, quoted in Hulbert, *Raising America*, 109. In turn, mothers, in particular, had to carefully construct and monitor their children's social environments. As Peter Stearns explains, it was thought that "flaws could emerge in the best of homes, without the provocation of bad example, and could poison the adult personality." *Anxious Parents*, 22.

25 Ehrenreich and English, *For Her Own Good*, 234.

26 Plant, *Mom*, 88.

27 Ehrenreich and English, *For Her Own Good*, 231.

28 Rose, *Governing the Soul*, 168.

29 Rose, *Governing the Soul*, 160.

30 For example, in the *Parents' Magazine's Baby Care Manual* published in 1950, one article, entitled "New Techniques in Baby Care," sought to teach young mothers about their babies' "kinesthetic sense": here mothers were counseled to enfold the new techniques and methods of experts into their own "muscles." Gray, "New Techniques in Baby Care," 21. Another article suggested, "The best way to convince a tiny baby that you love him is to answer his urgent needs as they arise. . . . It is a method based on the baby's own feelings . . . which are totally dissimilar to ours, yet which we must interpret." Seery, "Self-Demand," 16. Another encouraged mothers to be flexible and patient with their baby's development, counseling careful monitoring of the inevitable unwanted affects of anxiety and competition: "No two babies are alike. No mother should follow too slavishly any hard and fast schedule of baby growth. Your baby may smile before your neighbor's baby; he may creep a little later. It's all right, you needn't worry. He is being himself and proceeding at his own rate of speed. The important thing is not to prod or push him, but to watch and encourage him and to be relaxed yourself and pleased with him." Littledale, "Congratulations to You," 59.

31 Martin, "Thirteen Mom Truths."

32   Ehrenreich and English, *For Her Own Good*, 231.

33   Inhabiting the ethopolitical milieu heightens sensibilities of individual autonomy and thus comes to require of women new modes of affective regulation. Sociological research shows that the rise of what Beck and Beck-Gernsheim call the "post-familial family"—a family defined less by the social and moral obligations of tradition and more by the elective affinities of self-enterprising and actualizing subjects—demands constant negotiation and communication, as mothers' sensibilities of individual autonomy often run counter to the entrenched and highly naturalized gender demands of mother love and domestic governance. See Rubin, *Worlds of Pain*; Stacey, *Brave New Families*; and Silva, *Coming Up Short*, 53–80. Many of the mothers we interviewed were working constantly to reconcile individual and family autonomy, balancing their own needs as women expected to make their own lives with the ever-mounting demands of neoliberal family autonomy.

34   Rose defines ethopolitics as "attempts to shape the conduct of human beings by acting upon their sentiments, beliefs, and values—in short, by acting on ethics." *Politics of Life Itself*, 27. Unlike the antimaternalist discourses discussed previously, ethopolitical discourses offer mothers distinctly maternal "technologies of the self."

35   For example, *Mothering*'s popular parenting guide, *Natural Family Living: The "Mothering" Magazine Guide to Parenting* urges an approach "based on trust rather than on fear": "above all, trust yourself to know what is best for your child. That trust is what is at the heart of natural family living." O'Mara, *Natural Family Living*, 1, 2. *Natural Family Living* promised to help mothers "develop a personal ethic of parenting," 2. While earlier parenting guides also urged mothers to trust their intuitions, *Mothering*'s concept of a personal ethic based on trust in oneself was based on an active distrust of dominant cultural institutions. As the guide describes it, "an ethic of parenting must be based on the true nature of your child. It must not be based solely on the prevailing beliefs of the culture, because such beliefs are too arbitrary, transitory, and tenuous to sustain an ethic that will determine, to a large extent, the life history of an individual" (2). It is important to see that ethopolitical demands cut across cultural politics. While *Mothering* articulates a countercultural sensibility, MOPS is premised on more traditional and conservative approaches to family government. However, in both cases, mothers are urged to cultivate a form of "mom gut" based on a personal ethic of parenting. The MOPS Mission/Vision sees this personal ethic as ideally animated by "a personal relationship with Jesus Christ," but, more importantly, it is a sensibility of capacity inherent to the situated experiences and knowledges of mothers. Mission/Vision, http://www.mops.org /about/mission-vision. *Momsense*, for example, is one of MOPS's terms for personal ethic; it emerges from combining *mom intuition* and *common sense*. Blackmer, *MomSense*, 15. Similarly, *Momology* centers on developing what it calls "core resilience" in mothers. Radic, *Momology*, 16.

36   Rose, *Politics of Life Itself*, 27.

37   Rose, *Powers of Freedom*, 176.

38   Rose, *Governing the Soul*, 203.

39   MumsPick, "What Makes Nearly 7 in 10 Women Change How They Shop? Mother-
     hood," http://www.mumspick.com/advertising?SID=01624af51d53de1fc4ac5c289f9
     f5d34.
40   On free labor, see Terranova, "Free Labor."
41   Rose, *Powers of Freedom*, 179.
42   Rose, *Powers of Freedom*, 178.
43   Paasonen, "Midsummer's Bonfire," 30–33.
44   Rose, *Governing the Soul*, 132.
45   See Mejias, *Off the Network*.
46   See Hansen, *Feed-Forward*.
47   See Friedman and Calixte, *Mothering and Blogging*; and Lopez, "Radical Act."
48   Van Cleaf, "*Of Woman Born*," 247.
49   See Andrejevic, *Infoglut*.
50   Dean, *Blog Theory*, 13.
51   See Stewart, *Ordinary Affects*.
52   Cooper, *Cut Adrift*, 20.
53   Cooper, *Cut Adrift*, 13–14; see also Lorey, *State of Insecurity*, 10–15.
54   Cooper, *Cut Adrift*, 22–23, 92–126.
55   Cooper, *Cut Adrift*, 22, 65–91.
56   Cooper, *Cut Adrift*, 13–18.
57   Cooper, *Cut Adrift*, 149–50, 23, 127–57.
58   The privatization of risk represents a profound rewriting of earlier liberal ideas;
     as François Ewald elaborates in his work on the rise of insurance, risk was not ini-
     tially a sensibility of danger or threat but rather a rationalized mode of constituting
     and managing the social. It was a calculus designed to discipline randomness and
     thereby insure capital against damage and depreciation. In Ewald's discussion,
     risks were calculable and collective, as insurance was about quantifying prob-
     abilities and distributing them across a population. See Ewald, "Insurance and
     Risk." However, neoliberalism and its government through insecurity dramati-
     cally rewrite the rationality of risk management. Mitchell Dean elaborates the
     privatization of risk as "the multiple 'responsibilization' of individuals, families,
     households, and communities for their own risks—of physical and mental ill-
     health, of unemployment, of poverty in old age, of poor educational performance,
     of becoming victims of crime." *Governmentality*, 166.
59   Martin, *Financialization of Daily Life*, 106.
60   Martin, *Financialization of Daily Life*, 110.
61   On micro-vigilantes, see Evans and Reid, *Resilient Life*, 16.
62   According to Binkley, happiness is a "hinge," "a point of transfer or a relay (albeit
     one that is ambivalent, polyvalent, and open to reversals) between a strategy for
     the government of large groups, populations, institutions, societies, and econo-
     mies, and an art of governing oneself, one's own subjectivity and emotional life
     through one's freely chosen practices." *Happiness as Enterprise*, 5.
63   Berlant, *Cruel Optimism*, 4.

CHAPTER 2. MAMAPRENEURIALISM

1   See, for example, Mompreneurs (http://themompreneur.com/). For analysis of these discourses, see Anderson and Moore, "'Doing It All.'"
2   Hays, *Cultural Contradictions of Motherhood*, 153.
3   Brown, *Undoing the Demos*, 30.
4   Dardot and Laval, *New Way*, 3.
5   Dardot and Laval, *New Way*, 11–13.
6   Brown, *Undoing the Demos*, 31.
7   Dardot and Laval, *New Way*, 106.
8   Burchell, "Liberal Government," 28–29.
9   Rose, *Powers of Freedom*, 164.
10 Foucault, *Birth of Biopolitics*, 229.
11 Foucault, *Birth of Biopolitics*, 241.
12 Brown, *Undoing the Demos*, 104–7.
13 Foucault, *Birth of Biopolitics*, 230.
14 Brown, *Undoing the Demos*, 105–7.
15 Brown, *Undoing the Demos*.
16 Brown, *Undoing the Demos*, 106–7.
17 Brown, *Undoing the Demos*, 104–5.
18 Zelizer, *Purchase of Intimacy*.
19 Illouz, *Saving the Modern Soul*, 93.
20 Illouz, *Saving the Modern Soul*, 32–34. In *Cold Intimacies* Illouz similarly argues that rationalizing domestic life "includes five components: the calculated use of means; the use of more effective means; choosing on a rational basis (that is on the basis of knowledge and education); making general value principles guide one's life; and, finally, unifying the previous four components in a rational and methodological lifestyle" (31–32).
21 As Jacob Hacker's work shows, families bear the brunt of privatized risk, as ongoing economic insecurity regularly disrupts and destabilizes the scenes of family; in the face of sudden job losses and other catastrophes, imagined or real, mothers are expected to absorb the shocks by continually adjusting their aspirations, rechanneling their desires, and renegotiating their relationships to work, including both paid labor and childcare. See Hacker, *Great Risk Shift*.
22 Evans and Reid, *Resilient Life*, 42.
23 Stephanie Morgan, "About," *Modern Parents Messy Kids*, n.d. http://www.modernparentsmessykids.com/about, accessed January 30, 2015.
24 Happy Family Habits Archive, *Modern Parents Messy Kids*, http://www.modernparentsmessykids.com/category/happy-family-habits.
25 Eldridge, "New Series: Happy Family Habits."
26 Eldridge, "Happy Family Habit #6."
27 Eldridge, "Happy Family Habit #4."
28 Power of Moms, "About Us," https://powerofmoms.com/about-us, accessed July 15, 2016.

29 Power of Moms, "About Us."

30 McClelland and Padilla, *Digital Mom Handbook*, 1.

31 Latvala, "New Stay-at-Home Mom."

32 McClelland and Padilla, *Digital Mom Handbook*, 28.

33 Sherman and Smith, *Mom, Incorporated*, 14–15.

34 Foucault, *Birth of Biopolitics*, 230.

35 Fabulessly Frugal, "All About the Fabulessly Frugal Team . . ."

36 As Diane Negra and Yvonne Tasker note in their introduction to *Gendering the Recession*, these sorts of gendered labors have garnered much media attention in recessionary culture, as evidenced by popular reality shows like TLC's *Extreme Couponing*, which forwards "a mixed discourse of praise and pathologization around figures inscribed on the one hand as bravura postfeminist housekeepers but on the other as intense over-consumers who speak of 'stockpiling'" (7).

37 Ouellette and Wilson, "Women's Work," 555.

38 Hochschild and Machung, *Second Shift*; and Hochschild, *Time Bind*.

39 Martin, *Financialization of Daily Life*, 55. For a more nuanced gender analysis, see Schowalter, "Financialization of the Family."

40 See McRobbie, *Aftermath of Feminism*.

41 On "can-do" capacity, see Harris, *Future Girl*.

42 The phrase "unavowed glue" comes from Brown, *Undoing the Demos*, 104–5.

43 To maintain anonymity, we have altered the name of the company Jenny works for.

44 Binkley, *Happiness as Enterprise*, 31.

45 Binkley, *Happiness as Enterprise*, 31.

CHAPTER 3. DIGITAL ENTANGLEMENTS

1 Ahmed, *Promise of Happiness*.

2 See Villalobos, *Motherload*. Villalobos's extensive ethnography of contemporary motherhood shows how mothers' intensive relationships with their children operate as a powerful "security solution."

3 Puar, "'I Would Rather Be,'" 61.

4 The phrase "composed and suffered" is from Stewart, *Ordinary Affects*, 5.

5 Stewart, "Interview with the Author."

6 In *Cut Adrift* Marianne Cooper argues that families cope with the rising but unequally distributed insecurities of neoliberalism by embarking on "security projects," which include "all the economic and emotion work done by a family to create, maintain, and further their particular notion of security" (20). As a result of the "inequality of security" (14), families in different socioeconomic positions enact security projects in vastly uneven ways. Upper-income families, in particular, "upscale," working to secure both the family's financial future and their children's futures. These projects are gendered: securing the children's future tends to fall on mothers' shoulders. Low-income families, on the other hand, "downscale," reducing their criteria for feeling secure and cultivating an optimistic outlook.

7   A division of SheKnows Media, which boasts 21,000 "content creators," BlogHer pays its bloggers a share of the revenue generated through advertisements on their blogs and provides advertisers access to "influencers" and their followers. Promising to empower women writers, BlogHer claims, "We believe [women bloggers] should be paid for quality work. . . . Since 2009, BlogHer Inc. has paid out $36 million to 5,700 bloggers and social media influencers who embrace our editorial guidelines and produce community content." To marketers, BlogHer boasts of "creating the most authentic conversations and the safest possible environment for marketers" (BlogHer, "About BlogHer," www.blogher.com/about-this-network). Since 2011 BlogHer has hosted multiday conventions designed to connect bloggers with brands. Keynote speakers at these conferences have included Sheryl Sandberg, Kerry Washington, Ree Drummond (the Pioneer Woman), Gwyneth Paltrow, and Barack Obama. Members of the BlogHer network produce content ranging from eco-friendly parenting tips to product reviews, crafting and organizing ideas, and meditations on difficult parenting moments.

8   A popular social media platform that many of the mothers we interviewed used, Pinterest bills itself as "a tool for collecting and organizing things you love" and brags that it has "helped millions of people . . . plan life's important projects." Launched in March 2010, Pinterest quickly amassed a dedicated user base, and in 2013 the scrapbooking site had about fifty million users globally and was valued at $2.5 billion. Colao, "Why Is Pinterest?" Pinterest is a virtual inspiration board where a social network of "pinners"—the vast majority of whom are upper- and middle-class women—develop highly organized boards populated by "pins," images pulled from around the web and described in brief captions written by the pinners. See Guimarães, "Pinterest's Demographics."

9   Berlant, *Cruel Optimism*, 4.

10 Here Dana is "downscaling," Cooper's term for the kind of "security project" that low-income families enact amid neoliberal insecurities. Downscaling is a form of emotional labor that includes both adopting an optimistic outlook and reducing one's requirements for feeling secure.

11 See Terranova, "Free Labor."

12 Sasha and Erin were two of the mommy bloggers we interviewed early on in our research. Sasha lives outside of Washington, D.C., while Erin was a part of Emily's community when she lived in Georgia. To preserve their anonymity, we have adopted pseudonyms for both Sasha's and Erin's blogs.

13 BlogHer 2006 was the second BlogHer conference and the site of the unveiling of BlogHer's advertiser's network. While the ad network did indeed help some women to be compensated for their writing, it also sparked debate about the potential for bloggers to "sell out" to advertisers' influence. BlogHer 2005 and 2006 were also the site of debates about "mommy bloggers." While some sought to advance women bloggers' reputations by suggesting that many women should blog about more important material than the seemingly soft or too-personal "diary entries" of mommy blogging, others espoused the political importance of mothers sharing

their personal stories. One attendee in 2005 declared mommy blogging to be a "radical act." See Lopez, "Radical Act." See chapter 4 for more discussion of the politics of mothering communities and modes of collectivity that mommy blogs facilitate.

14 Sasha proudly reported sitting on panels with sports journalists and doing "blogger outreach" for a major pop music tour. She has blogged for Disney's Babble, and she has a contract with Procter & Gamble. Sasha earns an average of $50 per post, but she has, on occasion, earned up to $1,500 for a single post. Blogging also connects Sasha to other women, both at conferences and at social gatherings sponsored by companies in return for enthusiastic blog posts about the parties. When we interviewed Sasha via Skype from her home outside of Washington, D.C., in 2012, Nintendo had recently invited her to host a party for her blogger friends to promote the Wii. The company rented a swanky space, bought wine and cheese, and had the women bloggers play video games until late in the evening. Companies host parties like this for mommy bloggers all the time, Sasha said, and she's met many friends this way. "The first million people I met were all moms, because you'd have play dates, you'd have mom things. . . . A lot of companies do events for moms and have us all come out and watch *Kung Fu Panda*." Sasha's best friend is not a mom, but she is a blogger whom Sasha hit it off with at a BlogHer conference in Washington, D.C., where Sasha was speaking on a panel about audience measurement and marketing.

15 Microcelebrity is a celebrity practice where individuals use new media publishing tools to amplify their online personae by engaging in strategic self-branding and presentation. Microcelebrity involves complicated forms of mediated emotional and affective labor; see Senft, *Camgirls*. As Alice Marwick shows in *Status Update*, microcelebrity authenticity hinges on consistency.

16 In the coming years, Sasha told us, she hopes to find ways to better amplify herself and to quantify the long tail of her influence in order to gain more leverage with publishers, advertisers, and sponsors. Right now, she has "a pretty good relationship with my audience" and regularly responds to comments, particularly if a reader "say[s] something well thought out or something poignant or something that I think is funny. . . . If I have time I'll come see your blog if you have a link to it and I try to interact with my audience." But, she explained, "The people that are on top of it have a media agent with all their numbers, and you do surveys figuring out who your readers are and where they came from and where they live and how much money they make. . . . I need to do that. I have not done that yet."

17 Dean, *Blog Theory*.

18 *Green Mama* is devoted to educating other mothers about green and natural parenting, in particular, how to achieve green lifestyle goals on a budget. A prominent anti–consumer culture ethos animates the posts, and topics include how to respond to acquaintances' disgust with cloth diapers, the environmental hazards of plastic grocery bags, directions for homemade cleaning products, schooling choices, and the frustrations of daily life with small children. In the post "Where

Is Your Beef From?," for example, Erin wrote, "Once I tried grass fed I never went back. I know what many of you are thinking: 'Do you know how EXPENSIVE grass-fed beef is?' Yes, I do. I have been to Whole Foods, it is crazy expensive. Which is why I buy LOCAL." Erin's blog is earnest and informational, pitched as an honest and well-researched conversation with friends about how to make moms' lives easier and how to make them feel more valued.

19 As we discuss in chapters 1 and 4, attendant to the rise of neoliberalism has been the ascension of ethopolitical discourses that govern through individualized values and ethical codes. While ethopolitical governing empowers mothers and grants them autonomy, it also sets the stage for the mommy wars Erin is combating, for, as Nikolas Rose argues in *Powers of Freedom: Reframing Political Thought*, it engenders "wars of subjectivity" around lifestyles and values.

20 According to Ulrich Beck and Elizabeth Beck-Gernsheim, in advanced postindustrial societies, individualized acts of life planning and community building perform the structural social function that was once the purview of modern institutions. This individualized social structure, running on the creativity and life projects of individuals, rests, however, on an institutionalized asymmetry between individualized subjects and the increasingly globalized problems they must navigate. As Beck and Beck-Gernsheim put it, "the Western type of individualized society tells us to seek biographical solutions to systemic contradictions." *Individualization*, xxii. Thus, addressing persistent structural social inequalities becomes quite tricky, if not impossible, especially in the context of family life and gendered divisions of labor. They write, "As women move at least partly outside the family as a result of changes in education, occupation, family cycle, legal system, etc., they can no longer rely on men as providers. Instead, in ways that are naturally often contradictory, a perspective of autonomy and self-sufficiency is held out to them. The 'subjective correlate' of such changes is that women today increasingly develop, and must develop, expectations, wishes and life projects which relate not only to the family but also to their own persons" (90).

21 See Dean, *Blog Theory*.

22 See Terranova, "Free Labor."

23 Williamson, "Family, Education, Photography," 236.

24 Goodsell and Seiter, "Scrapbooking," 319.

25 Sontag, *On Photography*, 8.

26 Slater, "Domestic Photography," 138–39.

27 Slater, "Domestic Photography," 140.

28 Wilson and Yochim, "Pinning Happiness."

29 Hoevel, "Honest Toddler Revealed."

30 Dean, *Blog Theory*, 95.

31 Douglas and Michaels, *Mommy Myth*.

32 Martin, "About."

33 Martin, "Why Vacuuming."

34 Stewart, "Pockets," 365.

35 Berlant, *Cruel Optimism*, 5.

36 Evans and Reid, *Resilient Life*, 16.
37 Martin, "Why Vacuuming."
38 Berlant, *Cruel Optimism*, 4.
39 Berlant, *Cruel Optimism*, 199.
40 Berlant, *Cruel Optimism*, 199.
41 Berlant, Cruel Optimism, 199.
42 Niequist, "You're Never."

CHAPTER 4. INDIVIDUALIZED SOLIDARITIES

1 On the mommy myth, see Douglas and Michaels, *Mommy Myth*.
2 Melton, "About."
3 La Leche League, "Our Mission."
4 Eavenson, "Letter from the Editor," 4.
5 The official history of MOPS describes an initial meeting of just eight mothers in Colorado, where the mothers pooled resources for childcare and watched a craft demonstration and "a short devotional." The program reportedly spread via word of mouth and printed materials, and in 1981 the organization was established with a board of directors as MOPS Outreach and, later, as MOPS, Inc. In 1982 MOPS held its first leadership conference, with 150 women in attendance. In 1988 the program became MOPS International, Inc., and eventually hired a paid staff member. Teen MOPS groups were organized in 1995. The organization now publishes books and a magazine and hosts yearly conferences. Mothers of Preschoolers, "How Did MOPS Get Started?"
6 Rose, *Powers of Freedom*, 176.
7 Rose, *Powers of Freedom*, 172.
8 As Marianne Cooper's research shows, organized religion plays a significant role in neoliberal regimes and figures prominently in the lives of those who are experiencing the most devastating consequences of these regimes. Indeed, with the ongoing privatization of the state, religious organizations have emerged as key social welfare providers thanks to laws such as the Personal Responsibility and Work Opportunity Act, which allowed religious groups to receive public funds. See Cooper, *Cut Adrift*, 158–88.
9 "How to Survive Parenthood," 13.
10 Ahmed, *Promise of Happiness*, 45–49.
11 Eavenson, "Keeping a Perspective," 4.
12 Mothers of Preschoolers, "About MOPS."
13 Melton, "The Monkees of Momastery."
14 See Mezey and Pillard, "Against the New Maternalism."
15 Mothers of Preschoolers, "What Is MOPS?"
16 Melton, "The Monkees of Momastery."
17 We are referring here to the work of Nancy Fraser and Lisa Duggan, both of whom have theorized the rise of neoliberal identity politics whereby political-economic modes of oppression are obfuscated and extended through a politics of cultural

recognition. See, for example, Fraser, "From Redistribution to Recognition?"; and Duggan, *Twilight of Equality*. For a thoughtful consideration of feminism's own vexed relationship to motherhood during this time, see Umanksy, *Motherhood Reconceived*.

18 Van Cleaf, "*Of Woman Born*," 251.

19 The phrase "relief from the political" is from Van Cleaf, "*Of Woman Born*," 259.

20 Melton, "I Have No Idea."

21 Together Rising, "About."

22 Together Rising, "About."

23 Together Rising, "Holiday Hands."

24 Together Rising, "Love Flash Mobs."

25 Melton, "Meet Glennon."

26 Berlant, *Female Complaint*, viii.

27 The quotations are from Berlant, *Female Complaint*, viii.

28 Melton, "One Letter to Read."

29 Melton, "One Letter to Read."

30 On collective intelligence, see Jenkins, *Convergence Culture*.

31 Melton, "Don't Carpe Diem."

32 Melton, "Don't Carpe Diem."

33 Melton, "Don't Carpe Diem."

34 The quoted comments are from the original post on Momastery, at http://momastery.com/blog/2012/01/04/2011-lesson-2-dont-carpe-diem.

35 The phrase "close gaps" is from Ahmed, *Promise of Happiness*.

36 Alvarez, "Brave Collective."

37 Alvarez, "Brave Collective Conversation Guide."

38 Evans and Reid, *Resilient Life*, 41–42.

39 Melton, "Cool Ashes."

40 Melton, "5 Ways to Secure."

41 Melton, "5 Ways to Secure."

42 Melton, "5 Ways to Secure."

43 Melton, "5 Ways to Secure."

44 This and the following comment are found at http://momastery.com/blog/2014/01/06/5-ways-secure-happyish-ever.

45 The phrase "insecure intimacies" is from Silva, *Coming Up Short*, 53.

46 The phrase "affect alien" is from Ahmed, *Promise of Happiness*.

47 Evans and Reid, *Resilient Life*.

CONCLUSION. SOCIALIZING HAPPINESS

1 "Prismatic" comes from Stewart, "Interview with the Author."

2 Rich, *Of Woman Born*.

3 The phrase "pressure points" is from Stewart, "Interview with the Author."

4 Duggan, *Twilight of Equality*.

5 Ahmed, *Promise of Happiness*.

6   Ahmed, *Promise of Happiness*, 42.

7   Ahmed, *Promise of Happiness*, 49.

8   Ahmed, *Promise of Happiness*, 217.

9   Ahmed, *Promise of Happiness*, 217.

10 The phrase "sea legs" is from Berlant, *Cruel Optimism*, 4.

11 Coontz, *Way We Never Were*.

12 Rose, *Powers of Freedom*.

13 Erickson, *Class War*, 186.

14 Erickson, *Class War*, 189.

15 See Binkley, *Happiness as Enterprise*, 174.

16 For critical research on family autonomy, see, for example, Stack, *All Our Kin*; and
    Collins, "All in the Family."

17 Thurer, *Myths of Motherhood*, xxv.

18 Thurer, *Myths of Motherhood*, 300.

19 Hays, *Cultural Contradictions of Motherhood*.

20 See, for example, Douglas and Michaels, *Mommy Myth*; Glenn, Chang, and Forcey,
    Mothering; and Podnieks, *Mediating Moms*.

21 Mezey and Pillard, "Against the New Maternalism."

22 Together Rising, "Love Flash Mobs."

23 Duggan, *Twilight of Equality*.

24 On women's work as the new social safety net, see Duggan, *Twilight of Equality*.

25 See, for example, Alexander, *New Jim Crow*.

26 On the intersections of family, nation, and white supremacy, see Collins, "All in the
    Family"; on the quotidian existence of racism, see Holland, *Erotic Life of Racism*.

27 Erickson, *Class War*, 200.

28 The phrase "dog-paddling around" is from Berlant, *Cruel Optimism*, 199.

29 Ahmed, *Promise of Happiness*, 218.

30 On happiness as asphyxiating, see Binkley, *Happiness as Enterprise*.

31 Ahmed, *Promise of Happiness*, 219.

32 Ahmed, *Promise of Happiness*, 219.

33 Stewart, "Pockets," 365.

34 Ahmed, *Promise of Happiness*, 218.

35 Seigworth and Gregg, "Inventory of Shimmers," 2.

36 Gregg, "Mundane Voice," 368.

37 For the phrase "relief from the political," see Van Cleaf, "*Of Woman Born*," 259.

AFTERWORD. PACKETS AND POCKETS

1   Singley and Sweeney, "In League with Each Other," 73.

2   Singley and Sweeney, "In League with Each Other," 70.

Ahmed, Sara. *The Promise of Happiness*. Durham, NC: Duke University Press, 2010.

Alexander, Michelle. *The New Jim Crow: Mass Incarceration in the Age of Colorblindness*. New York: The New Press, 2012.

Alvarez, Jackie. "The Brave Collective." *Hello Dearest: This Is Motherhood*, January 2, 2015. http://www.hellodearest.org/blog/brave-collective.

Anderson, Gillian, and Joseph G. Moore. "'Doing It All . . . and Making It Look Easy!' Yummy Mummies, Mompreneurs and the North American Neoliberal Crises of the Home." In *Mothering in the Age of Neoliberalism*, edited by Melinda Vandenbeld Giles, 95–116. Bradford, Ontario: Demeter, 2014.

Andrejevic, Mark. *Infoglut: How Too Much Information Is Changing the Way We Think and Know*. New York: Routledge, 2013.

Andrejevic, Mark. *iSpy: Surveillance and Power in the Interactive Era*. Lawrence: University Press of Kansas, 2007.

Ang, Ien. "Ethnography and Radical Contextualism in Audience Studies." In *The Audience and Its Landscape*, edited by James Hay, Lawrence Grossberg, and Ellen Wartella, 247–62. Boulder, CO: Westview, 1996.

Apple, Rima. *Perfect Motherhood: Science and Childrearing in America*. New Brunswick, NJ: Rutgers University Press, 2006.

Beck, Ulrich, and Elizabeth Beck-Gernsheim. *Individualization: Institutionalized Individualism and Its Social and Political Consequences*. London: Sage, 2002.

Berlant, Lauren. *Cruel Optimism*. Durham, NC: Duke University Press, 2011.

Berlant, Lauren. *The Female Complaint: The Unfinished Business of Sentimentality in American Culture*. Durham, NC: Duke University Press, 2008.

Berlant, Lauren. "Time Out." *Supervalent Thought*, December 17, 2015. http://supervalent thought.com/2015/12/17/time-out/.

Binkley, Sam. *Happiness as Enterprise: An Essay on Neoliberal Life*. Albany: State University of New York Press, 2014.

Bird, Elizabeth. "Are We All Producers Now? Convergence and Media Audience Practices." *Cultural Studies* 25, nos. 4–5 (2011): 502–16.

Bird, Elizabeth. *The Audience in Everyday Life: Living in a Media World*. New York: Routledge, 2003.

Blackmer, Jean. *MomSense: A Common-Sense Guide to Confident Mothering.* Grand Rapids, MI: Revell, 2011.

BlogHer. "About BlogHer." *BlogHer.* http://www.blogher.com/about-this-network. Accessed July 15, 2016.

Brown, Wendy. *States of Injury: Power and Freedom in Late Modernity.* Princeton, NJ: Princeton University Press, 1995.

Brown, Wendy. *Undoing the Demos: Neoliberalism's Stealth Revolution.* New York: Zone Books, 2015.

Burchell, Graham. "Liberal Government and Techniques of the Self." In *Foucault and Political Reason: Liberalism, Neo-liberalism, and Rationalities of Government*, edited by Andrew Barry, Thomas Osborne, and Nikolas Rose, 19–36. Chicago: University of Chicago Press, 1996.

Children's Bureau. "A Healthy Personality for Your Child." 1952. Available via the Maternal and Child Health Library at Georgetown University.

Colao, J. J. "Why Is Pinterest a $2.5 Billion Company? An Early Investor Explains." *Forbes*, May 8, 2013. http://www.forbes.com/sites/jjcolao/2013/05/08/why-is-pinterest-a-2-5-billion-company-an-early-investor-explains/#16f32d9c168f.

Collins, Patricia Hill. "It's All in the Family: Intersections of Gender, Race, and Nation." *Hypatia* 13, no. 3 (1998): 62–82.

Coontz, Stephanie. *The Way We Never Were: American Families and the Nostalgia Trap.* New York: Basic Books, 1992.

Cooper, Marianne. *Cut Adrift: Families in Insecure Times.* Oakland: University of California Press, 2014.

Couldry, Nick. *Listening beyond the Echoes: Media, Ethics, and Agency in an Uncertain World.* Boulder, CO: Paradigm, 2006.

Couldry, Nick, "Playing for Celebrity: Big Brother as Ritual Event." *Television and New Media* 3 (2002): 283–93.

Couldry, Nick. *Why Voice Matters: Culture and Politics after Neoliberalism.* London: Sage, 2010.

Dardot, Pierre, and Christian Laval. *The New Way of the World: On Neoliberal Society.* London: Verso, 2009.

Dean, Jodi. *Blog Theory: Feedback and Capture in the Circuits of Drive.* Malden, MA: Polity, 2010.

Dean, Mitchell. "Foucault, Government, and the Enfolding of Authority." In *Foucault and Political Reason: Liberalism, Neo-liberalism, and Rationalities of Government*, edited by Andrew Barry, Thomas Osborne, and Nikolas Rose, 209–30. Chicago: University of Chicago Press, 1996.

Dean, Mitchell. *Governmentality: Power and Rule in Modern Society.* London: Sage, 1999.

Douglas, Susan, and Meredith Michaels. *The Mommy Myth: The Idealization of Motherhood and How It Has Undermined Women.* New York: Free Press, 2004.

Duggan, Lisa. *Twilight of Equality: Neoliberalism, Cultural Politics, and the Attack on Democracy.* Boston: Beacon, 2003.

E24Creative. "Brave Collective Conversation Guide." *Hello Dearest: This Is Motherhood*, July 15, 2015. http://www.hellodearest.org/brave-collective-host-guide.

Eavenson, Addie. "Keeping a Perspective." *Mothering* 11 (1979): 16.

Eavenson, Addie. "Letter from the Editor." *Mothering* 11 (1979): 4.

Ehrenreich, Barbara, and Deirdre English. *For Her Own Good: Two Centuries of the Experts' Advice to Women.* New York: Second Anchor Books, 2005.

Eldridge, Kristin. "Happy Family Habit #4: Staying Young (and Silly!) with Your Kids." *Modern Parents Messy Kids,* May 30, 2013. http://www.modernparentsmessykids.com /2013/05/happy-family-habit-4-staying-young-and-silly-with-your-kids.html.

Eldridge, Kristin. "Happy Family Habit #6: Taking the Time to Teach Your Kids Something New." *Modern Parents Messy Kids,* August 1, 2013. http://www.modern parentsmessykids.com/2013/08/taking-the-time-to-teach-your-kids-something -new.html.

Eldridge, Kristin. "New Series: Happy Family Habits." *Modern Parents Messy Kids,* March 28, 2013. http://www.modernparentsmessykids.com/2013/03/new-series -happy-family-habits.html.

Erickson, Megan. *Class War: The Privatization of Childhood.* London: Verso, 2015.

Evans, Brad, and Julian Reid. *Resilient Life: The Art of Living Dangerously.* Cambridge, UK: Polity, 2014.

Ewald, François. "Insurance and Risk." In *The Foucault Effect: Studies in Governmentality,* edited by Graham Burchell, Colin Gordon, and Peter Miller, 197–210. Chicago: University of Chicago Press, 1991.

Ezzo, Gary, and Michael Bucknam. *On Becoming Babywise: Giving Your Infant the Gift of Nighttime Sleep.* Sisters, OR: Parent-Wise Solutions, 2012.

Fabulously Frugal. "All About the Fabulously Frugal Team . . ." *Fabulously Frugal.* http:// www.fabulouslyfrugal.com/about. Accessed July 21, 2016.

Foucault, Michel. *The Birth of Biopolitics: Lectures at the Collège de France, 1978–1979.* New York: Palgrave Macmillan, 2008.

Foucault, Michel. "The Ethics of the Concern for the Self as a Practice of Freedom." In *The Essential Foucault,* edited by Paul Rabinow and Nikolas Rose, 25–42. New York: New Press, 1994.

Foucault, Michel. "Governmentality." In *The Essential Foucault,* edited by Paul Rabinow and Nikolas Rose, 229–45. New York: New Press, 1994.

Fraser, Nancy. "From Redistribution to Recognition? Dilemmas of Justice in a Post-socialist Age." *New Left Review,* 1st ser., no. 212 (1995): 68–93.

Friedman, May, and Shana Calixte, eds. *Mothering and Blogging: The Radical Act of the Mommy Blog.* Toronto: Demeter, 2009.

Given, Sara. *Parenting Is Easy: You're Probably Just Doing It Wrong.* New York: Workman, 2015.

Glenn, Evelyn Nakano, Grace Chang, and Linda Rennie Forcey, eds. *Mothering: Ideology, Experience, and Agency.* New York: Routledge, 1994.

Goodsell, Todd, and Liann Seiter. "Scrapbooking: Family Capital and the Construction of Family Discourse." *Journal of Contemporary Ethnography* 40:3 (2011): 318–41.

Gray, Agnes. "New Techniques in Baby Care." *Parents' Magazine Baby Care Manual.* New York: Baby Care Manual, 1950.

Gregg, Melissa. "A Mundane Voice." *Cultural Studies* 18, nos. 2–3 (2004): 363–83.

Grossberg, Lawrence. "Affect's Future: Rediscovering the Virtual in the Actual." In *The Affect Theory Reader*, edited by Melissa Gregg and Gregory J. Seigworth, 309–38. Durham, NC: Duke University Press, 2010.

Guimarães, Thiago. "Pinterest's Demographics Mean It Could Become the Next Social Advertising Platform." *Business Insider*, December 8, 2014. http://www.business insider.com/pinterest-as-a-brand-platform-2014-11.

Hacker, Jacob. *The Great Risk Shift: The Assault on American Jobs, Families, Health Care, and Retirement—and How You Can Fight Back*. Oxford: Oxford University Press, 2006.

Hansen, Mark B. N. *Feed-Forward: On the Future of Twenty-First-Century Media*. Chicago: University of Chicago Press, 2015.

Harris, Anita. *Future Girl: Young Women in the Twenty-First Century*. New York: Routledge, 2003.

Hays, Sharon. *The Cultural Contradictions of Motherhood*. New Haven, CT: Yale University Press, 1996.

Hillis, Ken, Susanna Paasonen, and Michael Petit. *Networked Affect*. Cambridge, MA: MIT Press, 2015.

Hochschild, Arlie Russell. *The Time Bind: When Work Becomes Home and Home Becomes Work*. New York: Holt, 1997.

Hochschild, Arlie Russell, and Anne Machung. *The Second Shift*. New York: Penguin Books, 2003.

Hoevel, Ann. "The Honest Toddler Revealed." CNN, March 5, 2013. http://www.cnn .com/2013/03/05/living/honest-toddler-revealed/.

Holland, Sharon Patricia. *The Erotic Life of Racism*. Durham, NC: Duke University Press, 2012.

"How to Survive Parenthood." *Mothering* 11 (1979): 13.

Hulbert, Ann. *Raising America: Experts, Parents, and a Century of Advice about Children*. New York: Alfred A. Knopf, 2003.

Illouz, Eva. *Cold Intimacies: The Making of Emotional Capitalism*. Malden, MA: Polity, 2007.

Illouz, Eva. *Saving the Modern Soul: Therapy, Emotions, and the Culture of Self-Help*. Berkeley: University of California Press, 2008.

Institute for Precarious Consciousness. "We Are All Very Anxious: Six Theses on Anxiety and Why It Is Effectively Preventing Militancy, and One Possible Strategy for Overcoming It." Reposted on *Plan C*, April 4, 2014. http://www.weareplanc.org/blog /we-are-all-very-anxious/.

Jenkins, Henry. *Convergence Culture: Where Old and New Media Collide*. New York: New York University Press, 2006.

La Leche League. "Our Mission," October 14, 2007. http://www.llli.org/mission.html.

Laditan, Bunmi. *The Honest Toddler: A Child's Guide to Parenting*. New York: Scribner, 2013.

Laditan, Bunmi. *Toddlers Are A**holes: It's Not Your Fault*. New York: Workman, 2015.

Latvala, Charlotte. "The New Stay-at-Home Mom." *Parenting*. http://www.parenting .com/article/the-new-stay-at-home-mom. Accessed July 21, 2016.

Leary, Megan. "A Letter to My Nursing Toddler." *Mothering*, February 13, 2014. http://www.mothering.com/articles/a-letter-to-my-nursing-toddler.

Littledale, Clara. "Congratulations to You." In *Parents' Magazine Baby Care Manual*, vol. 42. New York: Baby Care Manual, 1950.

Lopez, Lori Kido. "The Radical Act of 'Mommy Blogging': Redefining Motherhood through the Blogosphere." *New Media and Society* 11, no. 5 (2009): 729–47.

Lorey, Isabell. *State of Insecurity: Government of the Precarious*. London: Verso, 2015.

Martin, Rachel Marie. "About." *Finding Joy*. http://www.findingjoy.net/about. Accessed June 15, 2012.

Martin, Rachel Marie. "Thirteen Mom Truths." *Finding Joy*. http://findingjoy.net/13-mom-truths/#more-2554. Accessed July 21, 2016.

Martin, Rachel Marie. "Why Vacuuming Should Always Be Beautiful." *Finding Joy*. http://findingjoy.net/why-vacuuming-should-always-be-beautiful/. Accessed July 21, 2016.

Martin, Randy. *Financialization of Daily Life*. Philadelphia: Temple University Press, 2002.

Marwick, Alice. *Status Update: Celebrity, Publicity, and Branding in the Social Media Age*. New Haven, CT: Yale University Press, 2013.

McClelland, Audrey, and Colleen Padilla. *The Digital Mom Handbook: How to Blog, Vlog, Tweet, and Facebook Your Way to a Dream Career at Home*. New York: Harper, 2011.

McRobbie, Angela. *The Aftermath of Feminism: Gender, Culture, and Social Change*. London: Sage, 2009.

Mejias, Ulises Ali. *Off the Network*. Minneapolis: University of Minnesota Press, 2013.

Melton, Glennon Doyle. "About." Momastery. https://plus.google.com/+MomasteryG/about. Accessed July 21, 2016.

Melton, Glennon Doyle. *Carry On, Warrior: The Power of Embracing Your Messy, Beautiful Life*. New York: Scribner, 2013.

Melton, Glennon Doyle. "Cool Ashes Can't Burn Us." Momastery, January 30, 2015. http://www.momastery.com.

Melton, Glennon Doyle. "5 Ways to Secure Your Happyish Ever After." Momastery, January 6, 2014. http://momastery.com/blog/2014/01/06/5-ways-secure-happyish-ever/.

Melton, Glennon Doyle. ""I Have No Idea What to Title This. I'm Not Even Sure You Should READ It. Nets. We'll Call It NETS." Momastery, November 7, 2013. http://momastery.com/blog/2013/11/07/idea-title-im-even-sure-read-nets-well-call-nets/.

Melton, Glennon Doyle. "Meet Glennon." Momastery. http://momastery.com/blog/about-glennon/. Accessed July 21, 2016.

Melton, Glennon Doyle. "The Monkees of Momastery." Momastery. http://momastery.com/blog/who-are-the-monkees-of-the-momastery/.

Melton, Glennon Doyle. "The One Letter to Read before Sending Your Child to School." Momastery, August 21, 2014. http://momastery.com/blog/2014/08/21/the-one-letter-to-read/.

Melton, Glennon Doyle. "2011 Lesson #2: Don't Carpe Diem." Momastery, January 4, 2012. http://momastery.com/blog/2012/01/04/2011-lesson-2-dont-carpe-diem/.

Melton, Glennon Doyle. "Why I'm Prejudiced and So Are You." Momastery, October 28, 2015. http://momastery.com/blog/2015/10/28/why-prejudiced/.

Mezey, Naomi, and Cornelia Pillard. "Against the New Maternalism." Georgetown Public Law and Legal Theory Research Paper no. 11-38 (2012): 229–96. Georgetown Law Faculty Publications.

Mothers of Preschoolers. "About MOPS." MOPS. http://www.mops.org/about/about-us/. Accessed July 21, 2016.

Mothers of Preschoolers. "How Did MOPS Get Started?" MOPS. http://www.mops.org/about/history/. Accesed July 21, 2016.

Mothers of Preschoolers. "What Is MOPS?" MOPS. http://www.mops.org. Accessed July 21, 2016.

MumsPick. "What Makes Nearly 7 in 10 Women Change How They Shop? Motherhood." MumsPick. http://www.mumspick.com/advertising?SID=01624af51d53de1fc4ac5c289f9f5d34. Accessed July 21, 2016.

Negra, Diane, and Yvonne Tasker. Gendering the Recession: Media and Culture in an Age of Austerity. Durham, NC: Duke University Press, 2014.

Newsweek. "Mommy vs. Mommy." June 3, 1990.

Niequist, Shauna. "You're Never Going to Be Fully Ready." Storyline, February 5, 2015. http://storylineblog.com/2015/02/05/youre-never-going-to-be-fully-ready/.

O'Mara, Peggy. Natural Family Living: The "Mothering" Magazine Guide to Parenting. New York: Pocket Books, 2000.

Ouellette, Laurie, and Julie Wilson. "Women's Work: Affective Labour and Convergence Culture." Cultural Studies 25, nos. 4–5 (2011): 548–65.

Paasonen, Susanna. "A Midsummer's Bonfire: Affective Intensities of Online Debate." In Networked Affect, edited by Ken Hillis, Susanna Paasonen, and Michael Petit, 27–42. Cambridge, MA: MIT Press, 2015.

Papacharissi, Zizi. Affective Publics: Sentiment, Technology, and Politics. Oxford: Oxford University Press, 2015.

Pickert, Kate. "Are You Mom Enough?" Time. May 21, 2012.

Plant, Rebecca Jo. Mom: The Transformation of Motherhood in Modern America. Chicago: University of Chicago Press, 2010.

Podnieks, Elizabeth. Mediating Moms: Mothers in Popular Culture. Montreal: McGill-Queen's University Press, 2012.

Puar, Jasbir. "'I Would Rather Be a Cyborg Than a Goddess': Becoming-Intersectional in Assemblage Theory." philoSOPHIA 2, no. 1 (2012): 49–66.

Radic, Shelley. Momology: A Mom's Guide to Shaping Great Kids. Grand Rapids, MI: Revell, 2010.

Radway, Janice. "The Hegemony of 'Specificity' and the Impasse in Audience Research: Cultural Studies and the Problem of Ethnography." In The Audience and Its Landscape, edited by James Hay, Lawrence Grossberg, and Ellen Wartella, 235–46. Boulder, CO: Westview, 1996.

Rich, Adrienne. Of Woman Born: Motherhood as Experience and Institution. New York: W. W. Norton, 2005.

Richardson, Theresa. *The Century of the Child: The Mental Hygiene Movement and Social Policy in the United States and Canada.* Albany: State University of New York Press, 1989.

Rose, Nikolas. *Governing the Soul: The Shaping of the Private Self.* London: Free Association Books, 1999.

Rose, Nikolas. *The Politics of Life Itself.* Princeton, NJ: Princeton University Press, 2007.

Rose, Nikolas. *Powers of Freedom: Reframing Political Thought.* Cambridge: Cambridge University Press, 1999.

Rubin, Lillian. *Worlds of Pain: Life in the Working-Class Family.* New York: Basic Books, 1976.

Schowalter, Dana. "Financialization of the Family: Motherhood, Biopolitics, and Paths of Power." *Women and Language* 35, no. 1 (2012): 39–56.

Seery, Shirley. "Self-Demand: What Is It?" In *Parents' Magazine Baby Care Manual,* vol. 42. New York: Baby Care Manual, 1950.

Seigworth, Gregory J., and Melissa Gregg. "An Inventory of Shimmers." In *The Affect Theory Reader,* edited by Melissa Gregg and Gregory J. Seigworth, 1–25. Durham, NC: Duke University Press, 2010.

Senft, Theresa. *Camgirls: Celebrity and Community in the Age of Social Networks.* New York: Peter Lang, 2008.

Sherman, Aliza, and Danielle Elliott Smith. *Mom, Incorporated: A Guide to Business + Baby.* South Portland, ME: Sellers, 2010.

Silva, Jennifer. *Coming Up Short: Working-Class Adulthood in the Age of Uncertainty.* Oxford: Oxford University Press, 2013.

Singley, Carol J., and Susan Elizabeth Sweeney. "In League with Each Other: The Theory and Practice of Feminist Collaboration." In *Common Ground: Feminist Collaboration in the Academy,* edited by Elizabeth Peck and JoAnna Stephens Mink, 63–80. Albany: State University of New York Press, 1998.

Slater, Don. "Domestic Photography and Digital Culture." In *The Photographic Image in Digital Culture,* edited by Martin Lister, 129–46. New York: Routledge, 1995.

Sontag, Susan. *On Photography.* New York: Farrar, Straus and Giroux, 1977.

Spigel, Lynn. *Make Room for TV: Television and the Family Ideal in Postwar America.* Chicago: University of Chicago Press, 1992.

Stabile, Carol. *White Victims, Black Villains: Gender, Race, and Crime News.* New York: Routledge, 2006.

Stacey, Judith. *Brave New Families: Stories of Domestic Upheaval in Late Twentieth-Century America.* Berkeley: University of California Press, 1998.

Stack, Carol. *All Our Kin.* New York: Basic Books, 1974.

Stearns, Peter. *Anxious Parents: A History of Modern Childrearing in America.* New York: New York University Press, 2003.

Stewart, Kathleen. "Interview with the Author." Supplemental material to "Precarity's Forms." *Cultural Anthropology* 27, no. 3 (2012): 518–25. http://www.culanth.org /articles/138-precarity-s-forms.

Stewart, Kathleen. *Ordinary Affects.* Durham, NC: Duke University Press, 2007.

Stewart, Kathleen. "Pockets." *Communication and Critical/Cultural Studies* 9, no. 4 (2012): 365–68.

Strauss, Elissa. "The Tyranny of the Bad Mother." *Salon*, February 17, 2014. http://www
.salon.com/2014/02/17/the_tyranny_of_the_bad_mother_slacker_moms_are_just
_as_intimidating_as_perfect_ones/.

Tatum, Beverly Daniel. *Why Are All the Black Kids Sitting Together in the Cafeteria? And
Other Conversations about Race.* New York: Basic Books, 1997.

Terranova, Tiziana. "Free Labor: Producing Culture for the Digital Economy." *Social
Text* 18, no. 2 (no. 63) (2000): 33–58.

Terranova, Tiziana. *Network Culture: Politics for the Information Age.* London: Pluto,
2004.

Thurer, Shari L. *The Myths of Motherhood: How Culture Reinvents the Good Mother.* New
York: Penguin, 1994.

Together Rising. "About." *Together Rising.* http://togetherrising.org/about/. Accessed
July 21, 2016.

Together Rising. "Holiday Hands." *Together Rising.* http://togetherrising.org/holiday
-hands. Accessed July 21, 2016.

Together Rising. "Love Flash Mobs." *Together Rising.* http://togetherrising.org/love-flash
-mobs. Accessed July 21, 2016.

Turow, Joseph. *The Daily You: How the New Advertising Is Defining Your Identity and Your
Worth.* New Haven, CT: Yale University Press, 2011.

Umanksy, Lauri. *Motherhood Reconceived: Feminism and the Legacies of the Sixties.* New
York: New York University Press, 1996.

Van Cleaf, Kara. "*Of Woman Born* to Mommy Blogged: The Journey from the Personal
as Political to the Personal as Commodity." *Women's Studies Quarterly* 43, nos. 3–4
(2015): 247–64.

Villalobos, Ana. *Motherload: Making It All Better in Insecure Times.* Oakland: University
of California Press, 2014.

Walkerdine, Valerie. *Daddy's Girl: Young Girls and Popular Culture.* Cambridge, MA:
Harvard University Press, 1997.

Walters, Suzanna Danuta, and Laura Harrison. "Not Ready to Make Nice: Aberrant
Mothers in Contemporary Culture." *Feminist Media Studies* 14, no. 1 (2014): 38–55.

Warner, Judith. *Perfect Madness: Motherhood in the Age of Anxiety.* New York: Riverhead
Books, 2005.

Williams, Raymond. *Marxism and Literature.* Oxford: Oxford University Press, 1977.

Williamson, Judith. "Family, Education, Photography." In *Culture/Power/History:
A Reader in Contemporary Social Theory*, edited by Nicholas Dirks, Geoff Eley, and
Sherry Ortner, 236–44. Princeton, NJ: Princeton University Press, 1994.

Wilson, Julie, and Emily Chivers Yochim. "Pinning Happiness: Affect, Social Media,
and the Work of Mothering." In *Cupcakes, Pinterest, and Ladyporn: Feminized Popular
Culture in the Early Twenty First Century*, edited by Elana Levine, 232–48. Urbana-
Champaign: University of Illinois Press, 2015.

Zelizer, Viviana. *Pricing the Priceless Child: The Changing Social Value of Children.* Princeton, NJ: Princeton University Press, 1994.

Zelizer, Viviana. *The Purchase of Intimacy.* Princeton, NJ: Princeton University Press,
2005.

Lisa, 89–94
Lorey, Isabell, 20

Maggie, 54, 58–60
mamapreneurialism, 66–67, 71–72; as optimizing domestic life, 79–84. *See also* work-at-home motherhood
mamasphere, 16–19; government of mothers and, 52–57; mamapreneurialism and, 73–79; mothering communities and, 143; participatory governing and, 158–61
Martin, Randy, 62, 83
Massumi, Brian, 13, 17
maternal affect, 39–41; mommy instinct and, 44, 48–49; mother love and, 41–47, 171; self-reflexivity and, 173. *See also* anxiety
Mejias, Ulises Ali, 18
Melton, Glennon Doyle, 29, 139–42, 168, 184; as microcelebrity, 152–54
Mezey, Naomi, 178
Michaels, Meredith, 35
Modern Parents Messy Kids (*MPMK*), 73–76
Momastery, 139–41, 145–46, 150–54, 158–61, 164–68, 179
mommy blogs/blogging, 56–57, 115–23, 198–99n13; as communicative capitalism, 119–23; microcelebrity and, 118–19. *See also* Momastery
mommy wars, 11, 53–56, 146, 190n13
mompreneur, 66. *See also* mamapreneurialism
MomsRising, 178
Morris, Meaghan, 13
motherhood: antimaternalism and maternalism and, 43–44; citizenship and, 36–37; ethopolitics and, 47–51, 54–57, 121–23, 138–39, 200n19; as experience and institution, 29–30; "good" mothering and, 37, 41, 63; as idealized scene, 103–4; as naturalized to women, 22,

35–36, 104; precarity and, 4–5, 20–24, 33–34, 58–59, 69–71, 103–6, 193n24; as risk management, 61–64; as "security project" 59–61, 197n6, 198n10. *See also* neoliberalism, motherhood
Mothering, 45–46, 143–45, 194n35
mothering advice, 25–27, 40–47, 53–57, 63–64, 106–7, 193n30
mothering communities, 142; as affective community, 152–54, 180; collective affect and, 159–61; ethopoliticization of motherhood and, 142–43, 146, 149–50; family autonomy and, 144–46; as intimate public, 154; mamasphere and, 143; new maternalism and, 146–47; participatory governing and, 155–61; privatization of happiness and, 147, 163; resilience and, 140, 147, 150–52, 162–66, 168
Mothers of Preschoolers (MOPS), 9–10, 194n35, 139, 141–50, 155–57, 162–64, 201n5

Nancy, 169–75
Negra, Diane, 197n36
neoliberalism, 14; community and, 144; motherhood and, 4, 22, 49–51, 54, 68–71, 179–80, 183–84. *See also* precarity
new momism, 11–12, 35

On Becoming Babywise, 39–40
Ouellette, Laurie, 79

Papacharissi, Zizi, 17
Pillard, Cornelia, 178
Pinterest, 16, 75, 109–12, 125, 130, 139, 197n8
Plant, Rebecca, 43–44
postfeminism, 79, 87
Power of Moms, 76–78